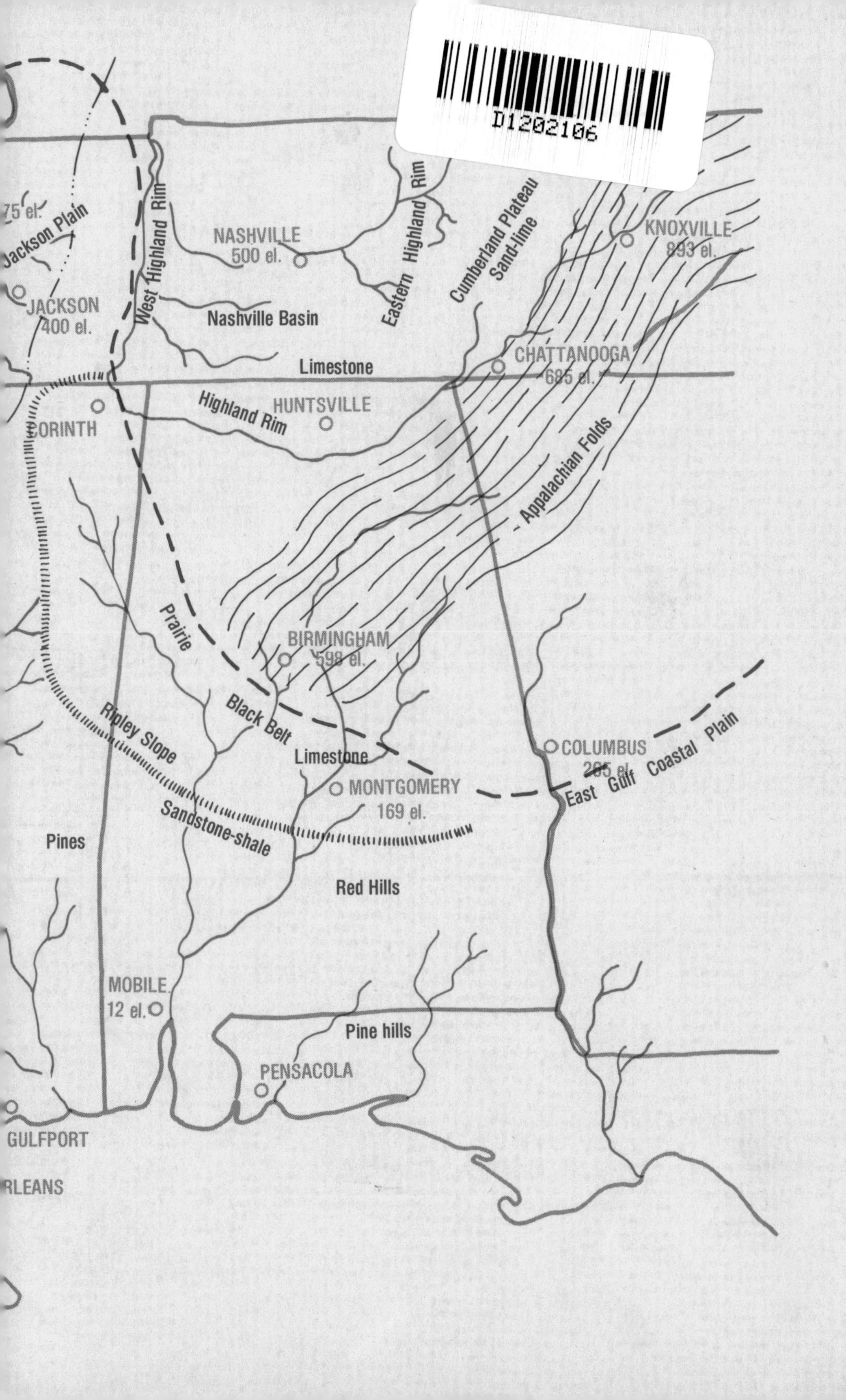

75 el.
Jackson Plain
JACKSON
400 el.
West Highland Rim
NASHVILLE
500 el.
Nashville Basin
Eastern Highland Rim
Cumberland Plateau
Sand-lime
KNOXVILLE
893 el.
CHATTANOOGA
685 el.
Limestone
Highland Rim
HUNTSVILLE
CORINTH
Appalachian Folds
Prairie
BIRMINGHAM
598 el.
Black Belt
Ripley Slope
Limestone
COLUMBUS
265 el.
East Gulf Coastal Plain
MONTGOMERY
169 el.
Sandstone-shale
Pines
Red Hills
MOBILE
12 el.
Pine hills
PENSACOLA
GULFPORT
RLEANS

D1202106

Happy Birthday, June,
from Gail & Ozzie
June 22, 1984

A Guide to WILDFLOWERS of the MID-SOUTH

A Guide to WILDFLOWERS of the MID-SOUTH

West Tennessee into Central Arkansas
and south through
Alabama and into East Texas

by
Arlo I. Smith

Memphis State University Press
The Press Of Mid-America

Copyright 1979 by Arlo I. Smith

All rights reserved. No part of this book may be reproduced or utilized in any form or by any means, electronic or mechanical, including photocopying and recording, or by any information storage and retrieval system, without permission from the publisher, except by a reviewer who may quote brief passages in a review.

Manufactured in the United States of America

International Standard Book Number 0-87870-076-5

Library of Congress Catalog Card Number 79-89883

Smith, Arlo I 1911-
A guide to wildflowers of the mid-South.

Bibliography: p.
Includes index.
1. Wild flowers—Southern States—Identification.
I. Title.
QK124.S64 582'.13'0976 79-23526
ISBN 0-87870-076-5

The front endpaper map and some pertinent information was redrawn, with permission of the publisher, as a composite of four Geologic Highway Maps published by the American Association of Petroleum Geologists, Tulsa, Oklahoma.

Contents

Preface

Over the many years of teaching college courses in field biology and ecology and talking to garden clubs and other interested groups, I have found that my extensive collection of color slides of wildflowers has filled a gap in plant identification in this area. The need for an illustrated nontechnical book to cover the Mid-South area flora has prompted the writing of this book which has received encouragement from students, wildflower enthusiasts, conservationists, and fellow botanists.

The approach to background information and plant developments over the ages was chosen to give the reader an understanding of plant relationships to each other and to their environment. Plant family names for the most part follow those used by Radford, Ahles, and Bell in their *Manual of the Vascular Flora of the Carolinas*. The unique combination of the relatively complete but simple plant descriptions, nontechnical keys for identification, and the color photographs will help both the student and the interested layman. For further studies the Supplementary Readings list refers the reader to both technical and nontechnical literature.

I wish to express my appreciation for the suggestions of Dr. Edward T. Browne, Jr. of Memphis State University for his review of the slides and Dr. H. R. DeSelm of the University of Tennessee, Knoxville, who reviewed the slides and carefully checked the manuscript. The project was aided through both the Sabbatical Program and the award of a Research and Creative Activity Summer Grant by Southwestern At Memphis. In the early stages Mrs. Anne McAuley aided in the difficult task of typing the first draft of the text material. Over the years my wife, Noreen, was a constant participant in the field and photographic endeavors. Her close scrutiny and clarification of the text, cross-referencing of the index, and typing of the final manuscript were especially helpful. The successful conclusion to our endeavors came when Memphis State University Press, with the endorsement of President Billy Jones, made possible the publishing of this book.

Arlo I. Smith

Part I. Introduction

Where Have All The Flowers Gone?

It is evident to many persons knowledgeable about our environment that the scene is rapidly changing. They often hear the question, "where have all the flowers gone?" Native habitats essential for the survival of plants and animals are rapidly disappearing as housing, industrial developments, dams, strip mines, and highways, as well as increasing acreage of farm lands opened for food production, are removing or seriously disrupting woodlands, streams, valleys, marshlands, and mountains.

Habitats develop slowly over many years of interaction between successive species of plants and animals in their physical environment. This represents an intricate web of interacting organisms all supporting each other, referred to as a climax condition. If a marsh is drained, a woodland clear-cut or burned over, a dam floods a valley or air and water pollution infiltrate the habitat, the destruction upsets the balance of nature for several hundred years. Such destruction often threatens the extinction of many species.

Why Another Book?

The lover of the out-of-doors in this area is hard pressed to find a book enabling him to identify the kinds of plants he encounters in our remaining natural areas. This book is meant to be helpful to the nonprofessional and beginning botany students who want to become more familiar with the plant life around them. As they stroll through a natural area, they see about them more than just the showy wildflowers, which often are few and far between, but also ferns, shrubs, vines, and trees that together make up the superstructure of the changing plant-animal-environmental complex. When they learn to "see" all of these plant types they can more easily understand environmental interrelationships. Thus, some of the more common ferns, shrubs, vines, and trees, not thought of as wildflowers, are also included in this book.

We have recorded in color and description over 475 species of plants representing 122 families of higher plants encountered in the south central part of the United States. The area covered includes Alabama into east Texas, the western half of Tennessee and into central and southern Arkansas. Most of the plants covered here extend beyond this area making the book useful in surrounding compatible habitats.

Technical terminology has been reduced to a minimum and translated into more understandable terms even if they are longer than technical ones. The more curious enthusiasts and outdoor leaders will be able to understand and use the basic characteristics for identification of most of the plants and plant types to be seen around them. A good 6 to 10 power pocket hand lens available at most university book stores will be needed to identify correctly some of the plants, especially the composites or sunflowerlike plants.

Plants are grouped together in their appropriate families, and are arranged in the increasing complexity that over the millions of years has been the result of adaptive modifications to their changing environment. In the overall view, one can appreciate the continuity of change and yet be aware of the similarities resulting from genetic continuity and adaptation. Features not usually found in a book like this are included to carry out this objective. Among them are discussions of climatic and soil conditions, and plant successions to climax types of vegetation, as well as plant variations through ages of time.

WHY DO PLANTS GROW WHERE THEY DO?

Climatic and Soil Conditions. One of the most important factors determining where plants will grow is precipitation. Our weather is largely determined by moisture-laden winds approaching this country in the Pacific Northwest, moving southeastward. As the air mass rises over the cold Olympic Range, moisture condenses, producing 100-200 inches of precipitation on the lower western slopes and resulting in the growth of a luxurious temperate rain-forest. As the somewhat drier winds again rise over the Cascade Mountains more moisture produces a luxurious coniferous vegetation. The air mass is quite dry as it then descends the eastern slope, where rainfall is only 5-10 inches and the vegetation is of the cold desert type. But the air picks up some moisture as it warms and deposits 10-30 inches at elevations of 6-10,000 feet on the western slopes of the Rockies, supporting coniferous vegetation. Continuing southeastward, the dry air mass moves across the Great Plains at 3-6,000 feet elevation, supporting sparse, short grasslands with 15-20 inches of rainfall per year. Gradually the air mass picks up moisture at lower elevations of 1-3,000 feet and the Central Plains get 20-40 inches, supporting our great prairie grasslands. This is our most fertile wheat and corn cropland, which is also rich in legume and composite plants. In the northern reaches of the midwest and east about 35 inches of precipitation supports the northern coniferous forest, while southward 40-60 inches and higher temperatures produce the eastern deciduous forests—beech-maple to the colder north and oak-hickory to the warmer south. The increased rainfall is the result of warm moist air from the Gulf of Mexico meeting cold fronts of air from the northwest, producing 40-60 inches of precipitation, or even over 80 inches along the lower coastal plain.

Rainfall and its distribution are important but temperature and humidity also play a great part in where plants will grow. Plants must be able to survive long hot dry spells during summers farther south and intense, below freezing temperatures farther north. High humidity and temperature promote many plant diseases and drier low temperatures kill many plants by dessication in winter.

Another factor in determining plant distribution is soil composition. Soils in the mid-central area of the South have been affected by past geologic history. The area was covered by an extension of the Gulf of Mexico beginning 100 million years ago when sandy and limy deposits occured. As seen on the map, sandstone and limestone rocks are exposed at the edges of the Appalachian folds and the Highland Rim. Other outcrops appear locally where rocks have been exposed by erosion. For the most part the delta region has fertile sandy-clayey soils enriched by soil deposition while the upland soils are depleted by erosion. Then there are freshwater swamps and marshes and, closer to the coastline, brackish swamps and marshes. These factors combine to produce a wide variety of species and plant families represented in the book's coverage. In addition special attention should be called to the "islands" of prairie vegetation noted on the map as the Black Belt in Alabama and Mississippi, and the coastal and inland black prairies of eastern Texas and Arkansas (see map inside front cover).

Soils which furnish minerals for plant nourishment also have a profound effect on the type of plants that grow in the area. They vary from flood-deposited soil to wind-deposited sand hills. Loose sandy soil holds little water and rains leach out the soil minerals. Tighter clayey-sandy soils hold more moisture, are found in bottom-lands with accumulated humus and support abundant growth. Soils with more clay, less sand and humus do not have the porosity to hold air for oxygen needed by plant roots. In response to such soils, roots grow close to the surface. In times of drought shallow-rooted plants often die when their roots dry out in the parched surface soil. Likewise, when heavy clay soil is water-logged for very long the roots die of suffocation. This is why trees in flooded lowlands die if the water level stays high for very long.

Thus one sees that wild plants must "make do" with conditions as they are in an area and adapt to them. Plants growing on limestone or calcareous soils are probably there because they have adapted to alkaline soils, and if planted elsewhere, may require addition of lime or limestone in order to grow. Usually it is difficult to transplant more specialized plants unless the proper conditions can be duplicated.

Plant Successions and Vegetation Types. Climax vegetation types are reached only after several hundred years by a continuous succession of predictable species. The climax species are determined by climatic and soil conditions, and are unable to survive in a raw, exposed area. After pioneer species modify the area other species move in, replacing those species that have gone before. This process continues until a stable or climax community is reached.

One type of succession may be seen in concentric zones of vegetation around a pond or lake. As silting-in of a lake occurs, conditions change, the body of water gets smaller and the zones of plants move inward, each zone being overtaken by the next outer one until the water is gone. The zones themselves are successively obliterated until only the outer zone covers the area and perpetuates itself indefinitely as a climax

Zonation around Reelfoot Lake in West Tennessee located in an oak-hickory climax forest region.

A Southern tupelo swamp forest with water tupelo the dominant tree, accompanied by bald cypress and/or pond cypress. The Anhinga or water turkey in the photo is/was a common inhabitant of southern lakes, ponds and adjacent swamps.

A climax oak-hickory forest with dominant canopy trees, understory trees, shrub and herb layers.

Leaves of white oak and mockernut hickory, common co-dominant trees of the climax forest.

type of vegetation. It could be desert, grassland or forest. If drastic changes occur, the climax condition could be wiped out or seriously set back.

In observing a lake giving way to an oak-hickory forest one might see the following zones from the lake outward: (1) in the shallow water—water lily, coon-tail, cut-grass and cat-tail; (2) at the water's edge—pickerel weed, sedges, rush, button-bush, alder, willow; (3) in moist soil—cottonwood, box-elder, ash, maple, sycamore; (4) in drier soil—hackberry, elm, sweetgum, tulip poplar; (5) in still drier soil—species of oaks and hickories mixed with previous stages of trees which will gradually die out as their seeds no longer germinate in the deeper shade and drier soil. In an oak-hickory forest there are also "understory" trees, such as dogwood, paw-paw, hornbeam, hop-hornbeam, and sassafras.

This vegetation is now climax, the lake is gone as well as stages (1)-(4). Larger surviving trees of stage 3 and 4 will die out in time. Abundant herbs appear on the forest floor. Most plants growing in the oak-hickory forest are deciduous and their leaves readily decompose, enriching the soil and thus supporting a great variety of plants which in turn support a myriad of animals both small and large. By the time trees leaf out, early-blooming spring plants have completed seed production and they are replaced by shade-loving plants. These later plants may include violets, trillium, Soloman's-seal, jewelweed, and fern, along with red buckeye and deciduous holly. Vines such as poison ivy, Virginia creeper, grape, and cross-vine spiral upward into sunlight. This has taken 500-600 years of species succession.

In drier, well-drained soils, pines are a subclimax to the oak-hickory forest. A recent practice of man is to maintain this subclimax condition by periodically burning the pine lands to kill the broadleaf seedlings, thus allowing the southern pine forests to grow in croplike stands. Coniferous forests support a scant variety of herbaceous plants since light for ground level plants is insufficient for their growth. Also, pine needles decompose slowly, and hardly enrich the soil beyond self maintenance. The soil is infertile and has little organic matter. There is little food source for support of animals. Unfortunately perhaps, the pressure to produce timber and pulpwood from pines is calling for our replacement of oak-hickory timber land with southern pines. This is one rather extensive way we are removing natural habitats and endangering the existence of many species of plants and animals. Regeneration of forests that have been clear-cut in lumbering follow what is called a secondary succession. Some of the requirements of the later plant stages remain and if the area is left alone, the climax condition can again be reached in 150-200 years.

River bottom and flood plain forests or swamps are controlled rather naturally and do not reach an oak-hickory climax because of periodic flooding, eroding and depositing of soil. Major species found in these areas are cypress, tupelo gum, sour gum, cottonwood, willow, sycamore, birch, hackberry, alder, elm, and ash. River bottom cane makes brakes and on their edges are found pecan (a hickory), swamp red oak, water oak, willow oak, and shagbark hickory. Among vines are included grape, Virginia creeper, pepper-vine, cross-vine, and yellow jasmine. Water smartweed and lizard's tail are common on the wet forest floor.

Forest edges or openings away from water may have prairie type vegetation with little bluestem grass, blackberry, and sumac in the opening. Around the lower coastal plain palmetto is said to "hold the sand together." There are several oaks here, especially turkey oak and live oak with its drapings of Spanish moss, as well as evergreens such as yaupon holly, wax-myrtle, and often sweetbay magnolia.

Conditions supporting prairie grasslands prevail in islands in much of the area covered here. These are in the Black Belt crescent of Mississippi and Alabama and islands in eastern Texas and Arkansas. Plains grasslands are found along the coastal plains of Louisiana and Texas. There is greater rainfall, 50-60 inches, in the coastal area but a clay hardpan close to the surface seems to prevent the water table below from reaching the prairie plants above it. Trees are supported where the hardpan is disturbed and their roots can reach the water table.

The more eastern prairie grassland is referred to as "tall grassland," primarily dominated by 5-6 foot tall big bluestem grass to the eastward and 3-5 foot little bluestem toward the west. These grade into the short grass plains of needle-grass and grama grass farther westward in drier areas. Thirty to forty inches of rainfall support the eastern prairies while 15-25 inches support the short grass plains. The most persistent grass in the south is Johnson grass, which is not limited to grassland but grows rampant over bottomlands throughout the area. It may be over 6 feet tall and is a perennial, spreading mainly by rhizomes. Grassland herbaceous species of plants found commonly with grasses are in the composite family represented by sunflowers, asters, thistles, blazing-star, and ragweed; the legume family includes clovers, partridge pea, vetch, and peas; and other plants such as milkweeds, mints, phlox, and verbenas.

Marshes are described as treeless grassland with standing water most of the time. If the water is fresh as opposed to salty then grass, sedges, rush, cat-tail, spatter-dock, water-hyacinth, water-lettuce, arrowhead and alligator-weed are found. If the water is salty, cord grass, salt grass, sedges, black rush, salt bush, glasswort, and sea ox-eye are found. Marshes are quite fertile and rank above prairie lands in productivity. This productivity and shelter make them the prime nurseries for marine life as well as for many birds and mammals.

Unfortunately under the pressures of today's technology and population growth, marshes and swamps are fast disappearing. For instance, 90 per cent of the delta swamplands of Arkansas have been channelized and drained to produce soybeans, and coastal marshlands are being converted to urban sprawl. It is estimated that 45 million acres of swamps and marshes in the U.S. have been lost to various developments and 75 million more are under siege. The water table in these habitats is being disastrously lowered in many areas. The remaining wetlands are being severely affected by urban, industrial, and agricultural pollutants to the detriment of marine and freshwater plants and animals. The use of pesticides, and especially herbicides, in agriculture and in the maintenance of rights-of-way for power lines, gas transmission, railroads, and highways is especially destructive to natural habitats as they affect vegetation miles away from the point of application.

Plant habitats are so imperiled everywhere that everyone should resist picking wild plants simply to enjoy them briefly. Transplanting wild plants to new locations involves the need for real knowledge of soil and other requirements for even a small degree of success. Transplanting during flowering time is seldom successful under the best of conditions and should not be done. If you want a wild flower garden you will have the most success with plants started from seed. Garden stores in most places carry wild flower seed that will be successful if care is taken to duplicate the major growing needs of that particular species.

Plant Life Through the Ages

Geologic evidence indicates that plants first existed as unicellular aquatic organisms about 3.1 billion years ago. Since then, in response to the interplay of heredity and environment, plants have become very diverse. The ability of a plant to achieve structural change is limited to the patterns of genes it has inherited, but through sexual reproduction some genes are replaced and incorporated in the heredity. These revisions may result in harmful, useless, or beneficial structural or functional changes. As environmental conditions change, certain adaptations enhance the plant's chances for survival. There have been many parallel lines of development since some "fossil" types of plants have found basic patterns that were versatile enough to succeed over the ages, while other plants have succeeded through modifications and refinements of patterns. The algae are still with us, a parallel to the complex flowering plants. In the following summary of plant development, stress has been on the sexual reproductive process with its modifications that have resulted in enough plant versatility to literally clothe the earth, even though the basic process has remained the same.

Fossil evidence indicates that the first abundant plant life was aquatic algae similar to our pond scums and seaweeds of today. These algae are abundant from 900 million years ago. They were simple cells and colonies of cells reproducing at first only by cell division and later by sexual reproduction.

When sexual reproduction came about each sex plant contributed a single set of heredity-determining chromosomes to the next generation. These genetic materials with genes on chromosomes were exchanged, shuffled, and reshuffled giving much more opportunity for a greater variety of plant forms to appear. Water served as a medium for fertilization outside the simple plant bodies.

Moss plants, similar to our common mosses now, were the first "amphibians" of the plant world. They became adapted for life on land but still their sperms had to swim in water (rain or dew) to reach the egg. Eggs and sperms are usually produced on the tops of separately sexed leafy moss plants called female and male gametophytes, literally meaning gamete (egg, sperm)-producing plants. These plants have single sets of chromosomes until fertilization of the egg by the sperm occurs. Fertilization produces a different structure, a sporophyte which is a leafless stalk with a tiny capsule on top and is attached to the top of the female gametophyte. Each cell of the sporophyte has a double set of chromosomes, one set from the egg, the other set from the sperm. Spores are produced in the capsule in a type of cell division which separates the double set of chromosomes into a single set in each cell or spore. In doing this, half the spores grow into female moss plants and the other half into male plants. This cycle from gametophyte to sporophyte and back again is called alternation of generations. The plant cycles shown in figure 1, p. 10-11, demonstrate this.

Not only do moss plants still reproduce this way in their life cycle, but also all of our higher plants. The reproductive cycle is the same but the size of the two generations has been reversed. The sporophyte plants you see today are the large leafy food-producing ferns, conifers, and flowering plants. The gametophytes have become reduced and (except for the ferns) are attached to, and mature on, the sporophytes; the tiny fern gametophyte is still separate from the large leafy sporophyte. The moss sporophyte does not have water and food conducting cells nor does it make much food for itself. Until the sporophyte became food producing and had a transport system for water and food, a large plant could not develop. The plants that first developed such tissues, called vascular tissues, are thought to be relatives of *Psilotum* or whisk fern, which is usually found in the tropics.

Psilotum is a 25-45 cm branching plant with no roots, only a green photosynthetic stem with tiny remote scales for leaves and 3-lobed spore cases about match-head in size along the sides. It may be found around the bases of palm trees in moist shady places in Florida. It had the first type of water conducting tissue, called xylem, and the first food conducting tissue, called phloem. Their fossil relatives are now found in Devonian deposits of 350 million years ago. Some grew quite large and resembled *Psilotum* and *Equisetum* (horse-tails) of today. Fossil stems several inches in diameter have been found. It seems quite fitting that these living "fossil" plants and *Lycopodium,* with the first veined leaves, be included in this book. They are illustrated in the first plate of the plant photos.

The ferns and their relatives developed leaves and increasingly extensive vascular tissues. They were, and are, the most abundant non-seed-bearing, spore producing vascular plants. They became coal deposits over 300 million years ago as a result of their incomplete decomposition over a period of about 100 million years. It is not surprising that the first seed plants looked like ferns and are called seed ferns. They be-

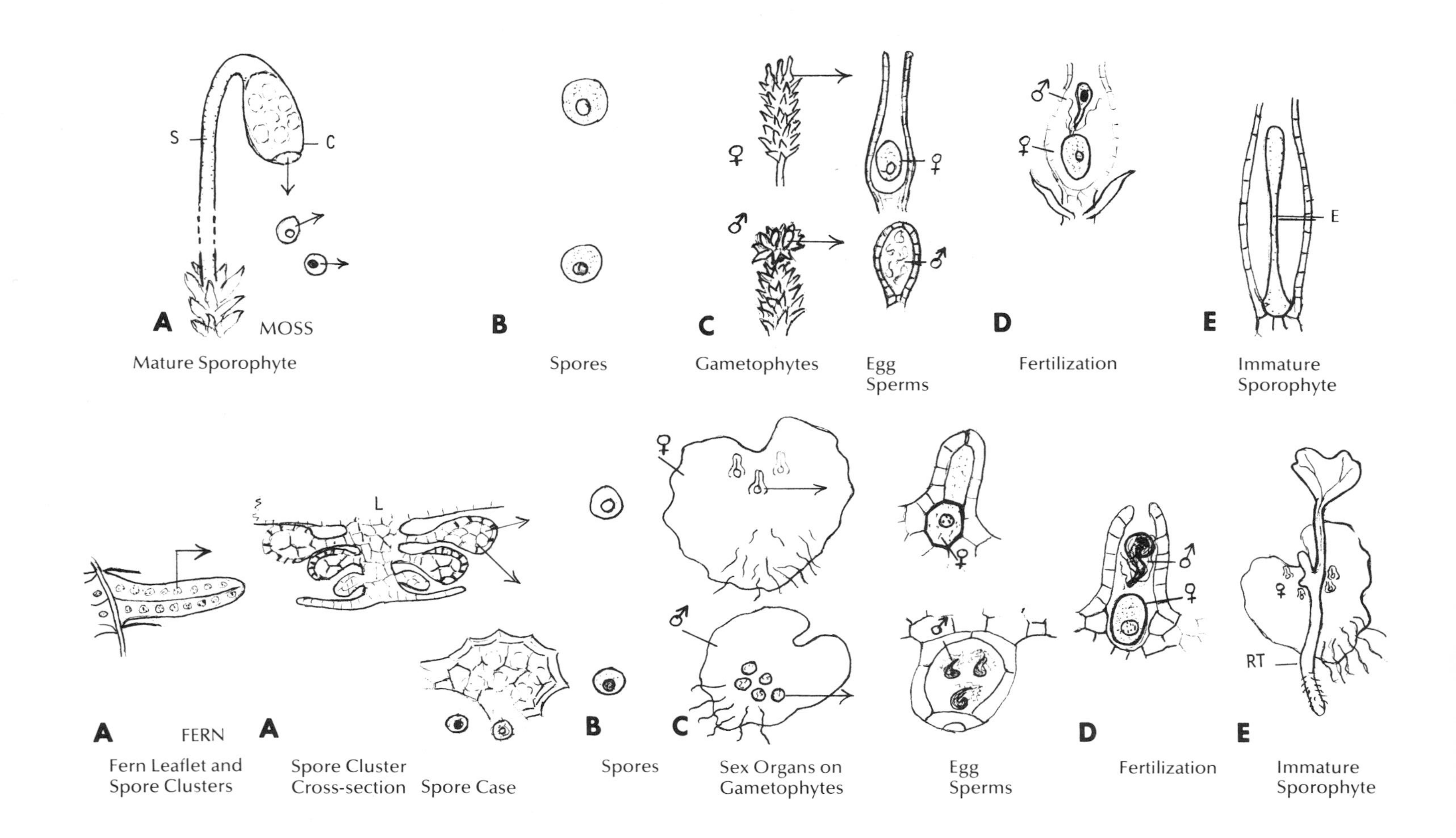
S
C
A
MOSS
Mature Sporophyte
B
Spores
C
Gametophytes
Egg
Sperms
D
Fertilization
E
E
Immature
Sporophyte
L
A
FERN
Fern Leaflet and
Spore Clusters
A
Spore Cluster
Cross-section
Spore Case
B
Spores
C
Sex Organs on
Gametophytes
Egg
Sperms
D
Fertilization
RT
E
Immature
Sporophyte

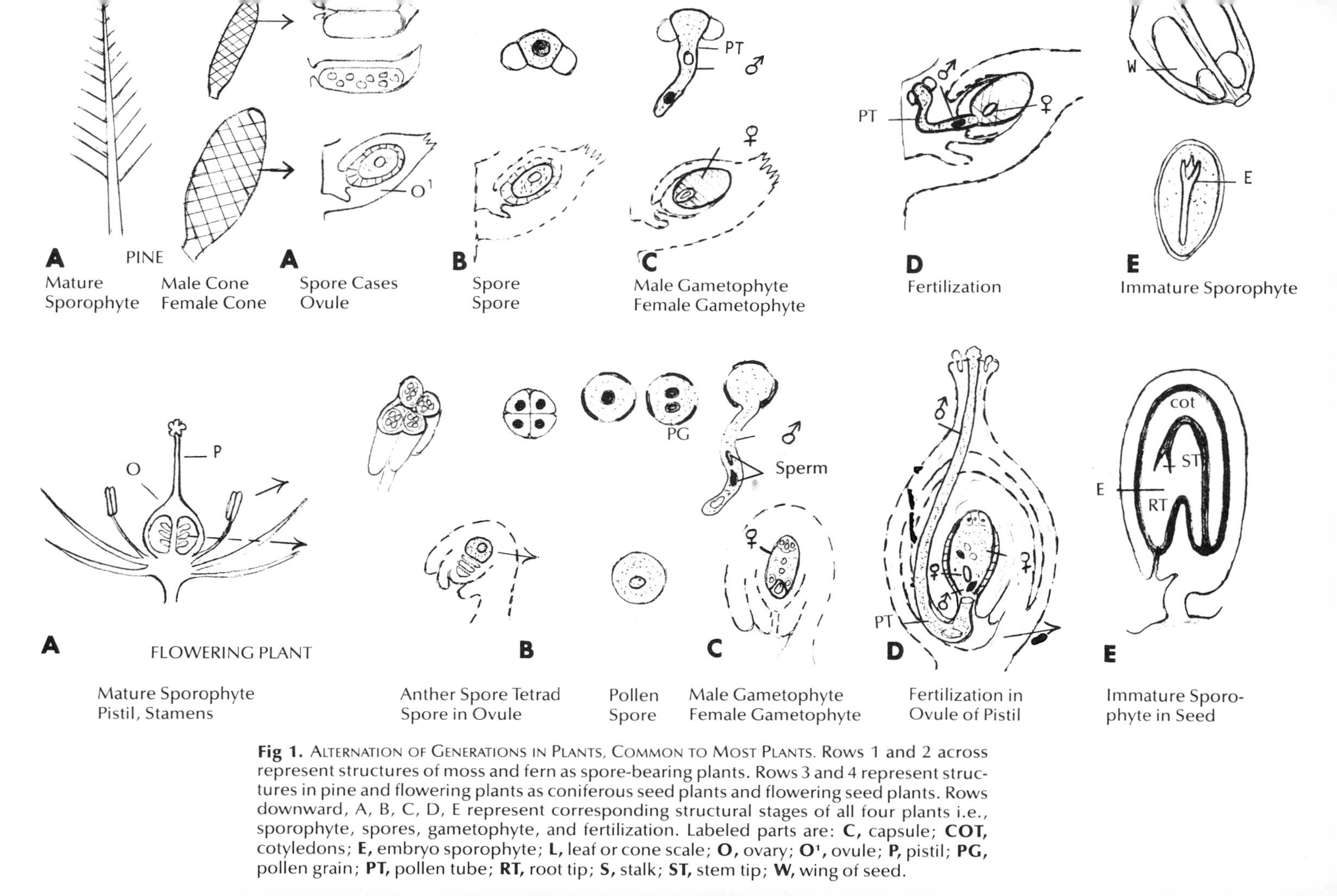

Fig 1. Alternation of Generations in Plants, Common to Most Plants. Rows 1 and 2 across represent structures of moss and fern as spore-bearing plants. Rows 3 and 4 represent structures in pine and flowering plants as coniferous seed plants and flowering seed plants. Rows downward, A, B, C, D, E represent corresponding structural stages of all four plants i.e., sporophyte, spores, gametophyte, and fertilization. Labeled parts are: **C,** capsule; **COT,** cotyledons; **E,** embryo sporophyte; **L,** leaf or cone scale; **O,** ovary; **O',** ovule; **P,** pistil; **PG,** pollen grain; **PT,** pollen tube; **RT,** root tip; **S,** stalk; **ST,** stem tip; **W,** wing of seed.

came extinct about 150 million years ago, having lived about 100 million years. They left, however, their pattern of development, the seed structure that is still followed by conifers and flowering plants. The seed is defined as a dormant embryo sporophyte plant with stored food material and a protective covering. Seeds help tide the plant over during unfavorable times and thus make possible the appearance and success of annual plants.

Another important contribution at this time was the development of the pollen tube (a male gametophyte) that comes from the spore or pollen grain. This tube grows through plant tissues and deposits a sperm at the site of the egg, producing a seed in conifers and flowering plants. For the first time this enabled plants to carry out fertilization without dependence upon water for the sperm to swim to the egg in the female gametophyte. Thus most land plants then became truly land plants. Most plants below the seed plants (algae, mosses, fungi, etc.) must still depend upon water for fertilization.

As seed ferns became extinct, the conifers became the dominant vegetation type for about 30 million years. One of the extensive patterns of development accomplished by the coniferous plants was the cylinder of cell-dividing formative tissue between wood and bark called the cambium. This cylinder is a thin tissue that continuously produces by cell division the water conducting xylem (wood) toward its inside and the food conducting tissue, the phloem, toward its outside. Phloem is the inner bark that transports food from the leaves to the stem and roots. It is this cambium tissue that enabled the stem and roots of the sporophyte to grow in girth.

The conifers produce cones which are composed of modified leaves called scales, that are specialized to produce spores. Small male cone scales produce spores which become pollen grains with pollen tubes (the male gametophyte) and sperms all with a single chromosome set. Large female cone scales produce spores which become female gametophytes that produce eggs inside the ovules, all with the single set of chromosomes. There are two of these ovules per scale on the upper side of each cone scale. The pollen grains fall on the female cone scale and grow a pollen tube which delivers a sperm to the egg inside the ovule. Upon fertilization the double chromosome sets are present in the embryo sporophyte which is surrounded by food tissue and a protective covering (seed coat). This is the conifer seed. The cycle is not really different from that of the moss plant, nor is it in the flowering plants, only the structures are modified. Conifers are also known as Gymnosperms which means "naked seed," and refers to the seeds that are exposed on the upper side of the cone scale without being enclosed in a pod or capsule.

The first of the flowering plants, or Angiosperms, were trees with annual rings of xylem (wood), a cambium of cell-forming tissue, and phloem in the bark as in the conifers. The tulip poplar, a magnolia, is one of the oldest of flowering plants, its relatives being found in late cretaceous fossil deposits of 100 million years ago. *Magnolia* shows resemblance to the conifers in that there is a female cone of scales arranged spirally on the stem axis. However, each cone scale folds lengthwise to become a pistil composed of stigma, style, and an ovary enclosing two ovules, each containing an egg. After fertilization of the eggs, the ovules become seeds enclosed in the pistil. This pistil develops into a dry fruit which splits open on one side and releases the seeds. Thus the term angiosperm means "covered seed" and this is the beginning of pistils. There are no male cones, but spirally arranged scales at the base of the female cone become modified into structures called stamens, thus setting the pattern of arrangement of pistils and stamens. Stamens are composed of a filamentous stalk tipped by a pair of spore cases called anthers. The anthers produce spores which become pollen grains. The pollen grains fall on the stigma of the pistil and grow a pollen tube which delivers a sperm to the eggs within the ovules in the ovary.

Another feature found in the magnolia that is not found until the development of flowering plants is the presence of many petals. They are spirally arranged somewhat following the pattern of many spiral cone scales. Both represent leaf modifications. The many petals as well as many stamens seem to follow an early pattern that has persisted with success in the magnolia. Other plants have found success in refinements of these patterns.

The flowering plants are composed of two great groups, the monocots and the dicots. The monocots have one seed leaf, or cotyledon, usually remaining in the seed and below ground upon germination. The succeeding leaves are usually narrow and have parallel venation. The flower parts are in threes and sixes. Monocots never developed a true cambium and do not have annual rings of xylem. As a result monocots are mainly herbaceous and small in comparison to the woody trees. The treelike palms are monocots that have patches of cells that do make vascular strands but are not woody with annual rings of xylem produced by cambium.

The dicots have two seed leaves (cotyledons) usually appearing above ground at germination. The successive leaves usually are broad and have netted veins. The flower parts are mainly in fours or fives. The dicots developed a true cambium and the woody flowering plants become shrubs and trees. Dicots also include herbaceous flowering plants which do have a cambium though it is not very active in producing xylem and phloem. As a result they are small and have a limited life span since their vegetative parts usually die back seasonally. Food for the next growing period can be stored only in their normally small root or underground stem systems. There are, however, many exceptions in the perennials and biennials.

The earliest flowering plant fossils were definitely present around 100 million years ago, perhaps even earlier, and they apparently developed rapidly into divergent forms. Both monocot and dicot plants seem to have had parallel existence from early times from similar ancestry. Herbaceous flowering plants probably appeared about 75 million years ago, apparently from woody, shrub-type ancestry. The seed containing the embryonic sporophyte made herbaceous plants possible and was a practical development in relation to the environment. They are able to produce seeds quickly in one or two seasons before unfavorable conditions for their limited hardiness come along.

In this book we have followed most authorities in treating the monocots first. In writing a linear presentation something has to come first. This does not imply that, because monocots never developed an active cambium and became treelike but remained small and mostly herbaceous, they are more primitive than dicots. It is perhaps only another parallel line of diversity. On the inside back cover of the book there is a chart which illustrates possible relationships and steps in development of flowering plant families. It is a modified version of one first presented by the botanist Charles E. Bessey in 1915. Fossil evidence as well as studies of plant structures, genetic and biochemical analysis, plus geographic distribution are the bases for this modified chart of evolutionary projection. There is still a great deal that is unknown and room for other projections, but most botanists are in agreement with it as a general view of family relationships. Usually development progresses from the simpler patterns at the bottom to the more complex higher on the chart. Only a representative number of the families found in this book are included.

Vegetative Parts of Vascular Plants

The vegetative parts of vascular plants are the roots, stems, and leaves of the sporophyte plant, originating in relatives of *Psilotum*, continuing through the ferns, seed ferns, the conifers, and flowering plants. The stems of ferns are mostly long horizontal underground rhizomes. Their internal anatomy is more primitive and quite diverse in pattern from those of the seed plants. The cambium is not well developed and there is not much woody xylem or other supporting tissue. The extinct seed ferns had erect stems and cambial activity producing more xylem tissue.

The embryo sporophyte in the seed of conifers closely resembles that of the flowering plants. This embryo sporophyte in flowering plants is essentially a central axis with the upper stem-producing tip, the epicotyl, above the attachment of one or two seed leaves or cotyledons and the root-producing tip, the hypocotyl, below the attachment of the cotyledons. It is from this axis that the adult sporophyte develops. The tips undergo constant cell division and differentiation producing the anatomical parts of stems and roots. Along the sides of the stem axis patches of cell-dividing tissue become lateral branches with cell-dividing tips, and the process is repeated. From these tips the arrangement of the internal tissue pattern is also determined, fixed to a given species pattern, whether they will be herbaceous annuals or biennials, or woody vines, shrubs or trees.

If the plant is to be a long-lived perennial (such as a tree), another cell-dividing cylinder of tissue similar to the cambium is developed out beyond the phloem. It is a cork cambium which produces layers of waterproof corky material in the bark which protects the living cells, such as phloem, from drying out and dying, which would be fatal to the tree.

Stems. The primary function of stems is to serve as a transport passage for water and minerals from the roots to the leaves and for food materials, mainly sugars, from the leaves to the living cells of stems and roots. If there is more food material than is needed for growth and activity of these organs the excess is stored in the stems, mostly in the form of carbohydrates or fats. It may be stored for a long period of time or only until needed in flowering or seed production. Stems also serve in the transport of chemical coordinators, the hormones of different kinds. Some of these are produced in the leaves and/or stem tips and carried to other tissues where, among other things, they help control the time of flowering, the stimulation of roots on cuttings, and the direction of growth and turning, bending or twining of stems, leaves, and roots. The terminal buds produce a hormone inhibiting the lateral buds from elongating unless the terminal bud is cut off or removed.

Stems are an additional means of propagating the plants beyond the production of seeds and have been modified in many ways, becoming more important than production of seeds in many plants. Above ground, horizontal or arching stems, called **stolons**, sprout new plants beyond the original one. Underground, stems may become modified in several ways for vegetative propagation, the most common forms being rhizomes, tubers, bulbs, and corms. Horizontal underground thickened and elongated stems are **rhizomes** which sprout roots and upright leaves at the nodes, as in ferns, grasses, and iris. **Tubers,** like the Irish potato, are short swollen stems stored with food material for use at the next growing season. Each eye of the potato is at a node of the stem from which sprouts out a new potato stalk. **Bulbs** are short upright, usually underground, stems which are really terminal buds. They have stored food in fleshy leaves, as in onion or hyacinth. The stem tips simply elongate into a new plant the next growing season. A **corm** has a structure similar to a bulb except that the short stem axis becomes fleshy with stored food instead of thin and papery leaves, as in crocus. In addition to these specialized adaptations, roots may appear near the end of a broken or cut stem and are called **adventitious roots.** Injury causes a flow of root promoting hormone to the cut or injured tissue where it stimulates root formation. This is hastened or even initiated by man when he treats stem cuttings with rooting compound, a commercial substitute for the naturally produced root promoting hormone.

Vegetative propagation through all of the above methods assures that the resulting plants will be of the same genetic composition as the parent plant. This is so since all of the parts involved contain the genes brought together at fertilization. The gene composition will not change until seeds

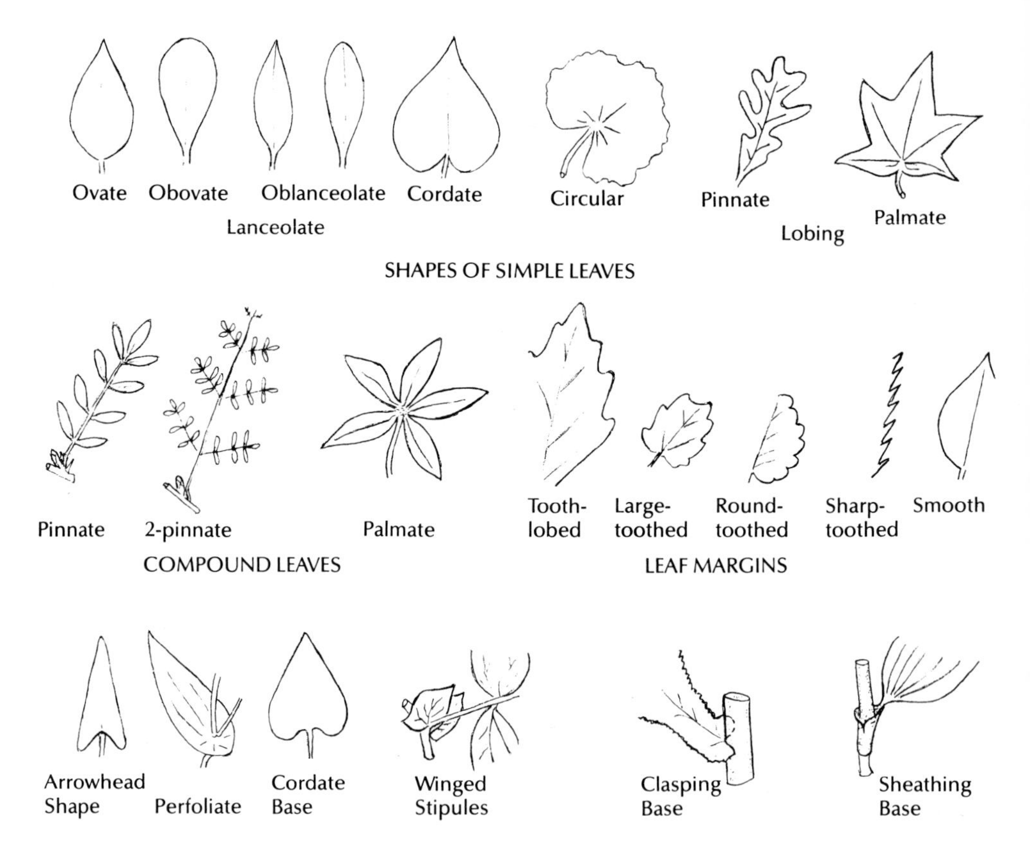

Fig. 2. Leaf Patterns. See glossary for terms not evident here.

Fig. 3. Flower Parts as Labeled. **br,** involucral bracts; **cc,** calyx cup; **cot,** corolla tube; **ct,** calyx tube; **d,** druplets; **g,** glumes or chaff, **k,** keel; **n,** nutlets; **o,** ovary; **pa,** pappus; **pe,** petal; **pi,** pistil; **r,** receptacle; **s,** stamen, **se,** sepal; **ss,** sterile stamen; **st,** stigma; **sta,** standard; **sty,** style; **ua,** united anthers; **us,** united stamens; **w,** wing.

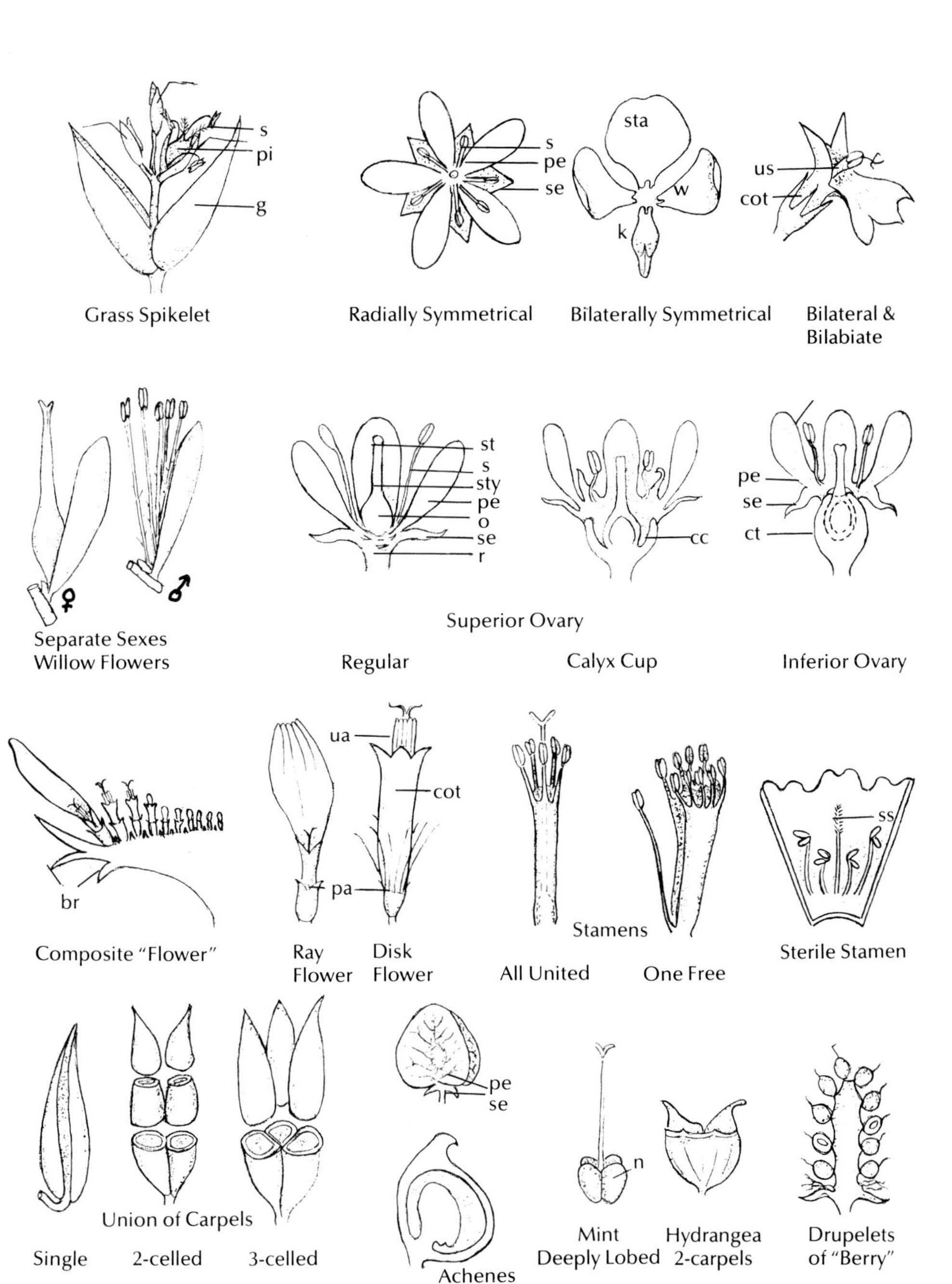
s
pi
g
Grass Spikelet
s
pe
se
Radially Symmetrical
sta
w
k
Bilaterally Symmetrical
us
cot
Bilateral &
Bilabiate
Separate Sexes
Willow Flowers
st
s
sty
pe
o
se
r
Superior Ovary
Regular
cc
Calyx Cup
pe
se
ct
Inferior Ovary
br
Composite "Flower"
ua
cot
pa
Ray
Flower
Disk
Flower
Stamens
All United
One Free
ss
Sterile Stamen
Union of Carpels
Single
2-celled
3-celled
pe
se
Achenes
n
Mint
Deeply Lobed
Hydrangea
2-carpels
Drupelets
of "Berry"

are again produced in sexual reproduction. One cannot plant seeds from a seedless orange but he can propagate the plant vegetatively by cuttings or stem grafting. So, although the primary function of stems is to produce and maintain a lifeline between leaves and roots, stems are also very important in vegetative propagation of plants.

Roots. The primary functions of roots are to absorb water and minerals from the soil and to anchor the plant in position. Root systems vary in form based upon their gross development. When the seed sprouts, the hypocotyl of the sporophyte axis becomes a primary root from which secondary roots may grow much as limbs on a tree, even forming annual rings in woody plants. In some plants the ends of young roots have numerous single microscopic epidermal cell extensions called root hairs. In these plants they are the main absorptive units by which water and minerals are obtained. In some plants the primary root does not branch extensively, but becomes a **tap-root** and serves as a reservoir for food storage as in beets, carrots, and turnips. These food plants are usually biennials which store food for the second seasons' production of flowers and seeds. The perennial sweet potato is another plant which stores food in thickened horizontal roots. The wild potato vine *Ipomoea pandurata*, pictured in the colored plates, produces a deep enormous edible root that may weigh from 5-20 pounds (2.27 kg-9.08 kg at 454 g/lb. and 1000 g/kg.

Roots, as well as stems, may serve as a means of vegetative propagation. The roots of some plants sprout stems which in turn produce new roots and thus a new plant. Some examples include willows and black locust trees whose roots sprout many stems resulting in the formation of dense thickets. Plants obtained from roots as from stems retain the heredity of the original plants.

Leaves. The primary function of leaves is to make food for the plant. This activity starts in the leaf blades where the green pigment chlorophyll is contained in microscopic chloroplasts within leaf cells. The upper of two layers between the two surface epidermal layers is compact and contains most of the chloroplasts where they are exposed to light. The lower layer is spongy and has air spaces connected by pores or stomates in the lower epidermis to the outside air. The veins in leaves are an extension of the transport system of the stems and deliver water and minerals to the cells. Water is used in the manufacture of food through photosynthesis after which the food and other products are carried back through the veins to living cells in stems and roots.

Photosynthesis is the name given to a two-fold process of food production in plants. Chlorophyll has the power to trap energy from light and convert it to energy used in plants in two ways. First the energy splits water molecules into hydrogen and oxygen. The oxygen is let free while more energy is used in the second process of tying the hydrogen to carbon dioxide in the leaf, thus making simple sugar such as glucose. In this way some of the energy from light has been converted to stored energy (in the form of sugar) in the cells. Further cell activity rearranges the carbon, hydrogen, and oxygen ratios, producing other carbohydrates like starches and cellulose, fats and oils. Elements such as nitrogen are brought to the leaf and combine with the sugars to produce the complex proteins which include living cell matter, the protoplasm. A visible example of the use of minerals in plants is the change of leaf color when a nitrate fertilizer is applied to the soil. Chlorophyll is a complex compound and the presence of a plentiful supply of nitrogen is used in the production of a plentiful supply of chlorophyll, making the leaf a dark green. These are the materials from which tissues, organs, and cells are produced in plant growth and development. There is no method other than photosynthesis by which inorganic materials are converted into foods animals can use; without plants there can be no animal life. It is also thought that nearly all of the oxygen in our atmosphere, about 20% of the air, has come from plants when oxygen is freed by the splitting of hydrogen from the water molecule.

In addition to their function as producers of food, leaves have been modified in some plants to other functions. Some leaves have been adapted into flower parts, or as food storage organs, as in the onion, or in some cases for vegetative propagation. Some leaves and leaflets may function as tendrils or spines. There is little particular functional significance attached to the many shapes and patterns of leaves, whether they are simple or compound, have teeth or not, whether they are alternate, opposite or whorled. These patterns will not be discussed here but may be found in the glossary and accompanying sketches. These features, though, are important in the identification of plants. These patterns and their various combinations are carried by the genes in the plant and remain relatively stable in each succeeding generation of the same species. These in combination with other plant characteristics are clues to species, genera, and family relationships.

Patterns of Flower Variations

Flowering plants are relatively recent plant forms but over the past ten million years they have developed many variations of the basic theme. There is really no typical flower; there are only basic patterns of many diverse flowers and even these patterns overlap and intergrade. Flower parts and their arrangements are of greater interpretive significance however, than are the vegetative parts since flower patterns vary less within families. This is why in plant identification the family relationships are based largely upon reproductive parts. Before attempting plant identification it is helpful to understand how flowers are constructed and the sequence of their modification.

Flowers are usually borne singly or in clusters at the tips of branches, in the axils of leaves that have become reduced in size and are called bracts. Sometimes flowers are axillary along the main stem. The bracts may vary in size and color from the normal (small and green) to red in poinsettia or white as in the dogwood with the size greatly increased.

A flower bud may be thought of as a shortened stem axis bearing specially modified leaves. The cell-dividing tip of the stem ceases to elongate and instead initiates four whorls of leaf-developing patches of cells. The lower or outer whorl becomes sepals, the next petals, then stamens, and finally pistils or carpels. The patterns these flower parts develop in shape, position, number of parts and degree of union is programmed in the heredity of each plant. Each of the floral parts is discussed below relating to variations and patterns through the ages (see Fig. 3).

Sepals. The sepals are the outermost whorl of flower parts which collectively are the calyx. The sepals are usually green but often are colored and petallike, as in the tulip or buttercup. Sepals are sterile and their main function seems to be as a protective layer around the fertile inner parts. The most primitive pattern of arrangement is a spiral of many separate leaflike bracts coming off the stem tip or receptacle. Later, fewer parts are arranged in whorls. Succeeding development patterns progressively find sepals becoming united, first only at their base, and then farther up forming a cuplike calyx, and finally becoming tubelike with only the tips of the sepals free. The tubelike calyx usually surrounds and becomes attached to the ovary of the pistil. This is the origin of the inferior ovary and the petals and stamens arise separately from the top of the calyx tube. Before the development of the fused sepals the ovary was free and above the attachment of sepals, petals, and stamens, a condition making a superior ovary (see Fig. 3, Row 2).

The number of sepals is usually constant in threes in the monocots and in fours and fives in the dicots. Sepals are usually radially symmetrical if the petals are, and somewhat bilateral if the petals are bilateral.

Petals. The second whorl of floral parts is the corolla with its bright or soft colors and its myriad shapes which make it the showy part of the flower. The petals of the corolla are sterile, in that they are not directly reproductive in function; however, they seem to play an accessory part in aiding the process of fertilization.

Petals, like sepals, follow the line of development from many separate petals arranged in a close spiral to a few petals with their edges joined together forming a tube with only tips free. In most patterns there are various modifications as, for an example, that shown in the water-lilies, when some of the many petals changed in shape and intergraded with stamens. As patterns modified, the number of petals decreased in more modern plants and the spiral arrangement was modified into whorls of petals.

Symmetry of petals and corollas may be either radial or bilateral, with radial being considered more primitive. In the variation of patterns from primitive to the more recent, some patterns in different genera were later than others. As an example, bilateral symmetry and united petals are both later developments, but often a flower will have only one advanced feature, as in violets which have bilateral symmetry but still have separate instead of united petals. Another variation appears in the legumes with bilateral symmetry and two lower petals fused into a keel while the other petals are separate. In another line of pattern development in symmetry there are many corollas that are radially symmetrical with the later feature of united petals, as seen in the phlox and the morning-glory. There are many such examples and it appears to indicate that petals (and other flower parts) have been modified independently of each other. When a flower has a greater number of features that are considered primitive it is placed lower than one that may have fewer such features (see Fig. 3, Row 1).

Corolla parts in monocots are in threes and in most dicots are usually in fours and fives, though sometimes the normal pattern is not followed and there are only two petals or even none. Some flowers have no sepals or petals, but if only one is absent, it is usually the petals.

Petals seem to serve as an accessory to fertilization in several ways, especially for plants seemingly dependent on insects for cross-pollination. On the upper surfaces at the base of the petals there are often sugar-secreting nectar cells, hairs or glands that attract insects. While getting the nectar the insects brush pollen on/off their bodies and carry it from flower to flower. The shape of the corolla may also make it necessary for an insect to go deep within to reach the nectar at the base of the petals, thus increasing the possibility that pollen will be dislodged. Color of the petals may also play a part in attracting insects.

Stamens. The third whorl of modified leaves are the stamens, each composed of a filament or stalk tipped by the anther. The stamen is fertile in the sense that it produces spores which contribute half the chromosomes that will make up the sporophyte plant after fertilization. The spores are developed in the anther by the special cell division that separates the double sets of chromosomes into single sets. These spores become the pollen grains seen when the anther splits open and releases them. Pollen grains are usually yellow though some are other colors, such as red or brown.

Stamens, like sepals and petals, were produced in great numbers on each flower in primitive plants and such plants living today include, among others, the magnolias and buttercups. In later developments the numbers became reduced, sometimes to only two. Some plants, such as the *Penstemon,* will produce five stamens but one will have no anther and be sterile. Other species may have only two fertile stamens with the rest sterile, having no anthers, and often only rudimentary filaments. Some of these developments may have paralleled increased abundance of insects which sought nectar and served as vehicles in cross-pollination by carrying pollen on their bodies from flower to flower. Species of plants whose flowers are wind pollinated, such as willows, oaks, and grasses, produce an abundance of pollen but also produce an abundance of male flowers rather than many stamens on one flower (see Fig. 3, Row 2).

The union of stamens occurs in several patterns, one of which is the joining with petals, probably as they arise from patches of petal-stamen initial cells in the bud. Other patterns involve stamens being joined together by their filaments, beginning at the base of the filament in a narrow band or ring. Other filaments fuse all the way up forming a staminal column, as in mallows. Both filaments and anthers are fused in the lobelia. Another variation occurs in the composites with only the anthers united. The Legume Family flower parts seem to exhibit some variation from most patterns in every case. In this one family the stamens of some species may all be separate, in other species all the anthers are united by their filaments, or in many species, nine stamens are united by their filaments and one is separate.

Pistils. The pistils are leaves modified to produce spores in the ovules of the ovary, by the same cell-dividing method as in anthers, separating the double set of chromosomes into a single set. Each spore then produces the female gametophyte, which in turn produces an egg to be fertilized, after which each ovule becomes a seed (see Fig 1, Row 4).

The pistil originated from a spore-bearing leaf folding lengthwise and making a pod or structure surrounding the ovule or ovules. The tip of this leaf becomes glandular, secreting a sugary material in which pollen grains may sprout tubes after pollination. This specialized leaf tip is the stigma.

A simple pistil (carpel) represents a single leaf not united with another. When two or more leaves on a single receptacle form pistils they may join together to make a compound pistil. Compound pistils usually produce a cavity from each pistil; if there are two pistils (carpels) they form a two-cavity or two-celled ovary. Should the pistils not join completely by their tips, the lobes of the stigma indicate how many pistils were joined, though in some cases an ovary may have two or more cavities with no stigma lobes. In other cases pistils may simply join by the edges of each leaf not folding inward all the way to the center, leaving a single cavity or cell of the ovary. In this case the rows of attachment of ovules to the ovary wall indicate how many carpels or pistils produced the compound ovary. Each cavity may have one to many ovules or seeds. Many separate pistils on a single receptacle of a single flower indicate the primitive pattern (see Fig. 3, Row 4).

The kinds of fruits produced by the ovary are important in genus and species determination, but are less so for family indication. In the Buttercup Family the buttercups have fruits that are achenes; but other members of the family may produce follicles as in the columbines, or even a berry as in doll's-eyes.

The superior ovary is considered the earlier development pattern before the stem-calyx tube union surrounded and embedded most of the ovary. This latter condition results in an inferior ovary. In this case the sepals, petals, and stamens appear to be attached above the ovary as in the more complex, perhaps later, families such as the iris and orchids of the monocots and the evening primroses, bellflowers, and composites of the dicots (see inside back cover for chart of relationship patterns).

Flowers with both stamens and pistils are said to be perfect. Those with stamens missing are called pistillate or female flowers. Those with pistils missing are called staminate or male flowers. Unisexual wind-pollinated flowers, as in the willows and oaks, are thought to represent a primitive condition, very likely long preceding insect-pollinated adaptations of flowers. Their exact position relative to a time frame is unknown. These flowers have no sepals or petals, only a scale or two, which is also considered a primitive condition. There is the possibility that some more recent unisexual forms could have appeared due to a loss of stamens or pistils from formerly perfect flowers.

Plant Names

In 1753 the Swedish naturalist Carl von Linné (Carolus Linnaeus) published the important work *Species Plantarum* in which he set forth an orderly system of classifying plants. The importance of his work can scarcely be overrated and it has been said "he found biology a chaos; he left it a cosmos." Linné classified each plant by giving it a latinized two-part name composed of a "genus" (noun) and a "species" (commonly an adjective). Related plants were placed in the same genus and each plant in that genus had a particular species name. By definition members of a species have common distinctive characteristics, they commonly interbreed and reproduce fertile offspring. In turn, related genera make up plant families. From the work begun by Linné international rules of nomenclature have been established and only one scientific name is officially recognized the world over. This does not mean that these names have been unchanged if further studies warranted it, but when changed, international rules are followed and the name officially recognized.

The text describing the illustrated plants lists the family name, the scientific name and one or more common names for each plant. Note that following the scientific name there is an initial or abbreviation(s). It represents the name of the botanist(s) who first described the plant and named it. If one initial or abbreviation is in parentheses followed by another name it indicates that further study resulted in the plant name being changed by the last botanist listed. As knowledge increases some change is inevitable, but in general, scientific names are relatively stable and the orderly grouping of species in related genera helps us learn recognizable characteristics for plant identification. It is well worth the effort to learn the scientific name. Common names vary greatly from one locality to another and often one name is used for several different plants which can be very confusing. Despite these obvious disadvantages, common names are often quite descriptive of the plant and of its historic use in earlier years, as well as being the only name by which the uninitiated will recognize a plant you are describing. Thus a common name is useful as long as these limiting factors are recognized.

SUGGESTIONS FOR COLLECTING AND IDENTIFYING PLANTS

One should be prepared to handle properly the plants he wishes to collect and identify. Take along opaque plastic bags which are ideal for keeping plants fresh. Add a little water along with the plants to keep them from drying out, and keep as cool as practical. Plants left in the bag in a refrigerator or cool place will keep for several days, but try to work on them as soon as possible since fresh plants are best to assure accurate identification.

Be judicious and conservative when collecting plants; if they seem to be scarce do not pick whole plants, take only a small representative branch. Observe the whole plant before collecting any of it and make note of its size, habit of growth, i.e., bushiness, erectness, etc., and especially of leaf arrangements on the stem, since once they are removed it is impossible to tell whether they are alternate, opposite, or whorled. Be sure to get a few buds, full flowers and some fruiting stages where possible. Make your collections away from roadsides and trails; save plants there for others to enjoy. Be as unobtrusive as possible or your activity might be considered needless plundering.

Before starting to use the plant key, first examine your specimen to get as much information as possible while it is still fresh from your collecting bag. Note the shapes and arrangements of leaves, their margins and surfaces; check the flower to see if it is complete with sepals, petals, stamens, and pistil; count the numbers of the different flower parts and note whether or not they are united to each other as stamens or petals often are, or whether some stamens are sterile having no anthers; whether the ovary is compound or simple, superior or inferior. It may help to write down your findings so that when you start using the key you will have the information you need. When you have keyed a few plants you will learn which parts need the most attention.

There are four keys provided: one for spore-bearing plants, mainly those ferns in the book; one for monocots, one for dicots, and one for the composites, the ASTERACEAE. The key for spore-bearing plants is not complicated and leads directly to the species of ferns included here. The other keys are more complicated because there is a greater number and variety of plants to be considered. The keys are based upon making choices from two or more observable features of the plant. These options are in series denoted by similar numbers and letters with the same marginal indentation. At the ends of lines may be the notation "(cf. A-D)," which means for you to compare the options of lines A-D and to pick the most appropriate one to fit the plant in question. In the monocot and dicot keys there are additional sets of choices where numbers and letters are not used, only the same indentations; these are close together and should not be confusing. Upon reaching the end for your plant, you will find either its generic name, or the family to which it belongs, or one or two others that are related. You should compare detailed descriptions and pictures for resemblance to your plant for an accurate species identification.

The key to the composites is a simplified one and will take the user only to related groups of genera. In order to identify composites it is necessary to examine the pappus atop the achene, which is not difficult with the use of a 6-10 power hand lens or magnifier. The dandelion "parachute" resembles that shown for *Erechtites* which is made up of fine capillary bristles. The pappus on other species may be feathery bristles, awn-like scales or missing. It is usually present in one or two rings or series on the top of the achenelike fruit. When you get as far as you can go in this key you will find one or more genera listed. Turn to the pages noted and compare descriptions and pictures to determine which is the plant you have. There are very many composites in the area of coverage by this book, but it is hoped that the 65 species that have been described include those that will be most often encountered.

A glossary of terms is included. If you are in doubt about a term, check the glossary so you will not get lost in the key options. You might also refer to the sketches in figure 3.

Metric Measurement. The metric system of measurement is used in the plant descriptions, as it is much easier to use millimeters than fractions of inches for measuring small parts of plants. In addition, we are near conversion to the universal metric system and will be using it exclusively in the future. The metric system progresses in multiples of ten: there are 10 millimeters (mm) in a centimeter, 10 centimeters (cm) in a decimeter, 10 decimeters (dm) in a meter (m). Decimeters are not used in this book. We may use mm and cm either as 0.7-1.2 cm or as 7-12 mm in stating a variable range of the size of a part. For comparison:

1 inch = 2.5 cm	1 yard = 91.5 cm (+/−90 cm)
1 foot = 30.5 cm (+/−30 cm	1 meter = 100 cm (39.3 inches)

(approximate estimates in parentheses)

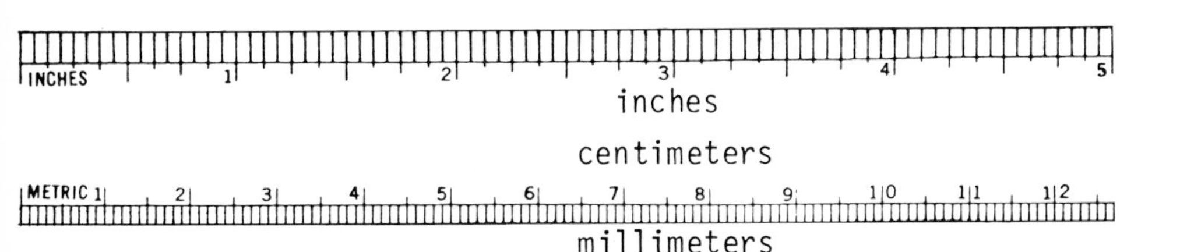

Glossary

Achene. A hard, dry, 1-seeded nonsplitting fruit from a single pistil.
Acuminate. Tapering to a gradual point at the end.
Aggregate fruit. A cluster of small fruits from many separate pistils of a single flower, as the blackberry is a cluster of tiny drupes.
Alternate. Located singly at nodes along a stem.
Angiosperms. Flower bearing seed plants.
Annual. Producing flowers and seeds in one year or growing season, then dying.
Anther. The pollen producing portion at the tip of the stamen.
Appressed. Closely pressed against, as stem or leaf hairs to the surface.
Ascending. Rising upward indirectly or slanting.
Awn. A slender bristle usually at the tip of a part.
Axil. Angle between two structures, as between a leaf and the stem.
Axillary. Located in the axil or angle, as a bud between leaf and stem.

Barbed. With minute, backward projecting points as on some pappus bristles.
Beaked. Having a firm elongate slender tip; i.e., on a pod, capsule, or achene.
Beard. A cluster of hairs or bristlelike structures.
Berry. A fruit in which the ovary wall is fleshy enclosing many seeds, as a tomato.
Bi-. Indicating two, double, or twice.
Biennial. Requiring two seasons to produce flowers and seeds, then dying.
Bilabiate. Two-lipped, as in the corolla of mints.
Bilateral. Having a mirror image on opposite sides.
Bipinnate. Twice-compound, as leaflets of a once-divided leaf being again divided.
Blade. The flat expanded portion of a leaf.
Bract. A small leaflike structure usually below a flower or cluster of flowers.
Bristle. A long, usually stiff, hair.
Bud. An unelongated stem; an unopened flower.
Bulb. An underground, short, vertical stem having fleshy leaves, as an onion.

Calyx. A collective term for sepals, the outer parts of most flowers.
Calyx cup. A cuplike structure formed by sepals uniting by their edges.
Calyx tube. A tubelike structure formed by sepals uniting by their edges.
Campanulate. Being bell-shaped, as a corolla or calyx.
Capillary. Slender and hairlike.
Capsule. A dry fruit from 2 or more carpels, each splitting open separately.

Carpel. A simple pistil or each segment of a compound pistil.
Catkin. A drooping spikelike cluster of flowers usually of one sex, as in willow.
Cauline. Located on the stem as opposed to basal.
Cell. A term denoting cavities in an ovary or fruit, as 3-celled in lily capsules.
Chaff. Papery or scalelike parts, as in grasses and composites.
Cilia. Short hairs usually marginal on leaf or flower parts.
Clasping. Partly or wholly surrounding; as a leaf base around a stem.
Claw. The narrow elongate base of a petal or sepal attaching it to the receptacle.
Cleft. Blades cut more than half way to the mid-rib.
Complete flower. Having 4 parts present: sepals, petals, stamens, and pistil.
Composite. A plant of the ASTERACEAE having a compact head of many separate flowers.
Compound. Made up of 2 or more similar parts of a whole, as leaflets of a blade or carpels of a pistil.
Cone. A cluster of seed- or pollen-bearing scales in a spiral arrangement.
Cordate. Heart-shaped, usually with notched base and pointed tip.
Corm. A short, vertical, underground solid stem enlarged in food storage.
Corolla. The second series of flower parts: all the petals, united or separate.
Corona. A crownlike appendage rising from petal bases or a tube, as in daffodil.
Crest. Ridge or elevation on a surface, as on a petal.
Crisped. Crinkled or twisted, as leaf or petal edges.
Crown. An inner appendage to a petal or to the throat of the corolla; also, base of clustered stems at ground level.

Deciduous. Shedding as opposed to persistent, as leaves in fall.
Decumbent. Reclining or lying on the ground with their tips ascending.
Dehiscent. Splitting open of some dry fruits to release seeds.
Deltoid. Triangular in shape.
Dicots. A plural abbreviation of dicotyledonous plants which have two seed leaves, and broad leaves, netted veins, and flower parts in fours and fives.
Dioecious. Having male and female flowers on separate plants.
Disk flower. The central tubular flowers in composite heads of ASTERACEAE.
Dissected. Deeply cut into fine lobes or divisions even to compound in some leaves.
Drupe. A stone fruit, as plum; the inner wall of the ovary being stony while the outer walls are fleshy.

Elliptic. A flattened circle (oblong) with the ends equally rounded.
Emergent. Growing in water but with stems and/or leaves rising above the surface.
Entire. A smooth margin without teeth.
Epiphyte. A plant growing upon another plant but not feeding upon it.
Erect. Often used for simple unbranched upright stems.
Exserted. Projecting beyond surrounding parts, as stamens beyond a corolla tube.

Family. A group of plants more similar to each other than to other plants; it may contain one or more genera.
Fascicle. A cluster or close bundle, as of leaves or pine needles.
Fertile. Producing reproductive cells.
Filament. The stalk supporting the anthers of stamens; any threadlike structure.
Follicle. A dry single-ovary fruit opening by a single slit, as in larkspur.
Frond. Refers specifically to fern leaves, which may be several times divided.
Fruit. The mature ovary of the pistil in which seeds develop.

Glabrous. Free of pubescence or hairs, smooth.
Glandular. Having secretory cells, such as nectar glands or gland-tipped hairs.
Globose. Spherical or nearly so.
Glume. The scaly bract at the base of a grass spikelet of 1-several flowers.
Gymnosperms. Plants bearing naked seeds in a cone, such as pine, fir, and juniper.

Head. A dense cluster of stalkless flowers; specifically as in the composites.
Herbaceous. Not shrubby or woody, more fleshy and dying back to ground seasonly.
Hirsute. With rough, coarse bristlelike hairs.
Hyphen. Denotes variability such as leaf shape, ovate-lanceolate; and in distance from, to and including (at least in part) as Florida-Texas.

Indehiscent. Not splitting open to release its contents, as in some fruits.
Indusium. A cover, shield, or flap over a spore cluster in ferns.
Inferior ovary. An ovary below petals and stamens, three-fourths or more surrounded by, and attached to, the calyx.
Imperfect flower. Having either stamens or pistil, but not both.
Inserted. Attached to or growing from another part, as stamens upon a corolla tube.
Internode. The portion of stem between two nodes.
Involucral bracts. Specifically the bracts surrounding the flower head in composites.

Involucre. A series or whorl of bracts at the base of a cluster or single flower.
Irregular flower. A flower with bilateral symmetry as opposed to one with radial symmetry.

Keel. The lower two united petals opposite the upper petal in pealike flowers.

Laciniate. Divided into narrow, nearly equal strips, as in the fringed orchid.
Lanceolate. Much longer than wide, broad at the base, and tapering to the tip.
Lateral. On or at the sides as opposed to terminal or basal.
Leaflet. Any one of the blade segments of a compound leaf.
Legume. Species of FABACEAE; the pod from a single pistil splitting in two places.
Linear. Long and very narrow with parallel sides, as in most grass leaves.
Lip. The upper or lower segment of a bilateral flower, as a snapdragon; also the apparent lower petal of some orchids.
Lobe. A mostly rounded portion of an irregular margin of leaf or petal, not more than one-fourth the depth of the part.

Margin. The edge of the blade of a leaf or petal.
Monocots. A plural abbreviation of monocotyledonous plants which have 1 seed leaf and have mostly narrow, parallel-veined leaves, with flower parts in threes.
Monoecious. Having separate female and male flowers on the same plant, as in corn.

Nodding. Bending downward; usually flowers whose stalks curve downward.
Node. The place on the stem from which leaves and lateral buds arise.
Nut. A dry, 1-seeded, nonsplitting fruit with a hard outer wall.
Nutlet. A small, hard, 1-seeded fruit, usually a segment of a deeply lobed 4-carpel ovary, as in the mints.

Ob-. A prefix signifying reversal of a shape, as oblanceolate which is tapered at the base instead of the tip.
Opposite. Located in pairs, as of leaves on two sides of a stem.
Ovary. The basal part of the pistil in which seeds develop.
Ovate. Egg-shaped in outline, the narrow end toward the tip of a leaf or petal.
Ovule. The structure in which the egg is fertilized and becomes the seed.

Palmate. Simple lobed leaves or divided compound leaves diverging like fingers from a hand are palmately lobed or palmately compound.

Pappus. A modification of sepals in the composites, as hairs, bristles or awns atop the achene fruits.
Pectinate. Toothed like a comb.
Pedicel. The stalk supporting a single flower, usually in a cluster.
Peduncle. The main stalk supporting a flower cluster or the stalk of a solitary flower.
Peltate. A leaf whose petiole is attached at or near the center lower surface of the blade, as in *Nelumbo* and *Hydrocotyle*.
Perennial. Continuing to live year after year.
Perfect flower. Having both stamens and pistil in each flower.
Perfoliate. Sessile leaf blades that clasp or surround the stem making the stem appear to pass through the leaf, as in boneset and bellwort.
Petiole. The stalk that usually attaches the leaf blade to the stem.
Pinnate. Compound, with leaflets scattered along two sides of main axis or rachis.
Pinnatifid. Deeply divided almost to mid-rib axis, appearing nearly compound.
Pistil. The female reproductive organ as a modified leaf with stigma, style and ovary.
Pistillate. Female flowers with pistil but with either no or sterile stamens.
Plumose. Featherlike; an axis with fine side parts; a pappus type in composites.
Pod. A dry splitting fruit; a single pistil opening by two slits, as in peas.
Polygamous. Having both perfect and separate sexed flowers on the same plant.
Pome. A fleshy accessory fruit, as an apple; the fleshy part is the stem around the inferior ovary, the core.
Prostrate. Lying flat on the ground, as many creeping stems.
Puberulent. Minutely pubescent with barely elongate hairs.
Pubescent. Covered with soft short hairs; often used as opposed to glabrous.
Punctate. With colored, translucent, or black dots, as in *Hypericum punctatum,* or pits on leaves and petals.

Raceme. An elongated flower cluster with stalked flowers along a main axis, the youngest at the top.
Rachis. The axis of a flower cluster or of a pinnately compound leaf.
Ray. The ribs of an umbel of flowers or the marginal flowers of head in composites.
Receptacle. The end of the stem to which the flower parts are attached.
Recurved. Gently or gradually curved downward or backward.
Reflexed. Abruptly or sharply bent downward or backward, as sepals of evening primrose.
Regular. Flowers with the members of each part alike in size and shape.
Rhizome. A horizontal underground stem rooting at the nodes and producing upright leaves, as in iris and many ferns.

Rootstock. A synonym for rhizome.
Rosette. Circular cluster of leaves on a short stem, as in dandelion or mullein.

Sagittate. Arrowhead shape, with basal lobes pointing backward.
Samara. Winged, nonsplitting fruits, as in elm, maple, and ash.
Scape. A leafless elongate nonbranching flower stem of a cluster or single flower.
Seed. A dormant embryo plant with stored food and a protective cover.
Sepal. The single unit of the calyx, the lower or outer whorl of flower parts.
Serrate. Having teeth pointing forward.
Sessile. Stalkless, as in leaves with no petiole or flowers with no pedicel.
Sheath. A cylindric structure around another, as the lower part of grass leaves.
Shrub. A woody perennial with several stems at the base and without a main stem.
Simple. Single; of one piece, as a stem with no branches or leaf with no leaflets.
Smooth. Glabrous or without hairs; sometimes a leaf margin without lobes or teeth.
Spadix. A fleshy stem axis in which flowers are embedded, as Jack-in-the-pulpit.
Spathe. A usually large bract enclosing a spadix or flower cluster, as calla lily.
Spatulate. Somewhat spoon-shaped, narrowed below, and widened at the tip.
Spike. An upright, nonbranching flower cluster of closely spaced stalkless flowers.
Spikelet. A small spike. In grasses, 1-several flowers above two empty scales.
Spore. Reproductive cell; indirectly, sperm and egg producing cells.
Spur. A tubular projection of the calyx or corolla, as in larkspur or columbine.
Stamen. The male reproductive organ composed of a stalk and pollen producing anther.
Staminate. Having stamens and no or rudimentary pistils. Male.
Standard. The upper large petal in the pealike legume flower.
Stellate. Star-shaped, as hairs on surfaces of *Solanum*.
Sterile. Producing no reproductive cells; or stamens without anthers.
Stigma. The tip of the pistil adapted to receive pollen for fertilization.
Stipule. A pair of structures at the base of a leaf or petiole. They can be leafy, minute, spines, or tendrils.
Style. The short to elongate structure between the stigma and ovary of a pistil.
Subtend. A structure just below another, as flowers subtended by bracts.
Superior ovary. An ovary above and not enclosed by the calyx tube.

Tendril. A coiling twining structure usually modified from leaves, as in vetches.
Terete. Circular in cross section.
Throat. The area of the corolla where the tube flares widely into lobes.
Toothed. Having marginal, variously pointed projections on leaves or petals.
Tri-. In composition, three or three times, as in pinnately compound leaves.
Trifoliolate. Having three leaflets, as a compound leaf in clover.
Tuber. A short horizontal underground stem for food storage, as in the potato.
Tuberous. Swollen or thickened.

Umbel. An umbrellalike cluster of flowers, as in the parsley family.
Unisexual. Flowers or plants of one sex only, staminate (male) or pistillate (female).
United. Growing together of similar parts, as petals into a corolla tube.

Vascular. The water conducting (xylem) and food conducting (phloem) tissues of plants.
Vein. The strands of vascular tissue as seen in leaves, usually in a network.
Villous. Having long, unmatted hairs.
Vine. A plant usually climbing by tendrils or twining stems.

Weed. A plant growing where it is not wanted, usually but not necessarily troublesome.
Whorl. Three or more leaves at a stem node, or several flowers encircling a stem.
Wing. A flat appendage on a seed or fruit, or down a stem, or lateral petal of legumes.
Winter annual. A plant bearing seeds in late winter-early spring from a previous seed crop.
Woolly. Having long matted hairs over the surface.

Part II. Identification Keys

Key to Spore-Bearing Vascular Plants

I. Very small floating plants with scalelike, overlapping leaves—p. 54 *Azolla caroliniana*

II. Plants terrestrial or epiphytic on other plants (cf. A-D):

- A. Stems hollow, jointed; leaves scalelike in a whorl at nodes, spores in terminal conelike structure—p. 46 *Equisetum hyemale*
- B. Leaf part stemlike, viny, with 5-7 palmately lobed leaves—p. 50 *Lygodium palmatum*
- C. Stems green, branching by twos; leaves minute scales, 3-lobed spore case at nodes—p. 46 *Psilotum nudum*
- D. Stems mostly underground rhizomes; leaves upright:
  - 1. Leaves not compound, long-tapered from a broad, heart-shaped base; sprouting new plants at leaf tips—p. 54 *Asplenium rhizophyllum*
  - 2. Leaves pinnately compound (1-, 2-, or 3-divided):
    - a. Large, coarse ferns, 90-100 cm tall (cf. b, c, d):
      - (1) Fertile fronds separate from sterile fronds—p. 48 *Osmunda cinnamomea*
      - (2) Fertile leaflets on same fronds as sterile leaflets:
        - (a) Fertile leaflets at middle of the fronds—p. 48 *Osmunda claytoniana*
        - (b) Fertile leaflets terminating the fronds—p. 48 *Osmunda regalis*
        - (c) Most leaflets spore-bearing, leaf margin rolled under, covering the spore cases—p. 50 *Pteridium aquilinum*
    - b. Medium, coarse ferns, 50-70 cm tall:
      - (1) Leaves once compound, evergreen; spore-bearing leaflets terminal on leaf with sterile leaflets—p. 52 *Polystichum acrostichoides*
      - (2) Leaf above not completely divided into leaflets as below; fertile fronds of beadlike leaflets separate from the sterile fronds—p. 52 *Onoclea sensibilis*
    - c. Medium, delicate ferns (30-45 cm tall):
      - (1) Red-brown leaf stalk forked into two circlets of flat horseshoe shaped fronds of leaflets—p. 50 *Adiantum pedatum*
      - (2) Upper of three or four segments of leaf spore-bearing with beadlike leaflets—p. 48 *Botrychium virginianum*
      - (3) Leaf outline triangular shape with base leaflet pair usually pointed backward—p. 52 *Thelypteris hexagonaptera*

(4) Fronds once-compound, narrow, leaf tapering at both ends; leaf stalk black; sterile fronds shorter—p. 54 *Asplenium platyneuron*

d. Smaller ferns (15-30 cm tall):

(1) Leaves once-compound, evergreen, leathery, leaflets blunt-tipped, gray-green below; often on trees and logs—p. 54 *Polypodium polypodioides*

(2) Leaves twice-thrice compound, variously lobed, leaflets wide-spaced below:

(a) Leaflet edges rolled under, covering spore cases—p. 50 *Cheilanthes lanosa*

(b) Spore cases scattered below, covered by a one-sided membranous cover—p. 52 *Cystopteris fragilis*

Key to Monocotyledonous Plants

Plants in this group usually have relatively narrow leaves with parallel veins and sheathing petioles. Flowers have parts in 3s or its multiple. Exceptions are broad leaves in some, though still with essentially parallel veins, and grasses and sedges with chaffy scales as sepals and petals (cf. *Cocculus, Asimina*).

I. Plants usually aquatic or in marshy places (cf. II):

A. Floating, minute leafless plants—p. 66 LEMNACEAE

B. Anchored or larger plants:

1. Leaves grasslike or straplike (cf. 2):

a. Flowers not in small spikes subtended by scales or glumes (cf. b):

(1) Minute flowers in large dense terminal spikes, leaves straplike—p. 58 TYPHACEAE

(2) Minute flowers in a small, disklike head; leaves grasslike—p. 66 *Eriocaulon*

(3) Small flowers in globular heads, pistillate heads more obvious—p. 58 SPARGANIACEAE

b. Flowers in small spikes subtended by chaffy scales or glumes:

(1) Stems round and hollow—p. 60 POACEAE

(2) Stems 3-sided and solid—p. 62 CYPERACEAE

(3) Stems round and solid (not represented herein) JUNCACEAE

2. Leaves broader, not grasslike:

a. Sepals and petals united below, 2-lipped, 6 parts, blue:

(1) Petioles inflated, free-floating—p. 70 *Eichornia*

(2) Petioles not inflated—p. 70 *Pontederia*
b. Sepals and petals none, or separate in 2 series or whorls:
(1) Flowers in a dense golden spike—p. 64 *Orontium*
(2) Flowers not as above, leaves basal, petals white:
(a) Flowers with both stamens and pistils, leaves ovate—p. 58 *Echinodorus*
(b) Flowers separate, male above and female below:
Head in whorls—p. 60 *Sagittaria*
Flowers missing, or rare, rosette of floating leaves—p. 66 *Pistia*

II. Plants usually terrestrial:
A. Plants epiphytic on trees or elsewhere—p. 68 BROMELIACEAE
B. Plants not epiphytic:
1. Plants grasslike, stems round, hollow—p. 60 POACEAE
2. Plants not grasslike:
a. Plants trees or vines—p. 64, 78 ARECACEAE, DIOSCOREACEAE
b. Plants herbaceous:
(1) Ovary superior:
(a) Flower cluster not in fleshy leafy bract—p. 70 LILIACEAE
(b) Flower cluster enclosed in fleshy leafy bract:
Flowers in a dense spike—p. 64 ARACEAE
Flowers not in a dense spike—p. 68 COMMELINACEAE
(2) Ovary inferior:
(a) Flowers radially symmetrical:
Stamens 6—p. 88 AMARYLLIDACEAE
Stamens 3—p. 82 IRIDACEAE
(b) Flowers bilaterally symmetrical—p. 86 ORCHIDACEAE

Key to Dicotyledonous Plants

Plants in this group usually have relatively broad leaves with a network of veins, with or without a stalklike petiole. Flower parts are usually in 4s or 5s or multiples thereof. Exceptions include missing parts, especially some petals and stamens, or sterile stamens, thus altering the basic numbers (cf. *Cocculus, Asimina*).

I. Petals not united or not present (cf. II):
A. Petals usually not present (cf. I-B):
1. Petals none, sepals none (cf. 2, 3):
a. Herbaceous marsh plant, flower spikes with drooping tips, heart-shaped leaves—p.90 *Saururus*

b. Trees separate sexed, flowers in drooping catkins, leaves simple—p. 90 SALICACEAE
c. Shrub-tree, simple evergreen aromatic leaves, orange beneath—p. 90 *Myrica*

2. Petals none, sepals present, catkins present, trees:
a. Separate male and female catkins, bark smooth or shreddy—p. 92 BETULACEAE
b. Only male flowers in catkins:
(1) Leaves simple, fruit in a bur or cup—p. 92 FAGACEAE
(2) Leaves pinnately compound, fruit in a husk—p. 92 JUGLANDACEAE

3. Petals usually none, sepals present, flowers not in catkins, not solitary but clustered (petals present in PORTULACACEAE, CARYOPHYLLACEAE):
a. Flowers usually of separate sexes, ovary superior and 1-celled (cf. 3b):
(1) Trees with alternate leaves, milky juice, 2 stamens—p. 96 MORACEAE
(2) Trees with alternate leaves, juice not milky, 4-8 stamens—p. 94 ULMACEAE
(3) Seashore herb with opposite, fleshy elongate leaves—p. 102 *Batis*
(4) Seashore shrubs, with opposite matted branches, minute leaves—p. 100 *Salicornia*
b. Flowers mostly with stamens and pistils:
(1). Inferior ovary, no petals, 12 stamens, capsule several-celled, herbs—p. 98 ARISTOLOCHIACEAE
(2) Superior ovary, often separate sexed flowers:
(a) Fruit a 3-sided, 1-seeded achene, leaf petioles sheathe the stem—p. 98 POLYGONACEAE
(b) Fruit not a 3-sided achene:
Fruit a 1-seeded papery bladder—p. 102 AMARANTHACEAE
Fruit a red or black berry—p. 102 PHYTOLACCACEAE
Fruit a capsule:
Capsule 2-several celled, leaves whorled—p. 102 *Mollugo*
Capsule 1-celled, petals present:
Sepals 2—p. 104 PORTULACACEAE
Sepals 4 or 5—p. 104 CARYOPHYLLACEAE

B. Petals present, sepals present, neither united:
1. Ovary superior, free from sepals (except *Crataegus, Amelanchier)* (cf. I-B2):
a. Pistils per flower few to many, not united; stamens separate and more numerous than the separate sepals (cf. b, c, d):
(1) Aquatic herbs (cf. (2)):
(a) Pistils 3 or more and separate:

Pistils not embedded in receptacle, leaves mostly dissected—p. 108 CABOMBACEAE
Pistils embedded in spreading receptacle, leaves circular, depressed at center—p. 108 NELUMBONACEAE
(b) Pistils united into a compound ovary, stigma a disk, leaves notched at base—p. 106 NYMPHAEACEAE
(2) Mostly terrestrial herbs (cf. LAURACEAE):
(a) Stamens many, petals usually present, sepals separate (cf. (2)-(b)):
Opposite leaf shrubs with a hollow receptacle enclosing pistils—p. 118 CALYCANTHACEAE
Alternate leaf plants (except *Clematis)*, receptacle not hollow (cf. *Cocculus* below):
Flowers perfect (cf. *Clematis, Thalictrum):*
Fruits conelike, trees—p. 114 MAGNOLIACEAE
Fruits not conelike:
Sepals 3, petals 6, trees—p. 116 ANNONACEAE
Sepals 3-15, variable number of petals when present, herbs—p. 108 RANUNCULACEAE
Fruits a berry, 1 pistil, leaves umbrellalike—p. 114 *Podophyllum*
Fruits a capsule with lidlike opening, leaf blades of 2 winglike parts—p. 114 *Jeffersonia*
Flowers separate sexed, 6 sepals and 6 petals, vines—p. 114 *Cocculus*
(b) Stamens 9 or 12 in series of 3s, no petals, sepals 4-6, trees or shrubs—p. 118 LAURACEAE
b. Pistils 2 or more united into a compound ovary as seen in cross-section, or number of stigma lobes, sepals separate (cf. c):
(1) Not insectivorous plants:
(a) Sepals mostly only 2:
Flowers radial, stamens 8-many—p. 118 PAPAVERACEAE
Flowers bilateral, stamens 6—p. 120 FUMARIACEAE
(b) Sepals 4; petals 4; stamens 6, usually 4 long, 2 short—p. 120 BRASSICACEAE
(2) Insectivorous plants, flowers long stalked:
(a) Leaves hollow, ovary 3-5 celled, flowers nodding—p. 124 SARRACENIACEAE
(b) Leaf blades flat rosette (*Pinguicula* has united petals, not keyed here, cf. LENTIBULARIACEAE)
c. Pistils single or several separate or united, sepals united into a cup or tube where stamens arise (cf. d):
(1) Herbaceous plants (cf. (2), (3)):
(a) Pistils 4 or 5, as many as sepals and separate or united below, stamens 8-10—p. 126 CRASSULACEAE
(b) Pistils mostly 2, united below, stamens 5 or 10—p. 126 SAXIFRAGACEAE

(c) Pistils many, stamens many—p. 130 ROSACEAE
(d) Pistils single, flowers bilateral, stamens mostly 10, fruit a pod—p. 134 FABACEAE
(2) Shrubs:
(a) Leaves opposite, outer flowers of cluster often sterile and showy—p. 126 *Hydrangea*
(b) Leaves alternate, small flowers in long, narrow terminal clusters, 2 pistils united, 2 stigmas—p. 126 *Itea*
(3) Trees or shrubs:
(a) Leaves alternate, palmately lobed, flowers of separate sexes, trees (cf. (b), (c)):
Bark furrowed, gray; male catkins, female flowers in spherical head, woody at maturity—p. 128 *Liquidambar*
Bark smooth, white; male and female flowers in globose heads, not woody—p. 130 *Platanus*
(b) Flowers radial, perfect with stamens and pistils:
Ovary inferior, pistils united, sepals united into calyx tube, fruit a pome as an apple, leaves simple—p. 132, 134 *Crataegus, Amelanchier*
Ovary superior, compound pistil in calyx cup, 15-20 or more stamens present:
Fruit fleshy, leaves simple—p. 134 *Prunus*
Fruit a pod, leaves 2-compound—p. 134 *Schrankia, Albizzia*
(c) Flowers bilateral, perfect:
Tree with heart-shaped leaves—p. 136 *Cercis*
Tree with pinnately compound leaves—p. 142 *Robinia*
Shrub with pinnately compound leaves, spikes of tiny purple flowers—p. 140 *Amorpha*
d. Pistils united into a compound ovary, sepals usually separate:
(1) Stamens few, rarely over twice the number of sepals (cf. (2)):
(a) Herbaceous plants (cf. (b)):
Stamen filaments separate or partially united at their bases:
Leaves not pinnately compound, fruit a long beaked capsule—p. 146 GERANIACEAE, OXALIDACEAE
Leaves pinnately compound, fruit of 5 2-spined nutlets—p. 148 ZYGOPHYLLACEAE
Stamen filaments all separate:
Flowers bilateral:
Sepals 3, 1 petaloid and spurred; 5 petals; 5 stamens—p. 156 BALSAMINACEAE
Sepals 5, petals, 5, stamens 5—p. 162 VIOLACEAE
Sepals 5, petals 3, flowers in spike—p. 148 POLYGALACEAE
Flowers radial, often without petals, mostly with milky

juice—p. 150 EUPHORBIACEAE
Palmate-lobed leaves, stinging hairs—p. 150 *Cnidoscolus*
Leaves not palmate-lobed, fruit on a stalk from the calyx cup—p. 150 *Euphorbia*
(b) Trees, shrubs or vines:
Leaves simple, opposite:
Shrub with purple capsule, red seeds—p. 154 *Euonymous*
Tree with paired winged fruits—p. 156 *Acer*
Leaves simple, alternate:
Tree with black or red berries—p. 158, 154 *Rhamnus, Ilex*
Shrub with a 3-lobed drupe—p. 158 *Ceanothus*
Leaves, pinnately compound:
Vine, inflated capsule with 3 black seeds with heart-shaped scar—p. 156 *Cardiospermum*
Vine, fruit a black berry—p. 158 *Ampelopsis*
Vine or shrub, fruit a drupe—p. 152 *Rhus*
Leaves palmately compound, tree or shrub—p. 156 *Aesculus*
(2) Stamens usually very numerous (5 in *Passiflora*):
(a) Trees, shrubs or vines (cf. (b)):
Trees with broad, evergreen leaves, white flowers 5-7 cm broad—p. 160 *Gordonia*
Shrubs:
Flowers 8-10 cm broad, many stamens united into a tube, alternate leaves—p. 158 *Hibiscus*
Flowers smaller, stamens nearly separate, leaves opposite—p. 160 HYPERICACEAE
Vines with alternate, 3-lobed simple leaves, crown on petals—p. 164 *Passiflora*
(b) Herbs with opposite leaves with tiny black dots, flowers radial—p. 160 *Hypericum*
2. Ovary inferior, enclosed partly or wholly by a calyx cup or tube with 4 or 5 lobes, and has 4 or 5 separate petals:
a. Aquatic plants with leaves in whorls:
(1) Herbaceous, leaves finely pinnate—p. 168 *Myriophyllum*
(2) Shrub with lanceolate leaves—p. 164 *Decodon*
b. Terrestrial plants:
(1) Herbs:
(a) Floral parts usually in 4s:
Calyx tube free of ovary, leaves opposite—p. 166 *Rhexia*
Calyx tube attached to ovary, leaves alternate—p. 166 ONAGRACEAE
(b) Floral parts usually in 5s, many small flowers in flat-topped

clusters—p. 170 APIACEAE
(2) Trees or shrubs:
(a) Trees:
Leaves alternate, simple—p. 130, 172 ROSACEAE, *Nyssa*
Leaves opposite, simple—p. 174 *Cornus*
(b) Shrub with stout spines on stems:
3-pinnately compound leaves—p. 168 *Aralia*
1-pinnately compound leaves—p. 130 ROSACEAE

II. Petals when present united at least below (except in *Monotropa*, scarcely so in *Chionanthus*):
A. Overay superior (except inferior in *Vaccinium*), (cf. B):
1. Stamens separate, not attached to the corolla tube, alternate with corolla lobes, or twice as many (cf. 2, 3):
a. Petals 5 or 6, not united, flowers solitary, stamens 10, not a green plant—p. 174 *Monotropa*
b. Petals united, 5 or 10-lobed; ovary superior (except in Vaccinium), green trees or shrubs—p. 174 ERICACEAE
2. Stamens attached to the corolla tube, equal or more than the number of corolla lobes:
a. Herbs with 5 stamens, fruit a capsule—p. 178 PRIMULACEAE
b. Trees with 8-16 stamens, fruit 2- or 4-winged—p. 180 *Halesia*
3. Stamens attached to the corolla tube, equal or fewer than the number of corolla lobes:
a. Ovaries 2-celled or nearly separate in pistil (cf. b.):
(1) Stamens 2, trees or shrubs of separate sexes or not—p. 182 OLEACEAE
(2) Stamens equal to number of corolla lobes:
(a) Stigmas 2-4 lobed, juice not milky:
Ovary a 2-celled capsule—p. 182 LOGANIACEAE
Ovary a 1-celled capsule—p. 184 GENTIANACEAE
(b) Stigmas united, juice milky, fruit of 2 follicles:
Styles united, stamens separate—p. 184 APOCYNACEAE
Styles separate, stamens united—p. 186 ASCLEPIADACEAE
b. Ovaries 1, of 2-4 united carpels:
(1) Corolla radially symmetrical:
(a) Ovary not deeply 4-lobed:
Ovary 2-lobed or 2-celled—p. 190 CONVOLVULACEAE,
—p. 224 PLANTAGINACEAE
Ovary 3-celled, 3 stigma lobes—p. 192 POLEMONIACEAE
Ovary 1-celled, 2 stigma lobes—p. 194 HYDROPHYLLACEAE
(b) Ovary deeply 4-lobed, fruit of 4 nutlets, (*Heliotropium* 2-4 grooved)—p. 196 BORAGINACEAE
(2) Corolla mostly bilateral (except in SOLANACEAE, slightly so

in *Verbena, Callicarpa, Ruellia*):

(a) Ovary carpels or sections 1-2 seeded (cf. (b)), stamens 4, mostly 2 long, 2 short, or only 2; leaves opposite:

Ovary not lobed but 2-4 celled, stems not 4-sided—p. 198 VERBENACEAE

Ovary 4-lobed, stem 4-sided—p. 202 LAMIACEAE

(b) Ovary sections several/many-seeded, fruit a berry or a 1-2 celled capsule, mostly 4 stamens:

Flowers radial, 5 fertile stamens—p. 208 SOLANACEAE

Flowers bilateral, 4 fertile stamens, usually 2 long, 2 short:

Trees, shrubs or woody vines—p. 218 BIGNONIACEAE,

—p. 210 *Paulownia*

Herbs:

Insectivorous plants, only 2 stamens—p. 220 LENTIBULARIACEAE

Parasites on roots, not green, 4 stamens—p. 220 OROBANCHACEAE

Neither insectivorous nor parasitic:

Anther bearing stamens 4 (2 in *Justicia*)—p. 222 *Ruellia*

Anther bearing stamens 2 or 4; if 4, 2 long, 2 short—p. 210 SCROPHULARIACEAE

B. Ovary inferior, sepals and petals united:

1. Stamens not united by their anthers:

a. Flowers radially symmetrical or nearly so:

(1) Sepals-petals-stamens number 4-4-4—p. 224 RUBIACEAE

(2) Sepals-petals-stamens number 5-5-5—p. 232 *Campanula, Specularia*

(3) Sepals-petals-stamens number 5-5-3—p. 230 *Valerianella*

b. Flowers usually bilateral, bilabiate; sepals-petals-stamens number 5-5-5—p. 228 CAPRIFOLIACEAE

2. Stamens united by their anthers, filaments free or united:

a. Stamens also united by their filaments into a tube, bilateral—p. 232 *Lobelia*

b. Stamens usually with separate filaments:

(1) Flowers not in heads surrounded by involucral bracts as in the Composite family, 5 sepals, 5 petals, 3 stamens; vines with tendrils—p. 230 *Sicyos*

(2) Flowers in heads of ray and/or disk flowers surrounded by involucral bracts in 1-several series—p. 234 ASTERACEAE

Key to Asteraceae

I. Both ray and disk flowers present (cf. II, III):
- A. Rays yellow, orange or red (cf. B):
  - 1. Pappus of many fine bristles:
    Senecio, p. 238; *Solidago*, p. 254.
  - 2. Pappus of few bristles or scales:
    Grindelia, p. 248; *Borrichia*, p. 258; *Helianthus*, p. 260; *Verbesina*, p. 262; *Coreopsis*, p. 262; *Bidens*, p. 264; *Gaillardia*, p. 266; *Helenium*, p. 266.
  - 3. No pappus evident:
    - a. Leaves alternate:
      Silphium, p. 256; *Rudbeckia*, p. 256; *Ratibida*, p. 258; *Echinacea*, p. 260; Borrichia, p. 258.
    - b. Leaves opposite:
      Polymnia, p. 256; *Silphium*, p. 256.
- B. Rays pink, purple, lavender, or white:
  - 1. Pappus of many fine bristles:
    Aster, p. 252; *Erigeron*, p. 252.
  - 2. Pappus of few bristles or scales:
    Coreopsis, p. 262; *Galinsoga*, p. 264.
  - 3. Pappus not evident:
    - a. Leaves finely dissected:
      Achillea, p. 266; *Anthemis*, p. 266.
    - b. Leaves not finely dissected:
      Polymnia, p. 256; *Echinacea*, p. 260; *Chrysanthemum*, p. 268.

II. Only disk flowers present, no ray flowers (cf. III):
- A. Bracts papery or with white margins:
  Antennaria, p. 250; *Gnaphalium*, p. 250.
- B. Bracts mostly prickly or spiny:
  Xanthium, p. 236; *Centaurea*, p. 240; *Cirsium*, p. 242.
- C. Bracts not like either A or B:
  - 1. Pappus of numerous capillary bristles:
    - a. Flowers pink to purple:
      Vernonia, p. 242; *Liatris*, p. 244; *Eupatorium*, p. 246.
    - b. Flowers pink to white:
      Erechtites, p. 240; *Eupatorium*, p. 246; *Mikania*, p. 248; *Pluchea*, p. 250; *Pterocaulon*, p. 252.
    - c. Flowers yellow to red:
      Senecio, p. 238; *Bidens*, p. 264.
  - 2. Pappus of few bristles or scales:
    Elephantopus, p. 248; *Eupatorium*, p. 246; *Verbesina*, p. 262; *Bidens*, p. 264.
  - 3. Pappus not evident:
    Ambrosia, p. 234; *Centaurea*, p. 240; *Polymnia*, p. 256.

III. Only ray flowers, no disk flowers:
 A. Flowers yellow to orange:
  1. Pappus of two series of outer scales, inner bristles; involucral bracts 1 series, scapes simple or branched, p. 238 *Krigia*
  2. Pappus of capillary bristles:
   a. Heads 3-5 cm broad, single on hollow scape, p. 236 *Taraxicum*
   b. Heads 2-4 cm broad, 1-few on branching stems, pappus reddish-tan, p. 238 *Pyrrhopappus*
   c. Heads 2-2.5 cm broad, several-many; spiny, clasping leaves, p. 236 *Sonchus*
 B. Flowers not yellow to orange:
  1. Pappus of minute scales, flowers bluish, p. 236 *Cichorium*
  2. Pappus of unbranched capillary bristles, flowers bluish, p. 236 *Lactuca*

Part III. Plant Descriptions

PSILOTACEAE
(Whiskfern Family)

Psilotum nudum (L.) Beauv.
Whiskfern

This plant is seldom seen in this area but has been reported in Lousiana and South Carolina, more commonly in Florida and Georgia. It may be terrestrial or epiphytic in sheltered places under or upon trees or in humus. The only leaves are tiny remote scales along the green, 3-angled stem. From the axils of the upper scales, April-September, arise single 3-lobed spore cases about 2 mm in diameter. The green stems branch by twos and may grow to a height of 45 cm from a short, creeping rhizome. There are no roots from the rhizome. This plant is considered representative of the first type of vascular plants and predecessor of the horsetails, club-mosses and ferns. It is in this interest that this plant is presented here. The plant grows well under greenhouse conditions.

EQUISETACEAE
(Horsetail Family)

Equisetum hyemale L.
Common Scouring Rush

This is an evergreen perennial from branching underground stems producing many 0.8-1 cm diameter, to 2 m high, single unbranched stems in colonies. The slender, jointed hollow stems are solid at the nodes where membranous gray-black sheaths 0.8-1 cm long, tooth-margined above, becoming deciduous, are its only "leaves." The green stems produce food and have pores or stomates in the surface which is many-grooved and sandpapery surfaced. Another species *E. arvense,* produces stem branches in whorls at the nodes; when turned base upward the stem resembles a horse's tail. Not having these branches, the sandy surface of this species makes a good scouring pad. This is a spore-bearing plant kin to the ferns. Spores are seldom produced in black terminal cones 1-1.5 cm tall, but most propagation is vegetative. Cones may appear May-June, in dry or wet sandy soils. Georgia-New Mexico and north into Canada.

LYCOPODIACEAE
(Club-moss Family)

Lycopodium lucidulum Michx.
Shining Club-moss

Lycopodium obscurum L.
Ground-Pine

These spore-bearing club-mosses are a step beyond *Psilotum* and *Equisetum,* as they represent the first type of broader photosynthetic leaves. These leaves are simple, scalelike structures with a single unbranching vein of conducting tissue, which precede the leaves of fern plants. These two species have underground stems or rhizomes and upright aerial stems 20-40 cm tall. The evergreen leaves are to 15 mm long in *L. lucidulum* (photo, left) with crescent shape spore cases in leaf axils. *L. obscurum* (photo, right) has only 5 mm long vegetative leaves and separate spore-bearing leaves in a terminal conelike arrangement. These plants are mostly found in cooler wooded areas at higher elevations, some bordering on this area. These are included here, as was *Psilotum,* to show ancestral relationship to the higher plants.

lotum nudum

Psilotum nudum

uisetum hyemale

Equisetum hyemale

copodium lucidulum
Lycopodium obscurum

OPHIOGLOSSACEAE
(Adder's-tongue Family)
Botrychium virginianum (L.) Schwartz. **Rattlesnake Fern**

The genus *Botrychium* is called "grapefern" and of these the rattlesnake fern is more common. Usually a single leaf per year arises from a vertical rhizome. The lower part of the leaf is sterile and the upper part is fertile or spore-bearing. The sterile part is dissected into three dissected blade sections, while the fertile upper part becomes spore-bearing balls of leaflets. The plant may grow 25 cm to over 75 cm tall. Spores form April-June in rich woodlands over most of the U.S. This fern is kin to the adder's-tongue fern, *Ophioglossum,* which usually produces a single fleshy elliptic-ovate "leaf" about 4 cm wide by 9 cm long at the base of the upper spore-bearing portion. The latter is found in somewhat more open areas but is not common.

OSMUNDACEAE
(Cinnamon Fern Family)
Osmunda claytoniana L. **Interrupted Fern**

This luxurious fern, with 60-130 cm long fronds is aptly named; for 30 cm or more along the mid-length of the fronds, smaller spore-bearing leaflets are produced. These leaflets brown and wither as the spores mature, leaving sterile green leaflets both above and below them. Sterile leaves of this fern closely resemble those of the Cinnamon Fern but there is much less wool on the mature leaf stalk. "Fiddlenecks" are very woolly and brown. This is one of the earliest of the large, coarse ferns to appear in the spring. Spores are produced March-June in swamps, marshes, and wet woods; Georgia-Arkansas and north into Canada.

OSMUNDACEAE
(Cinnamon Fern Family)
Osmunda cinnamomea L. **Cinnamon Fern**

This 0.9-1 m high fern has coarse pinnately compound leaves with leaflets nearly divided again. At the leaflet bases is found a tuft of brownish woolly hairs and the leaf stalks are quite hairy. Separate spore-bearing leaves appear in spring ahead of the sterile leaves and are stiffly erect. Fertile leaves, March-May, appear deformed and are cinnamon colored; all its leaflets produce spores. Leaflets only midway of the leaf of the interrupted fern produce spores. Both species of *Osmunda* may be found in swamps, marshes and stream beds; Georgia-Arkansas and north into New England-Kentucky.

OSMUNDACEAE
(Cinnamon Fern Family)
Osmunda regalis L. **Royal Fern**

This large unfernlike, coarse fern may grow 0.6-1.4 m high and has bipinnately compound leaves with toothless elliptic-elongate leaflets in widely-spaced nearly opposite pairs. During March-June, smaller fertile leaflets appear at the tip several inches of each frond or leaf and are stiffly erect on the plant. The 5 to 7 pairs of lanceolate leaflets per section are more widely spaced than in most ferns and one may hardly recognize that it is a fern. The underground stem (rhizome) is vertical rather than horizontal as in most ferns. This fern is usually found in swampy acid soils and water; Florida-Texas and north into Newfoundland.

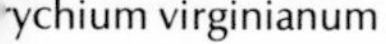

ychium virginianum

Osmunda claytoniana

Osmunda cinnamomea

Osmunda regalis

SCHIZAEACEAE
(Climbing Fern Family)
Lygodium palmatum (Bernh.) Schwartz **Hartford Fern, American Climbing Fern**

The leaflets of this climbing, viny fern are palmately lobed into 5-7 fingers and are about 5 cm across. Spore-bearing leaflets resemble sterile ones but are much smaller and appear July to September toward the tips of the "branches." Leaves arise from a slender creeping rhizome in the soil, as viny leaf stalks which climb over weeds, shrubs, and small trees in swamps, stream beds, and ravines; Georgia-Florida into Tennessee and north into Ohio. Another climbing fern, *L. japonicum,* has pinnately compound leaves, is apparently a garden escape, and may be found in the same range.

PTERIDACEAE
(Bracken Fern Family)
Adiantum pedatum L. **Maidenhair Fern**

From horizontal rhizomes, bare, upright, shiny red-brown 25-50 cm high leaf stalks branch into two rather horizontal curving segments bearing 5 to 10 branchlets. Each of these then has many pinnate fan-shaped leaflets spread to the light. As in members of this family, the edges of these leaflets fold under and produce spores there in protected sporangia. Spores appear June to August on plants in rich woods, along streams and ravines; Georgia-Louisiana and Oklahoma and north into West Virginia-Kentucky. A rare related species *A. capillus-veneris,* Venus'-hair fern, is found along wet limestone walls, near waterfalls, or seepage areas. Its leaves are only twice compound, and have alternate, somewhat 3-lobed leaflets.

PTERIDACEAE
(Bracken Fern Family)
Cheilanthes lanosa (Michx.) D. C. Eaton **Hairy Lipfern**

This small fern of rocky ledges gets its name from the abundance of hairs on the leaf axis and leaflets, giving them a blue-green color. There are 10-12 pairs of nearly opposite leaflets on 10-25 cm long leaves. The leaflets are again divided and lobed. The leaf axis is reddish-brown to purple and the lower leaflets are widely spaced. Spores are borne under the rolled-under edges of the upper leaflets June to September. Although the leaves are evergreen they may appear dead during droughts. *Cheil* refers to marginal, in reference to the rolled-under leaf edges, and *lanosa* refers to lanate or woolly. Mostly found on rocky ledges of foothills; Georgia-Texas and north into West Virginia-Kentucky-Oklahoma.

PTERIDACEAE
(Bracken Fern Family)
Pteridium aquilinum (L.) Kuhn. **Bracken Fern**

This large, stiffly erect, coarse fern rises to 1.5 m high from a widely creeping rhizome deep in the soil. The tall, smooth leaf stalks branch into three thrice-compound triangular, nearly horizontal leaf sections. These smaller sections vary from divided to only lobed toward their tips. All leaflets may produce spores under the rolled-under leaflet edges July to September. This common fern may become a pest in open, usually unfertile, soils because of its spread by deep rhizomes. The leaves are killed back by frost but new growth occurs in the spring and continues until frost. Found in poorer soils over most of the country.

Lygodium palmatum

antum pedatum

Pteridium aquilinum

anthes lanosa

ASPIDIACEAE
(Shield-fern Family)

Cystopteris fragilis (L.) Bernh. **Fragile Fern**

This is a small, bright green, fragile-looking fern, mostly of early spring, drying up somewhat during summer and reviving in the fall. The leaves may reach 30 cm long by 8 cm wide and in outline are broadest near the middle. They are variably dissected compound, nearly hairless, and have about 12 pairs of nearly opposite variously shaped leaflets. Spores are produced in a few clusters on veins on the underside of the leaflets. Spore clusters may be partially covered by a membranous flap or bladder. The term "cysto" refers to this and the group is called the bladder-ferns. Most members of this family have a shield or indusium as a covering of spore clusters. Rock crevices, rich shaded soil, tree trunks, and stumps are its favored habitats. Several varieties are distributed widely in our area, Alabama-Texas and north into Missouri-Illinois. If bulblets are found on the underside of leaflets, the plant is a related species *C. bulbifera,* the bulblet fern. Its leaves are broadest at the base.

ASPIDIACEAE
(Shield-Fern Family)

Polystichum acrostichoides (Michx.) Schott. **Christmas Fern**

The once pinnately compound leaves of this fern are evergreen and may reach a length of 90 cm. The near opposite leaflets are lanceolate and have a triangular lobe on the upper base of each leaflet. Leaflets are toothed and the fertile upper 12-20 pairs are much smaller than the sterile ones. In June to October there are two rows of spore clusters on the under side, nearly covering the surface. The covering of the spore cluster is circular and attached at the center. The short leaf stalk and axis are covered with brownish scales. Some leaves are sterile and remain through winter, thus are often used in Christmas decorations. The rhizome is perennial and may be erect or horizontal. These ferns are found in shaded ravines, slopes, swamps, and semiopen areas; Florida-Texas and north into Canada.

ASPIDIACEAE
(Shield-fern Family)

Thelypteris hexagonaptera (Michx.) Weath. **Broad Beech-Fern**

This fern has triangular shaped, pinnately compound leaves, with its basal pair of leaflets pointing backward. Adjacent leaflets run together at their bases of attachment to the stalk, making it "winged." This feature includes the lowest pair of leaflets; if not winged it would be the northern beech-fern, *T. phegopteris.* Tiny uncovered sporangial dots are found at the vein ends on the under surface of the leaflets. Leaf blades may be 13-30 cm long on somewhat longer stalks. These ferns frequent our oak-hickory forests where beech trees are often found, Florida-Texas, and are not limited to northern beech forests.

ASPIDIACEAE
(Shield-fern Family)

Onoclea sensibilis L. **Sensitive Fern**

This attractive fern with leaves up to a meter long is apparently sensitive only to early frost. Both fertile and sterile leaves arise near each other from a branching horizontal rhizome producing an extensive colony of leaves. Reproductive leaves to 0.5 m are shorter than vegetative leaves to 1 m high and persist through winter. The 12-16 nearly opposite segments of vegetative leaf blades are separated from each other only near the leaf base. Leaflets and segments have wavy margins. Fertile leaves have leaflets rolled up into little balls of spore cases similar to grape-fern. They remain dry and standing through winter. Found in low, open-wooded wet areas; Florida-Texas and north into Canada.

Cystopteris fragilis

stichum acrostichoides

Polystichum acrostichoides

lypteris hexagonaptera

Onoclea sensibilis

ASPLENIACEAE
(Spleenwort Family)

Asplenium rhizophyllum L. **Walking Fern**

The name of this fern comes from its ability to sprout new plants from the tips of its 5-30 cm long leaves where they touch the ground. The long-petioled leaves are not compound as in most ferns, but they are heart-shaped at the 2.5 cm wide base, long tapering, and evergreen. Plants grow in flat-spreading tufts close to the ground and arch upward from an erect rhizome. Spore clumps are elongate and scattered in a netted pattern along the veins on the leaf's under surface. Plants are commonly found on damp moss-covered boulders and banks; Georgia-Oklahoma and north into Maine-Minnesota.

ASPLENIACEAE
(Spleenworth Family)

Asplenium platyneuron (L.) Oakes **Ebony Spleenwort**

This common fern from an erect rhizome has once-pinnately compound leaves of two sizes. The fertile leaves are 10-60 cm long by 2-10 cm wide and are deciduous. The sterile leaves are shorter, spreading or prostrate, and evergreen. Stalkless leaflets are shorter at the two ends of the leaf than those in the middle. Most of the 25-50 pairs of leaflets have a triangular lobe on the upper base and the edges are toothed. As in members of this family spore clusters are elongate along the veins and have a membranous flaplike covering on the basal side of the leaflet. Spores may be seen April to frost on plants in open areas from Florida-Texas and north into Canada. This is one of the most widespread of the spleenworts, so called because it was thought to prevent troubles of the spleen.

POLYPODIACEAE
(Polypody Fern Family)

Polypodium polypodioides (L.) Watt. **Polypody, Resurrection Fern**

This small evergreen fern, to about 20 cm high, is a common epiphyte found on tree trunks over our southern area. During drought the leaves curl up but remain alive and uncurl in more humid weather. Small rhizomes are usually embedded in accompanying moss and lichens on the substrate. Leaves are once-pinnately compound and are 10-20 cm long by 3-5 cm wide, with blunt, narrowly elongate stalkless leaflets. The grayish appearance of the leaves is due to a covering of dark scalelike hairs, especially on the lower surface. Uncovered spore clumps are rather large, in two rows on the lower surface, June-October; Florida-Texas and north into West Virginia-Kentucky.

AZOLLACEAE
(Water-fern Family)

Azolla caroliniana Willd. **Water-fern, Mosquito fern**

The smallest of our ferns is this floating aquatic *Azolla,* which is 0.5-1 cm across. Its scalelike, 2 rounded-lobed leaves are in 2 rows along a branching horizontal stem and are 0.5-1 mm long. Leaves may turn reddish in the fall before the plant dies. Roots hang from the horizontal stem and spore clusters appear at stem branches. Plants are often in dense mats in shallow ponds and ditches, Florida-Lousiana and north into Georgia-Kentucky, sporadically farther north. Three of our smallest flowering plants, of the Duckweed Family, Lemnaceae, are seen here with the purple *Azolla.* The largest is *Spirodela polyrhiza* about 5 mm in diameter, *Lemma minor* about 3 mm and *Wolffia columbiana* about 1.5 mm. See page 66 for these species.

Asplenium rhizophyllum

ypodium polypodioides

Asplenium platyneuron

lla caroliniana

PINACEAE
(Pine Family)
Pinus palustris Miller **Long-leaf Pine**

This pine to 35 m tall has leaves 25 to 40 cm long in bundles of mostly 3 needles, each bundle within a sheath over 2.5 cm long at their base. Needles fall before the second season, leaving needles at branch ends, diagnostic of the species. Female cones purplish early, as seen here, are 15-20 cm long at maturity, are brown and attached stalkless to the branches. Male cones, 3-6 cm long, are many clustered, wither, and drop off. This native pine was the original main source of turpentine and pine oil production in the southeast. It is limited to sandy coastal plains; Florida and Georgia into East Texas, farther inland than the similar slash pine.

PINACEAE
(Pine Family)
Pinus virginiana Miller **Scrub Pine**

This scrub pine grows to 12 to 15 m tall, but may grow taller. It grows in poor, often sandy soils in open exposure. Its twisted needles are 2 per bundle, and 2 to 6 cm long. Subterminal clusters of yellow male or staminate cones appear in April-May. Mature female cones are needle length, produce a spine on each scale and may remain on the tree several years after maturing. Pines growing in the South are subclimax and may be replaced by more climax type hardwoods. Virginia pine is primarily a tree of the mountains, but it reaches sea level; Georgia-Alabama-Mississippi, north into Pennsylvania-New Jersey.

TAXODIACEAE
(Bald Cypress Family)
Taxodium distichum (L.) Rich. **Bald Cypress**

Of all plants typical of an area, this tree deserves recognition here; coastal plain and river valley swamps are dominated by bald cypress. Trees may live 1000 years, grow to 45 m tall and 3.5 m in diameter. Single 1.2-cm long flat needle-leaves grow outward in 2 ranks on 6-8 cm long drooping branchlets which are shed in fall. Female cones and male catkins of flowers appear in spring. The catkins drop off and the spherical, woody cones become 2.5-3 cm in diameter. Numerous "knees," or emergent root branches, were once thought to help get oxygen from air above water-logged, oxygen-poor mud. Plants grown on dry land produce no knees. Found Virginia-Florida-Texas and north up the Mississippi Valley into Illinois.

TAXODIACEAE
(Bald Cypress Family)
Taxodium ascendens Brongn. **Pond Cypress**

Scalelike, 0.8 cm long leaves of this cypress are appressed to the upright projecting branchlets. In bald cypress, the leaves are longer and spread outward from drooping branchlets. (Cones are similar to *T. distichum.)* Trunks bulge in a convex manner at the base, in contrast to the concave and buttressed appearance of *T. distichum*. By contrast pond cypress grows only about half the height of bald cypress. Limited to the coastal plain, Virginia-Florida-Alabama; cones form in March and April.

Pinus palustris

Pinus palustris

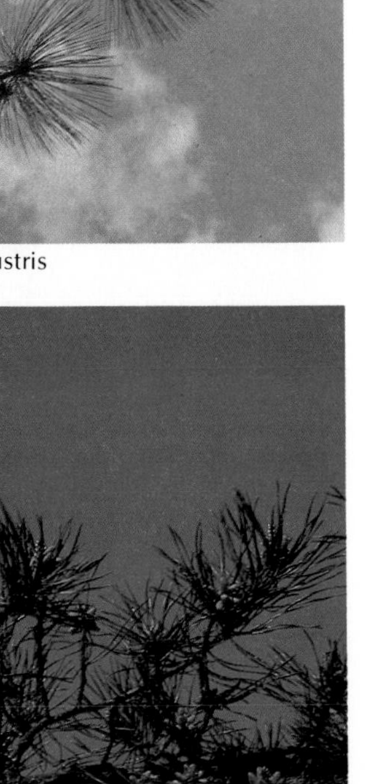

Pinus virginiana

Taxodium distichum

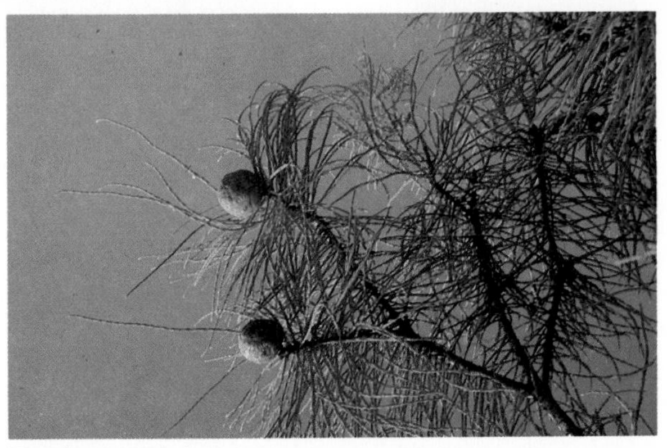

Taxodium ascendens

CUPRESSACEAE
(Cedar Family)

Juniperus virginiana L. **Eastern Red Cedar**

The Eastern red cedar and the Atlantic white cedar *(Chamaecyparis thyoides)* represent this family in the area. Female cones of both have 3-10 fleshy scales and in red cedar become berrylike 5-9 mm spheres, fleshy and bluish with a white waxy coating. White cedar cones are dry and woody. Red cedar seeds are simply pitted and those of white cedar are 2-winged on the edges. Separate male and female cones appear on separate trees in red cedar but separately on one tree in white cedar. Male "flowers" are hard to recognize as 2-4 mm long cones in both cedars. Red cedar produces both small appressed, overlapping pairs of scalelike leaves, as seen here, and larger, sharp, wide-spreading, separate scales on younger branches. White cedar produces only appressed scalelike leaves and flattened clusters of branches. Female cones are seen in the photo as they appear in late spring after pollination. Distribution is mainly in dry soils over most of the eastern U.S., while the Atlantic white cedar is limited to wet coastal plains; Mississippi-Florida-Maine.

TYPHACEAE
(Cat-tail Family)

Typha latifolia L. **Common Cat-tail**

The cat-tail is one of the most common plants along margins of fresh-water ponds, streams, and ditches over most of the country. Its leaves vary from 1 to 2.5 cm wide on plants 1 to 2 m tall from perennial rhizomes below. The flowering stalk is composed of a 5 to 25 cm long spike of female flowers immediately below a thinner spike of male flowers. Flowers have no recognizable petals and sepals. Two other narrower leaf species, *T. angustifolia* and *T. domingensis,* have a space on the stem between the male and female flowering sections. Latifolia means broad leaf and angustifolia means narrow leaf as applicable to the so-named species. Flowers appear May to July.

SPARGANIACEAE
(Bur-reed Family)

Sparganium americanum Nutt. **Bur-reed**

This perennial aquatic or marsh plant, in shallow water or mud, has alternate grasslike leaves, 2-ranked from 2 sides of the stem, growing upright from a creeping stem. It grows to 1 m high and has thin, flat, soft leaves with parallel veins, ascending or floating, 30-120 cm long by 6-18 mm wide. From the leaf axils, branches with a series of stalkless globular flower heads of many flowers, the lower 1-3 being female heads 1.5-2.5 cm diameter at maturity and the upper 1-6 being male heads drying up after maturity. Flower petals-sepals are reduced to only 3 chaffy scales, 3 mm long. Male flowers have only 3 stamens and female flowers only 1 single-seeded pistil becoming a long, beaked achene about 5 mm long by 2.5 mm broad. This is the only species of about 8 in the country that is native to this area. Flowers June-August; Florida-Mississippi-Oklahoma and north into Maine-Minnesota.

ALISMATACEAE
(Water-plantain Family)

Echinodorus cordifolius (L.) Griesb. **Burheads**

This emergent aquatic has long-stalked lanceolate to mostly heart-shaped 10-20 cm wide leaves with prominent curving veins. Flowering stems are arching or creeping and have whorls of white, 3-petaled perfect flowers arising from their nodes. Petals are about 0.5 cm long and surround a 0.5 cm globular head of 40 or more seedlike beaked fruits, hence the name burhead. The plants may resemble *Sagittaria* or arrow-leaf, but there are no arrowhead-shaped leaves on them. Plants are found around pond edges, swamps, and ditches along the coastal plain; Florida-Texas and north to Maryland and up the Mississippi River into Illinois.

erus virginiana

Typha latifolia

ganium americanum

Echinodorus cordifolius

ALISMATACEAE
(Water-plantain Family)

Sagittaria falcata Pursh. **Duck Potato**

A few species of *Sagittaria,* meaning arrow, have an arrowlike leaf, but leaves may even be narrowly grasslike. This plant has leaves tapered at both ends and up to 60 cm long by 8 cm wide. Flowers with 3 white petals and 3 green ovate sepals are borne in several whorls on tall stems. Lower flowers are pistillate or perfect while the upper flowers are staminate only. Fruits are in seedlike spherical heads similar to the burheads. Edible potatolike tubers are produced on horizontal rhizomes in the muddy bottom. Found flowering June to October in swamps, ponds, and ditches; Florida-Texas and north into Maryland-Illinois.

ALISMATACEAE
(Water-plantain Family)

Sagittaria latifolia Willd. **Arrowhead**

This emergent, mostly glabrous perennial from rhizome in mud produces basal leaves with varied arrowhead-shaped blades to 25 cm long on sheathing petioles to 100 cm long. Pointed leaf blade bases project backward ¼-½ the length of the blade, the blades being narrow to quite wide as herein, in different plants. Flowers are produced in 2-10 whorls on stalks to 6 cm long, from axils of 0.5-1.5 cm long, boat-shaped bracts, on scapes 10-150 cm tall. Flowers have 3 green reflexing sepals 5-12 mm long and 3 white circular petals 1.5-2.5 cm long. Lower flowers have numerous separate pistils only, while upper flowers have 25-40 stamens only, or both. Each pistillate head 1-1.8 cm diameter has many separate achenes 1.5-2.5 mm long with a tapered beak to one side. This is the commonest species and is found over most of the United States in shallow waters of swamps, streams, and ponds. Flowers July-September in our area.

POACEAE
(Grass Family)

Arundinaria tecta (Walt.) Muhl. **Switch-Cane**

This plant is the most common species of the bamboo tribe in our area. This perennial has 1-4 m tall by 2.5-3.5 cm diameter stems that are woody and hollow with prominent nodes. Leaves from the nodes are alternate, lanceolate, 15-20 cm long, 1-3 cm wide, with parallel veins and a sheathing petiole longer than the internodes of the stem. Spikelets of 7-10 flowers are 2.5-3.5 cm long and appear on shoots arising directly from the rhizome, but flowering is rare. Propagation is mostly vegetative by rhizomes which form thick cane brakes. Another, *A. gigantea,* giant cane, has stems which grown to 10 m high and to 7 cm in diameter, but is not very common. Both are along stream and river banks and in swamps. Flowers April-July; Florida-Texas and north into Maryland-Oklahoma.

POACEAE
(Grass Family)

Uniola latifolia Michx. **Wild Oats**

This member of the grass family is used in flower arrangements because of its attractive, strongly flattened spikelets often more than an inch long. Spikelets are loosely spaced along the upper 15-20 cm of the stem, each spikelet on a long pendulous stalk. The perennial clump grows 0.9 to 1.2 m high and has leaves 1.5-2.5 cm wide and to 20 cm long. Flowering stalks are loose, open and the spikelets resemble those of sea oats, *U. paniculata,* but those spikelets are in rather dense terminal clusters. Flowers July-September in low woodlands and shaded slopes; Florida-Texas and north into New Jersey-Kansas.

Sagittaria latifolia

ıdinaria tecta

Sagittaria falcata

ola latifolia

POACEAE
(Grass Family)
Poa annua L. **Annual Bluegrass**

Poa is the Greek word for grass or herbage, and there are several species of *Poa* in the area. This annual is the most common and grows abundantly for about 6-10 weeks in the spring before hot summer arrives. It is very common in lawns, gardens, and fields before other vegetation becomes abundant. Neither this species nor the rhizomatous perennial, *P. pratensis,* Kentucky bluegrass, survives summers in this area. The thick clumps are erect-decumbent 5-30 cm tall, with linear pointed blades 2-10 cm long by 2 mm wide, and overlapping sheathing petioles. There are 1-2 flower branches per node made up of loosely branching 2-10 cm long clusters of 3-4 flowered spikelets 3-7 mm long. Further flower details are difficult to see even with a hand lens. Flowers mostly April-May here, found over most of the United States.

POACEAE
(Grass Family)
Zizaniopsis miliacea (Michx.) D.&A. **Cut-grass**

This emergent perennial marsh grass is a common inhabitant of swampy areas of brackish or fresh water. This aquatic grass may get over 3 m tall, have blades 0.9 m long by 2.5 cm wide, and have terminal 60-cm long fruiting branches. Spikes are separate, male and female, the latter spikelets terminal. Grains produced are about 3 mm long, much shorter than wild rice which the plant resembles. The grass covers large acreages of wet lands and is an important food for wildlife. Leaf blades are razor-sharp and quickly inflict a cut, hence its common name. It is mainly coastal; Florida-Texas and north into Maryland-Missouri-Kentucky.

POACEAE
(Grass Family)
Andropogon scoparius Michx. **Little Bluestem**

This solid stemmed bunch grass makes a familiar scene in fall and winter when prairie fields are orange-tan where the grass abounds. Bunched stems grow 75-150 cm tall in close clusters, purplish blue at and near the nodes. Leaf blades are up to 25 cm long by 2-4 mm wide. From each upper bracted node a single raceme of spikelets arises, each spikelet 5-8 mm long is made up of 1 fertile and 1 sterile floret or flower. The lemma awn at the base of each floret is a bent-twisted awn 5-15 mm long. Big bluestem, *A. gerardii,* has leaf blades to 40 cm long and 2-6 mm wide; it grows 100-200 cm tall and has 2-6 racemes per bract, usually at the end of stems. It is not in abundance in our area. Both flower in August-October in fields, prairies, and barrens, and dry open woodlands; Florida-Texas and north into Massachusetts-Minnesota.

CYPERACEAE
(Sedge Family)
Cyperus esculentus L. **Nut-grass**

This perennial sedge propagates readily by seeds and also by 1.4 cm diameter tubers. It becomes a pernicious weed. The stems are 3-sided and leaves arise in 3 ranks. Flowers are scalelike and appear in spikelets similar to grasses. The 15-60 cm tall stem is terminated by a much branched loose head of spikelets just above a whorl of 3-7 long narrow bracts. Seeds are tiny 3-sided achenes. There are over 35 species of *Cyperus* and over 200 of *Carex* as sedges in eastern U.S., mostly in moist to marshy habitats. This species flowers April to October; Florida-Texas and north into Canada.

Poa annua

Zizaniopsis miliacea

Andropogon scoparius

Cyperus esculentus

CYPERACEAE
(Sedge Family)

Dichromena colorata (L.) Hitchcock **White-top Sedge**

The sedges are rather grasslike inconspicuous flowering plants. They can be distinguished by solid 3-sided stems as opposed to hollow, round stems of grass and solid, round stems of the rushes. This sedge is commonly seen along roadsides in the lower coastal plain, but it was reported in Middle Tennessee by Augustin Gattinger in 1901. Its "flowers" are seen because of the 5-10 green-tipped white bracts or leaves 5-8 cm long, which surround the inconspicuous scalelike flowers. This plant grows from a perennial rhizome up to nearly 1 m tall in swamps, calcareous or brackish shallow water, or low roadsides; Virginia-Florida-Texas.

ARECACEAE
(Palm Family)

Sabal minor (Jacq.) Pers. **Palmetto**
Serenoa repens (Bart.) Small **Saw Palmetto**

These rhizomatous monocot plants, creeping or upright, must be considered shrubs 1-2.5 m tall; however, forms growing in wet soil may become 8 m tall. Fan-shaped leaf blades to 1 m broad are cut into many linear pleated segments radiating from the somewhat longer leaf stalk. Leaf blade veins are essentially parallel. As seen in the photo of *Sabal* the leaf stalks are without spines along their edges; *Serenoa* has coarse spines at edges of stalk base. The *Serenoa* photo shows large branched flower stalks from the stem producing many yellowish perfect flowers. The calyx cup of 3 sepals is 1-2 mm long, and 3 separate triangular petals 3-5 mm long. There are 6 stamens and a small 3-carpel pistil, developing into a subglobose drupe fruit 6-8 mm diameter in *Sabal* and 15-20 mm in *Serenoa*. Flowers April-July on low sandy grasslands, and pinelands; North Carolina-Georgia-Florida-Texas.

ARACEAE
(Arum Family)

Arisaema triphyllum (L.) Schott. **Jack-in-the-pulpit**

The male and/or female flowers are found on the cylindrical stem (spadix) or "Jack" surrounded by the pulpit (spathe). Mostly either male or female flowers prevail, the female flowers being followed by a cluster of bright red berries. Plants 20-75 cm high have one or two 3-leafleted leaves arising from an underground corm or tuber. The corm stores abundant starch, edible when boiled (removing oxalic acid), thus its name Indian turnip. The spathe may vary from green to maroon striped, appearing April-July; rich woody, low, wet or boggy areas are preferred; Florida-Louisiana and north into Maryland-Minnesota.

ARACEAE
(Arum Family)

Orontium aquaticum L. **Golden Club**

This unusual, but locally abundant, plant of the small Arum family is found in acid bogs, swamps, and stream margins. Emergent leaves, to 30 cm or more long, are basally clustered, have ovate blades on long stalks and rise from a thick rhizome on the muddy bottom. The white flower stalk (spadix), 30-60 cm long, bears a spike of closely appressed golden perfect flowers above. The small four to six sepals-petals, 4 or 6 stamens, and an imbedded pistil are difficult to determine. Flowers March-April along coastal plains; Massachusetts-Florida-Texas, also rare in Tennessee and Kentucky.

Dichromena colorata

Serenoa repens

abal minor

risaema triphyllum

Orontium aquaticum

ARACEAE
(Arum Family)

Arisaema dracontium (L.) Schott **Green Dragon**

This plant, in the same genus as Jack-in-the-pulpit, particularly differs from the latter by its leaf shape and the "pulpit." The single compound leaf has its 5 to 15 leaflets spread out horizontally somewhat in a u-shape at the top of a stalk that may get 1 m tall. Also arising from the corm is a single flower stalk (dragon tongue?), a long tapering structure as high as the leaves. The lower part, producing the flowers, is surrounded by a short green, nonarching spathe. The fruit clusters are red berries ripening in the fall. Flowers May-June in low floodplain woodlands especially; Florida-Texas and north into Canada.

ARACEAE
(Arum Family)

Pistia stratiotes L. **Water-lettuce**

This common floating tropical plant, like the water hyacinth, is found Florida-Georgia into eastern Texas, a pest in some areas. The plant spreads both by buds branching horizontally and by producing small, 2-cm tall, flower spikes occasionally. The heavily rooted, floating plants have strongly ribbed leaves to 25 cm long, in rosettes, resembling garden lettuce. Plants may become rooted in mud when water of sluggish streams and ponds recedes. Its abundance may clog drainage ditches in the lower coastal plain. The Green Heron is feeding on insects and minnows sheltered in the water lettuce.

LEMNACEAE
(Duckweed Family)

Spirodela polyrhiza (L.) Schleid. **Greater Duckweed**
Lemna minor L. **Lesser Duckweed**
Wolffia columbiana Karst. **Duck-meal**

The floating green plants seen in the photo are in size as listed above, their lengths in mm being 5-10, 2-6, and 1-1.5. *Spirodela* has 5-10 rootlets hanging from the "leaf," *Lemna* has only 1, and *Wolffia* is rootless. The purple plant (green until fall) is the Water Fern, *Azolla,* described in the AZOLLACEAE. Duck-meal is the smallest of flowering plants and *Azolla* the smallest of ferns. As seen in high magnification each plant has a separate male flower of only a single stamen and a female flower of only a single pistil which may have 1-6 tiny seeds. These flowers are partially sunken in the surface of the "leaf." The plants are perennial, divide from a short stem and fall to the lake bottom, rising again in the spring. Found mainly in lakes and ponds over most of the United States, except *Wolffia* which is only eastern.

ERIOCAULACEAE
(Pipewort Family)

Eriocaulon compressum Lam. **Bog-buttons, Hatpins**

The separate-sexed flowers of this perennial plant are very tiny and are in a compact head at the end of a long 10-12 ridged stalk. Stalks arise from a rosette of grasslike leaves on a short, fibrous rooted stem. Flower stalks may reach 30 cm or more in height, flower heads 1-1.5 cm across, and basal leaves 10-20 cm long by 0.3-0.8 cm wide. Upon drying, flower heads remain intact and are used in dry flower arrangements. Flowers April-October in swamps, bogs, and roadside ditches mostly along the coastal plain; North Carolina-Florida-Texas.

Arisaema dracontium

Arisaema dracontium

Pistia stratiotes

Eriocaulon compressum

Spirodela, Lemna, Wolffia

BROMELIACEAE
(Bromelia Family)

Tillandsia usneoides L. **Spanish Moss**

This epiphytic plant, "growing" on trees and even wires around the lower coastal plain is not a moss; it and pineapple are members of this Family. The branching stems are covered with grayish scales which absorb water. Greenish 3-petaled flowers are 0.6-0.8 cm long, followed by a 2.5-cm capsule splitting into 3 linear valves as seen in the photo. The plant produces no roots and absorbs nothing from its "host." Flowers April-June in Florida-Texas and north into Virginia and south Arkansas. Several related species are found in south Florida and Georgia; most are tropical plants.

COMMELINACEAE
(Spiderwort Family)

Commelina erecta L. **Dayflower**

In contrast to *Tradescantia*, the dayflower has 3 fertile stamens rather than 6 and there may be 3 sterile ones. There are 2 petals of equal size instead of 3; the third (lower) petal is either translucent, quite small, or absent. In this species stems may be to 60 cm or more tall, have narrow linear leaves to 15 cm long, and petals over 1 cm long. Flower clusters are enclosed in a folded bractlike spathe to 2.5 cm long. Flowers last 1 day but in succession in a given cluster. Flowers June-October in dry sandy or rocky openings or woods; Florida-Texas and north into New York-Illinois-Kansas.

COMMELINACEAE
(Spiderwort Family)

Tradescantia virginiana L. **Spiderwort**

Contrast this species with *Commelina erecta* for generic differences. This plant grows to 60 cm tall, has smooth narrow leaves to 30 cm long, and flowers with 3 petals to 2 cm long. Flowers may be blue, purple, rose or white but usually are blue. Sepals may or may not have hairs. This species is a more southern one and is often cultivated. Another species shown here, *T. ohioensis* Raf. is equally as colorful and variable and may grow to 1.3 m tall. *T. virginiana* has hairy sepals but *T. ohioensis* does not. Flowers April-July in sandy open or woodsy moist areas; West Virginia-Georgia-Arkansas north into Maryland-Minnesota.

COMMELINACEAE
(Spiderwort Family)

Tradescantia hirsuticaulis Small **Spiderwort**

This hairy-stemmed (hirsuticaulis) spiderwort also has hairy leaves. The plant gets 45 cm tall and has 20-30 cm long-tapering leaf blades about 1.5 cm wide. Below the flower clusters are two, very unequal length, leaflike bracts somewhat shorter than the leaves. Flowers may be 3-4 cm across, the pink-purple to blue petals are undulate and broader than long. Sepals are quite hairy with some sticky-glandular ones among them. Flowers April-June in sandy woodlands and rocky ledges; Florida-Texas and north into North Carolina-Arkansas.

'landsia usneoides

Tradescantia virginiana

Commelina erecta

radescantia hirsuticaulis

Tradescantia ohioensis

PONTEDERIACEAE
(Pickerelweed Family)

Eichornia crassipes (Martius) Solms. **Water-hyacinth**

The water-hyacinth was probably introduced from South America, is now locally abundant and often a pest. Being free-floating, it clogs irrigation and drainage canals. It rapidly reproduces vegetatively by stolons. Ovate-reniform leaf blades, 8-12 cm long, usually have an inflated bulbous petiole equally as long. Flowering spikes to 25 cm tall have 5-10 flowers 5 cm across. Blooms have 6 similar blue petals-sepals, the upper one with purple veins around a yellow "eye." There are 6 curved stamens and a 3-lobed stigma; seeds are seldom produced in our area. Flowers June-September in quiet freshwater streams and ponds; Florida-Texas and north into Virginia; also seen in Missouri (Steyermark).

PONTEDERIACEAE
(Pickerelweed Family)

Pontederia cordata L. **Pickerelweed**

This coarse plant to over 1 m high is anchored by a short rhizome in the mud at pond or stream edges and marshes. Leaves with blades to 45 cm long by 5-11 cm wide are elongate heart-shaped. Flowering spikes with numerous 2-lipped flowers are about 15 cm long with a clasping bract at the base. Sepals-petals are united below into a tube, its 6 parts spreading to about 2 cm across; the upper lobe has a double yellow "eye"; color ranges from pale blue to purple, rarely white. Usually only one red seed 4-5 mm long develops in one of the three cells of the ovary. Flowers May-October; Florida-Texas and north into Nova Scotia-Minnesota.

LILIACEAE
(Lily Family)

Smilax bona-nox L. **Greenbrier, Catbrier**

This is a semiwoody, perennial, separate sexed, climbing vine with a pair of tendrils on the alternate leaf stalks, and a pair of spines below them. The flowers are greenish-yellow and have 6 similar greenish sepals-petals 4-8 mm long, borne in axillary clusters at the end of 1.5 cm long flower stalks. The leathery leaves are pointed and spread into basal lobes making an arrhowhead-shaped leaf 5 to 10 cm long; the edges are spiny toothed. Stems are 4-angled and main branches are stiffly prickly. Following flowering in May-June are black, 1-seeded berries about 1 cm in diameter, 12 to 15 in a roundish cluster. Several species appear in our area with red, blue, or black berries. Found in dry-moist sand-clay soils in fields and waste places; Florida-Texas and north into Maryland-Illinois.

LILIACEAE
(Lily Family)

Smilax smallii L. **Lance-leaved Greenbrier**

This high climbing woody perennial is usually not prickly on the stems, has alternate evergreen ovate-lanceolate leaves tapered to a petiole under 1 cm long with blades 5-6 cm long. The stipules at the petiole base become tendrils. Axillary flower clusters are umbels on a 0.5-1 cm long pedunele bearing few to many flowers with 6 greenish sepal/petal parts 3-6 mm long, on separate sexed plants. Each fruit in the cluster is a black globose 5-7 mm diameter, 1-3 seeded berry on a pedicel 3-7 mm long. A similar evergreen, more spiny species in the area is *S. laurifolia* with 1-seeded berries 6-8 mm diameter and 6-8 cm long leaves with sides nearly parallel, tapering quickly at leaf base and tip. Flowers June-July in low woodlands and bays of the coastal plain; North Carolina-Florida-Mississippi.

Pontederia cordata

ilax bona-nox

Eichornia crassipes

ilax smallii

LILIACEAE
(Lily Family)

Trillium grandiflorum (Michx) Salisb. **Large Flowered Trillium**

This is one of the largest-flowered trilliums and should be looked for in rich woods and thickets of Arkansas and Tennessee; it is not reported elsewhere in our area. Pointed sepals are 3-5 cm long. Petals are 4-8 cm long and the erect flower is elevated on a stalk 2-10 cm above the leaves. Color of the petals changes from white to pink, and the edges are crinkled. Several varieties of this species are found. Plants grow 45 to 60 cm high and seem to prefer alkaline soils. Leaves are ovate-elongate and long tapered 7-15 cm long by 5-12 cm wide; they are not mottled. Flowers April-June in rich wooded coves; Georgia-Arkansas and north from Maine-Minnesota.

LILIACEAE
(Lily Family)

Trillium cuneatum Raf. **Little Sweet Betsy**

The flowers of this plant are stalkless and the leaves are lightly mottled light and dark green or purple. Leaves are nearly sessile, ovate, to 10 cm wide by 17 cm long with a short tapered tip. Petals are variably ovoid 1.5 to 2.5 cm wide to 6 cm long and tapered to the base (cuneate). They range in color bronze to maroon. Shorter sepals may spread or stay erect but are not recurved as in *T. recurvatum*. Plants may grow 30 cm high from a short thick rhizome. Flowers March-April or later, particularly on wooded slopes; Florida-Mississippi and north into North Carolina-Illinois. A much shorter form, *T. underwoodii* Small, is found in Florida, Georgia, and Alabama, a separate species or a variety of *T. cuneatum*.

LILIACEAE
(Lily Family)

Trillium luteum (Muhl.) Harbison **Yellow Trillium**

This trillium resembles *T. cuneatum* and might be a yellow flowered variety of it, but petals are smaller and both petals and stamens are yellow. The leaves are strongly mottled. Some authorities think it might be a variety of *T. viride*. Whatever its identity, it is beautiful and makes masses of attractive flowers. It appears to prefer neutral to basic mountainous rich woods; Georgia-Arkansas and north into Kentucky and Missouri.

LILIACEAE
(Lily Family)

Trillium recurvatum Beck **Wakerobin**

This purple wakerobin is distinctive in that leaves narrow into petioles, the petals similarly into "claws," and the sepals are strongly turned down or recurved. Stems are 15-45 cm high, leaf blades are ovate and pointed, to 5 cm wide by 10 cm long; they are usually mottled. Flowers are stalkless, petals stand stiffly erect, 2-5 cm long, pointed at both ends, and are red-brown to maroon or purple as are the 6 stamens. Green sepals are 2-3 cm long and tapered. Flowers April-May in rich woods of plains and valleys; Alabama-Arkansas and north into Michigan-Nebraska.

Trillium grandiflorum

llium cuneatum

Trillium luteum

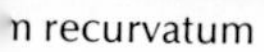

n recurvatum

LILIACEAE
(Lily Family)

Smilacina racemosa (L.) Desf. **False Solomon's-seal**

As in Solomon's-seal, this plant may be over 60-90 cm tall, erect, arching from a perennial rhizome. The 7-13 alternate short petioled leaves, 10-18 cm long, spread horizontally. It may be readily distinguished by its flower clusters at the tip of the stem. Flowers in the other similar species are axillary, as in Solomon's-seal. The yellowish perfect flowers with 3-4 mm long sepals and petals are followed by 8 mm diameter red berries, sometimes purplish spotted. Flowers April-July in rich deciduous woods, clearings, and slopes; Georgia-Mississippi and north into Canada.

LILIACEAE
(Lily Family)

Polygonatum biflorum (Walt.) Ell. **Solomon's-seal**

Solomon's-seal grows 20-200 cm tall from a perennial rhizome and has alternate, stalkless, ovate-lanceolate, hairless leaves 5-20 cm long by 2-10 cm wide. Usually two flowers are borne in leaf axils. Flowers are greenish-white, 1.2-2.2 cm long with petals and sepals united into a tube. The fruits are blue-black berries 8-12 mm in diameter. (False Solomon's-seal, *Smilacina racemosa,* has a terminal cluster of flowers with separate parts at the end of the stalk and produces red berries). Flowers May-June in moist woods, thickets, and roadsides; Florida-Texas and north into Connecticut-Indiana.

LILIACAEA
(Lily Family)

Aletris lutea Small **Colic-root; Star-grass**

Two other species of colic-root are found in our area, one with 1.2 cm long white flowers, *A farinosa,* and one with 0.8 cm long yellow flowers, *A. aurea. A lutea* has 1.2 cm long yellow flowers with features similar to *A. farinosa*; it could be a hybrid between those two. All flowers have 6 united sepals/petals 6-11 mm long and have a granular mealy appearance. Leafless flowering stalks arise to 75 cm tall from a rhizome and a basal rosette of narrow oblanceolate leaves tapered to tip and up to 17 cm long. Flowers May-June along the coastal plain in sandy wet meadows; Florida-Louisiana and north into Virginia. In the photo, the flowering stalk is separated from the plant base.

LILIACEAE
(Lily Family)

Chamaelirium luteum (L.) Gray **Fairy Wand; Blazing-star**

The name fairy wand well describes the plant's appearance, as well as being less confusing than blazing-star, which is also used for two other common plants. A bracted flower stalk 0.6-1.2 m tall arises from a basal rosette of evergreen leaves which are up to 20 cm long by 7 cm wide, broader toward tip, narrowed at petiole. Male and female flowers are borne on separate plants, the leaves upward becoming smaller bracts. The male spike of tiny flowers (see photo) reaches 13-15 cm long and curls over, while the female spike is shorter, 2-4 cm long but elongates to 25-35 cm as fruiting capsules mature. Flower sepals/petals, about 3 mm long are greenish to white, 6 in number and mostly separate. Female flowers may have 6 sterile stamens while the 6 stamens of male flowers are white and fertile. Flowers March-May in rich woods, thickets, and bogs; Florida-Mississippi-Arkansas north into Massachusetts-Michigan.

Chamaelirium luteum

Chamaelirium luteum

Smilacina racemosa

Aletris lutea

Polygonatum biflorum

LILIACEAE
(Lily Family)

Erythronium americanum Ker. **Dog-tooth Violet, Trout-Lily**
Erythronium albidum Nutt. **White Trout-Lily**

These two species are not in the violet family but are lilies. The name "trout" is of dubious origin. Dogtooth refers to the white small underground bulbs produced. The 3 sepals and 3 petals are 2-4 cm long, elliptic-lanceolate and recurved, more pronounced in the white species. The 6 stamens are of two lengths in both and the anthers usually are brown in the yellow lily. The stigma of the white lily is 3-lobed and recurved but it is unlobed and erect in the yellow lily. The two leaves are usually mottled in the yellow but rarely in the white lily. Flowers March-June in rich woods and thickets, barely reaching into our area from north and east; Georgia-Alabama-Arkansas-Oklahoma. *E. albidum* is considered an endangered species, not to be collected; protected by law—the Endangered Species Act.

LILIACEAE
(Lily Family)

Camassia scilloides (Raf.) Cory **Wild Hyacinth**

This is the only eastern species of *Camassia;* there are 4 western ones. Several narrow leaves 4-15 mm wide and 30-65 cm long arise from a bulb. There is a many-flowered leafless stalk 15-60 cm tall with blue to lavender sepals and petals about 1.2 cm long. The flower cluster is 10-30 cm long with a bract at the base of each perfect flower. The pistil has a 3-branched stigma and the fruit is a triangular-globose 3-celled capsule about 1.2 cm in diameter. Flowers April-June in moist open woods and meadows; Alabama-Texas and north into Pennsylvania-Iowa.

LILIACEAE
(Lily Family)

Ornithogalum umbellatum L. **Star-of-Bethlehem**

This European import seems to be a garden escape into waste places, fields, and woodlands. Leaves are all basal from a bulb, are 15-45 cm long by 0.8-1 cm wide and have a white mid-rib line on the upper side. Leaves tend to die back at their tips with onset of flowering. Flowering stalks 10-25 cm high are leafless, but are bracted and branching at top producing 5-6 flowers. There are 3 white petals and 3 white sepals, 1.5-2.5 cm long by 3-6 mm wide, with a green stripe on their undersides. The 6 anthers are on flattened filaments half the length of the petals. Fruits are a roundish 3-celled capsule. Flowers April-May, mostly uplands; Georgia-Mississippi and north-New York-Nebraska.

LILIACEAE
(Lily Family)

Uvularia grandiflora Smith. **Large-flowered Bellwort**

The 6 similar, yellow sepals and petals of this single stemmed bellwort may reach nearly 5 cm in length and have a twisted appearance. The inner (upper) surface of these parts is smooth rather than granular as in bellwort (*U. perfoliata),* which also has shorter petals 2-3.5 cm long. Flowers are borne singly in leaf axils. The upper leaves of both species may be perfoliate, the stem seemingly going through the leaf-blade. The ovate-lanceolate leaves of this species are hairy on the lower surface. The droopy appearing plant may reach 20-70 cm in height from a perennial rhizome. Flowers April-June, preferring alkaline soils; Georgia-Mississippi-Arkansas and north into Canada.

ythronium americanum

ythronium albidum

vularia grandiflora

Camassia scilloides

Ornithogalum umbellatum

LILIACEAE
(Lily Family)

Allium cernuum Roth **Nodding Onion**

This odorous onion is called "nodding" *(cernuum)* because its flowers, as their buds open, turn pendulous, as does the top of the main flower stalk. Stems are 20-60 cm tall and the narrow flat leaves 4-8 mm wide may get 40 cm long. Flowers with 6 similar sepals/petals are white, pink, or purple. The umbel terminating the stalk is composed of many 0.8 cm long flowers on individual pedicels 1.5-2.5 cm long. Sepals are usually shorter than the petals. No bulblets are produced on the umbel as on the more common wild onion, *A. canadense*. Flowers July-August in gravelly or rocky places; Georgia-Alabama-Missouri into Canada.

LILIACEAE
(Lily Family)

Allium canadense L. **Wild Onion, Wild Garlic**

In a few species of *Allium* the flower cluster may have bulblets instead of flowers, all flowers, or both flowers and bulblets as seen here. The stalkless bulblets are a means of vegetative propagation available in addition to seeds. Flowers with 6 similar sepals/petals, erect rather than nodding, may be white or pink, the southern variety having pink flowers and shorter individual pedicels than the more northern variety. Leaves are flat 10-30 cm long and less than 6 mm wide. These odorous plants are abundant along roadsides, in gardens, lawns and fields; flowers May-July; Georgia-Arkansas and north into Canada.

LILIACEAE
(Lily Family)

Allium bivalve (L.) Kuntze **Scentless Onion, Wild Garlic**

This onion is placed in the genus *Nothoscordum* by some as it has no onion odor. Then, too, there are several seeds per cavity rather than 1 or 2 as in most onions. Stems grow 15-45 cm high from a membranous covered bulb and are terminated by an umbel of 17 or fewer long-stalked erect flowers. Petals and sepals to 1.2 cm long are yellowish-green to white with green or purple mid-rib lines. Flower stalks are much longer than the flat, narrow leaves 10-40 cm long by 2-4 mm wide. Flowers February-May in lower piedmont fields and sandy soils; Florida-Texas and north into Virginia-Nebraska.

DIOSCOREACEAE
(Yam Family)

Dioscorea villosa L. **Wild Yam**

This is a climbing perennial with a semiwoody twining stem, usually with alternate, sometimes with opposite or whorled, long-petioled heart-shaped, 3 to 4 cm wide leaves with curving veins, as in dogwood. The male and female flowers are produced on separate plants on elongate branching clusters mainly in alternate leaf axils. The tiny flowers have 3 greenish sepals and 3 greenish petals all united by their bases. There are 6 stamens, aborted in the pistillate flowers. The fruits on the female plant are 3-winged, inflated capsules about 2 cm long. A similar plant called the Chinese yam, *D. batatas,* bears small potatolike tubers in leaf axils. Flowers April-June in wetter woodlands, swamps, and thickets; Georgia-Alabama-Texas and north into New York-Minnesota.

cernuum

Allium canadense

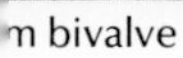

m bivalve

Dioscorea villosa

AMARYLLIDACEAE
(Amaryllis Family)
Hymenocallis occidentalis (LeConte) Kunth. **Spider-lily**

The spider-lily gets its botanical name from *hymen* or "membrane" and *callis* or "beautiful," *occidentalis* for "western." The membrane is the corona or crown arising as a tube made of united stamen bases. The tube gets 2.5-6 cm long while 3 sepals and 3 petals are alike, narrow and to 10 cm long. Flowers appear in a bracted umbel of 3 to 7 atop a leafless stalk about 60 cm high. Basal, linear leaves to 5 cm wide and 60 cm long arise from a bulb in swamps, wet meadows, and ditches. As in all of this family, the calyx tube grows up around the ovary making an inferior ovary. From this is developed a 3-celled capsule; in this plant the small capsule is 1-3 seeded. Flowers April-September; Florida-Louisiana and north into Georgia-Kentucky-Missouri.

AMARYLLIDACEAE
(Amaryllis Family)
Zephyranthes atamasco (L.) Herbert **Atamasco Lily**

Also known as Easter lily, the narrow basal leaves are 3-10 mm wide and 30-38 cm long. The single flowered stalk, without leaves except for a single bract subtending the flower, is fleshy and nearly 30 cm tall. The 6 petals/sepals are alike 8-10 cm long and white or pink tinged. Stamens are 5-8 cm long, the pistil is longer, and has a 3-branched stigma. Plants colonize from bulbs along wet roadside ditches and wet woodlands, mostly along the coastal plains. Flowers March-June; Florida-Mississippi and north into Pennsylvania.

AMARYLLIDACEAE
(Amaryllis Family)
Crinum americanum L. **Swamp Lily**

This is not a lily but is a relative of the amaryllis. Lilies have a capsule produced at the level of, or above (superior) the sepals. Amaryllids produced a capsule much below (inferior) the attachment of the sepals. The Crinums are mostly tropical in distribution, but this species and 2 others have entered our area. Three sepals and 3 petals are 8 mm wide, similar, and 8-10 cm long. The 6 stamens are reddish and quite long. Leaves from a bulb get 1-1.3 m long and 5-7 cm wide. The 1 m or more tall thick flower stalk has 3-5 flowers at its top. Flowers March-November in marshes, swamps, and roadside ditches; Florida-Texas.

AMARYLLIDACEAE
(Amaryllis Family)
Hypoxis hirsuta (L). Coville **Yellow Star-grass**

This plant resembles a grass only in its grasslike leaves 1-8 mm wide and 5-45 cm long. These leaves are long-hairy (hirsute), as are the buds and flower stalks. Petals and sepals are 3 each, united below, 0.5-1.5 cm long and yellow, as are the 6 stamens. The leaves arise from a perennial, underground upright stem or corm. Flowering stalks are several bracted, slender upright or reclining, 3-20 cm long and produce 2-9 flowers at their tips. Flowers March-September in open woodland and meadows; Florida-Texas and north into Canada.

Hymenocallis occidentalis

Crinum americanum

nenocallis occidentalis

Hypoxis hirsuta

Zephyranthes atamasco

IRIDACEAE
(Iris Family)
Belamcanda chinensis (L.) D.C. **Blackberry Lily**

This "lily" is really in the Iris Family, though it hardly resembles an iris except for its leaves. Leaves 2.5 cm wide to 40 cm long arise, irislike, from an orange rhizome. Upright stems 0.6-1 m tall producing flowers resemble those of iris. Flowers with 3 each, sepals and petals, all alike are orange and spotted with red; the flowers are about 5 cm across and have 3 stamens. Pistils are 3-cleft at the stigma, the branches simple and not like iris. The inferior ovary becomes a 2-3 cm capsule splitting and falling away exposing a clump of black "berries." Probably a garden escape naturalized from Asia. Flowers June-July in open wastelands; Georgia-Alabama and north into Connecticut-Nebraska.

IRIDACEAE
(Iris Family)
Alophia drummondii (Grah.) Foster **Herbertia**

This member of the family is rare on pineland and prairie soils, seldom pictured in recent works. There are 1-4 grasslike leaves about 30 cm long from a 2.5 cm thick bulbous rhizome; a scape about 30 cm long bears 1 or 2 flowers about 5 cm across, above a spathe 3-5 cm long. The sepals are large, pale purple with darker dots on a white background. Petals are much smaller, dark purple at the base and sharply pointed. Three branches of the pistil have each branch forked and arching over the 3 stamens opposite the sepals. (Dr. Clair A. Brown reports this plant rare in Louisiana; previously the genus was named *Herbertia*.) The accompanying photograph was of a plant in the Big Thicket of east Texas. Flowers April-May.

IRIDACEAE
(Iris Family)
Sisyrinchium atlanticum Bickn. **Blue-eyed Grass**

The Sisyrinchiums are not grasses and often have blue flowers with a yellow "eye." Also, flowers of 5-6 species in the area might be white, yellow or purple. With similar spreading sepals and petals, except for an inferior ovary, the flowers resemble a lily. Flowers are 2 cm across and arise from between 2 purple-tinged bracts or spathes, at the top of long scapes or leafless stems. These scapes are 2-winged, flat, each wing about 3mm wide. Tufted perennial plants from fibrous roots may grow 60 cm high. Flowers May-July in dry or wet meadows and open woods; Florida-Mississippi and north into Canada.

The Genus *Iris*

The genus *Iris* is widespread over the northern hemisphere and numbers more than 200 species. In our area, although there are few species (hardly a dozen), they reach their zenith in widespread abundance. They grace our low moist meadows, marshes, open woodlands, streamsides, and barrens in a gamut of color, heralding the arrival of spring. The many myths relating to Iris, the classic messenger of the gods, are a must reading for all iris plant lovers.

To describe the iris flower: the petals are usually erect and smaller than the "falls." The falls are the sepals which seem to be bent downward by the three arching, spreading lobes of the pistil branches, the stigmas. There is a stamen beneath each arching stigma lobe, also a nectar gland. All members of the family have an inferior ovary.

IRIDACEAE
Iris prismatica Pursh **Slender Blue Flag**
Iris virginica L. **Blue Flag**

Two irises *I. prismatica* and *I. virginica* have similar blue flowers about 7 cm across with the falls yellow blotched, the blotches being larger on *I. prismatica*. The capsule of *I. prismatica*, sharply angular, flat-sided, 3.5-4.5 cm long, is unique in the irises, as are the 2-4 grasslike leaves 5-9 mm broad, to 50 cm long. Its stems grow 20-75 cm in height. *I. virginica* has an ovoid-elliptic to cylindric capsule 5-7 cm long. Its leaves are to 3 cm broad and a meter long. Stems are also a meter long, weak and arching or reclining. The habitat of both species is in shallow fresh to brackish water, marshes and wet grasslands, though *I. virginica* is more often in water. Iris enthusiasts appear to be transplanting *I. prismatica* into our area, though its natural range is near the coast, Georgia-Nova Scotia and into North Carolina and Tennessee in a coarser variety. *I. virginica* ranges along the coast, Virginia-east Texas, reaching into Arkansas and, in the variety *Shrevei*, into Missouri and Kentucky. Both flower May-June.

ncanda chinensis

Iris prismatica

Alophia drummondii

inchium atlanticum

Iris virginica

IRIDACEAE
(Iris Family)

Iris cristata Ait. **Crested Iris**
Iris verna L. **Dwarf Iris**

The two dwarf irises in this area are the crested iris, *I. cristata*, and dwarf iris, *I. verna*. The crest of *I. cristata* is an elevated, 3-ridged, fringed, orange to white area on the falls partially covered by the over-arching stigma branches. Leaves may grow 2.5 cm broad and 30 cm long, taller than the 10 cm long, 1-2 flowered stem. *I. verna* has no crest but the corresponding area on it is orange-yellow, outlined with white. Leaves are 1.3 cm wide and about 20 cm long. Both species have blue to purple flowers about 5 cm across. The crested iris grows in rich woodlands and ranges from Georgia-Mississippi-Oklahoma and northeast to Indiana-Maryland. Flowers March-May. *I. verna* grows in acid, sandy pine barrens and damp peaty places, mainly coastal Maryland-Florida-Mississippi and northward into Kentucky. Flowers May-June.

IRIDACEAE
(Iris Family)

Iris brevicaulis Raf. **Zig-Zag Iris**

Iris brevicaulis, the zig-zag iris, has a weak reclining stem to 25 cm long which bends at a slight angle at the nodes from which arise leaves longer than the flower stalks and stem. Leaves are to 60 cm long by 3.5 cm wide. Large blue-purple flowers with falls 8-9.5 cm long appear on short, 2.5-3 cm long stalks or pedicels (brevi=short, caulis=stem, giving the species name) at stem nodes. Flowers May-June in swamps, streams, ponds, and wet woodland edges; Alabama-east Texas, north into Kansas-Ohio.

IRIDACEAE

Iris pseudacorus L. **Yellow Flag**

Iris pseudacorus, the yellow flag, is a European species, escaped from cultivation here into meadows and marshlands as well as roadside ditches and waterways. It is a tall species to 90 cm high, with leaves longer than the stem, bearing bright yellow flowers 7-9 cm across. The falls abruptly recurve and are contracted at the base. Flowers June-August; New York-Minnesota and south into Georgia-Louisiana.

IRIDACEAE

Iris fulva Ker **Copper Iris**

Iris fulva, the copper iris, has large coppery-red, flat, spreading flowers about 10 cm across and grows, with 1-several stems, to over 1.4 meter high. Two to four leaves along the stem grow 70-90 cm long with axillary flowers being produced above. Flowers March-May in marshland, pools, and along stream banks; Georgia-Louisiana and north into Missouri and Illinois.

cristata

s brevicaulis

pseudacorus

Iris verna

Iris fulva

ORCHIDACEAE
(Orchid Family)

Cypripedium acaule Aiton **Pink Lady's-slipper**

From an underground rhizome arises a pair of leaves 7-10 cm wide by 15-25 cm long and lower 1-3 1-flowered scapes to 50 cm tall. The flower has 3 petals; the pink one folds over to form the 4-7 cm long slipper, the 2 narrow lateral petals taper and are green, purple, or brown. Of 3 sepals the top one is narrow tapering over the slipper and under an arching green bract; the 2 lower sepals unite and project downward opposite the upper sepal. The inferior ovary is surrounded by the calyx tube and produces a 3-celled capsule (photo) fruit which is ellipsoidal and about 5 cm long. Flowers April-July in woodlands, bogs and swamps; Georgia-Alabama and north into middle Tennessee-Canada. This plant is considered rare and is protected by law.

ORCHIDACEAE
(Orchid Family)

Cypripedium calceolus L. **Yellow Lady's-slipper**

"Cypre" refers to Cyprus where Aphrodite, the goddess of love, was born, and "pedium" refers to sandal or slipper. "Calceolus" here means little shoe. The floral parts are the same as described previously. In lady's-slippers, stamens and pistil join into a "column," its parts hardly recognized. The yellow shoe, the lower petal, is shorter than the 2-6 cm long, greenish-yellow to purplish sepals and lateral petals. Upright stems to 60 cm high bear alternate leaves 10-20 cm long by 5-10 cm wide. Flowers April-June; Georgia-Texas and north into West Virginia and Kentucky.

ORCHIDACEAE
(Orchid Family)

Habenaria ciliaris (L.) R. Br. **Yellow Fringed Orchid**

The fringed orchids get their name from the much dissected, fringed lower petal or lip. This simple, erect plant grows 30-90 cm tall from fleshy or tuberous roots. Lower leaves, 1-3, are oblong-lanceolate, 15 cm long by 3-6 cm wide, being reduced upwards to just bracts. Loose to dense 5-12 cm long clusters of yellow-orange flowers terminate 5-12 cm of the stem. Sepals, 3, are widely ovate 6-9 mm long by 4-8 mm wide. Of the petals, 2 lateral ones are linear-lanceolate 6-7 mm long by 1-2 mm wide; the lower petal or fringed lip is 12-16 mm long by 6-10 mm wide. The lower lip has a 2.5-3 cm long spur at the rear. A similar yellow-orange species, *H. cristata*, the yellow crested orchid, has a 5-9 mm long spur. Flowers July-September in low swamps and meadows; Florida-Texas and north into Canada.

ORCHIDACEAE
(Orchid Family)

Pogonia ophioglossoides (L.) Ker **Rose Pogonia**

As seen in the picture, this rose-colored orchid may be found in pitcher plant bogs around the coastal plains. *Pogon* means "bearded" as is the lower petal, with raised projections, and *ophioglossoides* means "snake-tongue." The plant may get 60 cm tall and have a 10 cm long elliptic-ovate petioled leaf below the 1-3 fragrant flowers on the stalk. The lower lip is a fringed petal about 2.5 cm long, bearded on the upper side with light yellow hairs. Flowers April-June in bogs, peaty soils, and wet areas; Florida-Texas and north into Pennsylvania-Minnesota.

ripedium acaule

Cypripedium calceolus

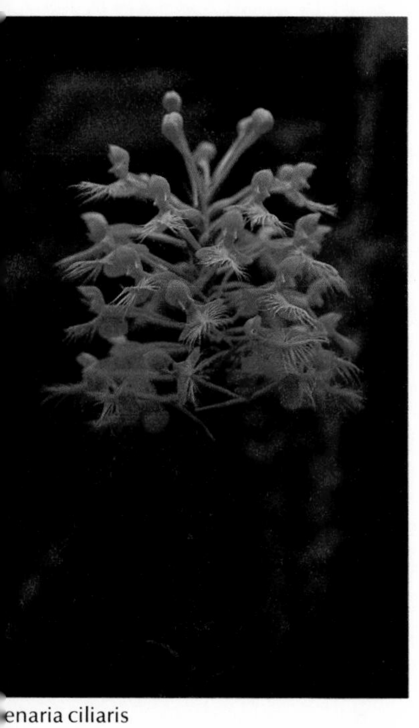

enaria ciliaris

Pogonia ophioglossoides

ORCHIDACEAE
(Orchid Family)

Calopogon pallidus Chap. **Pale Grass-pink**

This genus has a relatively simple flower but its petal arrangement is inverted compared with other orchids. The upper petal is the modified lip (bearded with yellow and pink hairs) and the two lower laterals are petals. The 3 sepals are the larger, ovate laterals and the narrower central lower sepal. The stigma-stamen column projects downward and broadens at its tip. Basal grasslike leaves 0.8 cm wide and up to 30 cm long come from a globose perennial corm surrounding a 1 to 10-flowered stalk which may get 60 cm tall. Flowers open successively over several weeks. Flowers June-August in damp, sandy pinelands and grasslands of the coastal plain; Virginia-Florida-Louisiana.

ORCHIDACEAE
(Orchid Family)

Spiranthes laciniata (Small) Ames **Lace-lip Spiral-orchid**

Most plants of this genus are called ladies' tresses of which there are 6 or 8 in our area, all having their flowers spirally arranged in the spike; "Spiranthes" means spiraled flowers. Both basal and stem leaves are 1 to 2 cm wide to 30 cm long. The stem may get 60 to 90 cm high from a fleshy cluster of roots, the upper 5 to 25 cm bearing the closely crowded spiral of flowers. The white fragrant flowers are about 2 cm long with the lower narrow lip finely toothed or laciniate. Flowers May-August in wet soil, marshes, and pools; Florida-Texas along the coastal plain and north into New Jersey.

ORCHIDACEAE
(Orchid Family)

Goodyera pubescens (Wild.) R. Br. **Downy Rattlesnake Plantain**

This wild orchid grows from thick fibrous roots to a height of 15-50 cm, most of the height being the flowering stalk. The basal rosette of 3-8 evergreen, 5-8 cm long, elliptic-ovate, short-petioled leaves are variegated. The mid-rib and veins are white on a blue-green background. The 0.7 cm long globose white flowers are crowded along the upper 2.5-10 cm of the hairy (pubescent) flowering stalk. Sepals and petals are glandular-hairy on the outside. Flowers July-August in dry to moist coniferous or hardwood areas; Georgia-Arkansas and north into Canada. This species has been collected for commercial use until it is now endangered in some areas; it must be protected.

ORCHIDACEAE
(Orchid Family)

Liparis lilifolia (L.) Richard **Twayblade Orchid**

This is also called the lily-leaf twayblade because of its two broadly ovate, lilylike basal leaves to 15 cm long. Its leafless flower stalk to 25 cm high has 5-30 flowers scattered loosely along it. The lower lip or petal is brownish purple, about shield-shape, 2 cm wide and about as long. Two other petals of same color are mere filaments about 0.8 cm long. Three narrowly linear sepals are greenish white to 0.8 cm long. Flowers June-July in wet swamps and rich woods; Georgia-Alabama and north into Maine-Minnesota. This plant is considered rare and should be protected.

Calopogon pallidus

Calopogon pallidus

Goodyeara pubescens

Spiranthes laciniata

Liparis lilifolia

ORCHIDACEAE
(Orchid Family)

Tipularia discolor (Pursh.) Nutt. **Crane-fly Orchid**

This "near nothing" orchid gets its name by its flower's resemblance to the crane-fly (family Tipulidae) which has long, slender legs and long, narrow wings. "Discolor" refers to the two-colored flowers, purplish bronze and yellow. A single slender-petioled, ovate leaf to 13 cm long, purplish underneath, grows from a horizontal tuber in the early fall and withers away before a leafless 30-60 cm flower stalk grows up the following summer. The slender sepals and petals are shorter than the 5-8 mm long spur. Flowers July-August in damp woodlands; Florida-Texas and north into New York-Indiana.

SAURURACEAE
(Lizard's-tail Family)

Saururus cernuus L. **Lizard's-tail**

Saur means "lizard" and *oura* means "tail"; *cernuus* means "nodding" or "drooping," thus the names above are explained. A stem 1-1.3 m tall arises from a perennial rhizome in the muddy substrate and has alternate heart-shaped leaves about 8 cm wide by 20 cm long. Opposite the leaves is produced a 10-13 cm long, nodding, spikelike raceme of "flowers" with no sepals or petals, having only 3-7 1-cm long white stamens and a shorter pistil. The fruit is a capsule with 3-4 carpels. Flowers June-August in swamps, marshes, and flood plains; Florida-Texas and north into Canada.

SALICACEAE
(Willow Family)

Salix nigra Marshall **Black Willow**

Willows are among the first to colonize a low wet area. This species is considered the most important of willows for wood use. A southern variety, *altissima*, grows 30-35 m tall, twice normal size elsewhere, in Arkansas, Louisiana, Texas, where most willow wood is harvested. Alternate leaves are narrowly lanceolate, often curved, 8-15 cm long by 1-2 cm wide, finely toothed, glabrous and green above and below. They have a petiole 2-8 mm long with stipules falling early. Young twigs are reddish brown and brittle. Separate sexed trees have flowers in catkins without sepals and petals. Male flowers in 4-5 cm long catkins are only a hairy scale with 3-5 stamens. Female catkins 4-8 cm long have only a scale with conical pistil with a bilobed stigma producing a capsule about 7 mm long; as seen in the photo the capsules are crowded on the axis. Found over the eastern half of the U.S. along stream banks and low woodlands.

MYRICACEAE
(Bayberry Family)

Myrica cerifera L. **Wax-Myrtle**

This large perennial shrub to tree 1-7 m tall is much-branched and bears alternate oblanceolate-elliptic deciduous to semievergreen leaves with smooth to remotely toothed edges. Leaf blades taper to a short petiole and are 3-8 cm long by 1-2 cm wide, dark green above, paler and pubescent, golden resinous below, are fragrant when crushed. Small staminate catkins 1-2 cm long, 4-6 mm wide, without sepals or petals, have 2-many stamens per flower. On the same or separate plant, female flowers in few flowered spikes have only an inferior ovary per flower, developing into a 2-mm globose, pale-green drupe covered with granules of bluish-white wax. They were boiled to get wax for candles and are eaten by many birds. This is a common shrub of coastal flat and upland pine woods and swamp edges. Flowers March-April; Florida-Texas and Arkansas-Oklahoma, north from Florida-Virginia.

Saururus cernuus

x nigra

Tipularia discolor

ca cerifera

JUGLANDACEAE
(Walnut Family)

Carya tomentosa Nutt. **Mockernut Hickory**

This is the most abundant of the co-dominant hickories of the southern oak-hickory deciduous forest and is the commonest one found in the coastal pine belt. The tree averages 22 m high with a trunk 30-60 cm in diameter and has a large round crown. Alternate leaves 20-30 cm long are pinnately compound with 5-9 ovate-lanceolate leaflets with finely toothed edges. The underside of the leaflets, the axis and petiole are covered with yellowish tomentose hairs, fragrant when bruised. Separate sexed flowers appear on the same tree, the male in clusters of 3 catkins, 10-13 cm long, each flower having 4 red stamens. The female flowers, 2-5 per cluster, have an inferior ovary surrounded by a 4-toothed calyx cup as a 4-ribbed husk enclosing the nut. The husk splits open exposing the stony ovary wall of the nut. Older catkins and 2 young fruits appear in the photo. The related pecan, *Carya illinoensis*, is a hickory native to the embayment area covered herein. Flowers April-May over most of the eastern half of the country to the Great Lakes and New York.

BETULACEAE
(Birch Family)

Carpinus caroliniana Walt. **American Hornbeam, Ironwood**

Except for the conifers, trees too are wild flowers. Hornbeam and hop-hornbeam, *Ostrya virginiana*, are abundant small trees of our southern forest. Their flowers have no sepals and petals but do have separate male and female catkins on the same tree. Male catkins are about 4 cm long and have several stamens just above each red and green small pointed scale. These are deciduous when pollen matures. Pistils appear in the axil of small, mitten-shaped lanceolate bracts, 3-lobed at the base, in catkins about 2.5 cm long. At maturity a small nutlet is present at each bract, which is 1-3 cm long in clusters 10-15 cm long. The hop-hornbeam female catkins at maturity have erect, more ovate bracts in clusters 4-8 cm long. Leaves of both hornbeams are much like elm leaves but with finer teeth. The bark is smooth and gray in the hornbeam, but brown and shreddy in hop-hornbeam. Rich woods and swamps, Florida-Texas north into Maryland and Illinois.

FAGACEAE
(Beech family)

Quercus stellata Wang. **Post Oak**

The post oak is so named because it is too knotty for timber and is used for fence posts. It is in the white oak group, having rounded rather than pointed leaf lobes. The terminal leaf lobes of this oak form a cross and epidermal hairs on leaves are stellate or star-shaped. Oaks form 5-10 cm long catkins of male flowers each with 3-12 stamens and several chaffy scales. Clusters of 2 or 3 tiny female flowers appear on main branches, each one a tiny pistil in a calyx cup of sepals producing an acorn if pollinated. Separate male catkins and female flower clusters appear on each tree. Description of the acorns is necessary to properly identify the species of most oaks. In this species, the leaf is adequate for identification. Mostly on dry rocky ridges, seldom in lowlands; Florida-Texas and north into Massachusetts-Iowa.

FAGACEAE
(Beech Family)

Quercus velutina Lam. **Black Oak**

A common dominant tree of our oak-hickory forests, one of over 25 species of oaks in the area. The tree may reach 1.8 m in diameter at the base of the trunk and over 30 m in height. The alternate petioled deciduous leaves are 8-13 cm wide and 13-18 cm long and have 5-7 bristle-tipped lobes, as do all of the black oak group. Staminate catkins are hairy, clustered, 10-15 cm long and appear with leaves in spring. Tiny female "flowers" of 2 or 3 pistils appear on short stalks in leaf axils. Acorns are ovoid, 1.5-2 cm long, vertical striped, and in cups with loose scales; they mature the second year. Acorns of white oaks mature in the first year. Florida-Texas and north into Canada.

Carya tomentosa

nus caroliniana

Quercus velutina

cus stellata

FAGACEAE
(Beech Family)
Quercus falcata Michx. **Southern Red Oak**

This is one of our common oaks of the oak-hickory forest. The curved falcate, basal leaf lobes are diagnostic. It is found in dry upland soils, often mixed with pines. It grows about 23 m high and is a good timber tree. The alternate leaves are 12-22 cm long, quite variable in shape and size. Leaves may be deeply 3-lobed or 5-7 lobed, all bristle-tipped on the same or different trees; the base is consistently rounded, as seen in the photo. Staminate catkins are 8-13 cm long and quite hairy. The pistillate flowers (seen in photo) on the same tree are 1-3 per cluster on short hairy stalks. Small orange-brown or striped globular acorns 10-15 mm diameter are in their shallow cups. The swamp red oak, Q. *pagodifolia,* is called cherry-bark oak as the bark closely resembles that of cherry. Its leaves are more uniformly 5-11 lobed and the leaf base wedge-shaped. Both reach their best development in this area. Found in lower bottomlands and higher grounds; Florida-Texas and north into New Jersey-Indiana.

FAGACEAE
(Beech Family)
Quercus marilandica Muench. **Black Jack Oak**

The black jack oak is a small tree to 9 m high, usually found in groves in infertile soil. The bark is quite dark and the branches droop somewhat. The 15-20 cm long 5-8 cm wide lustrous green shallowly 3-lobed, bristly-tipped leaves spread widely from a narrowly tapered-rounded base and a 1.2-cm long leaf stalk. Male catkins 5-10 cm long appear with the leaves and female pistils with no petals or sepals appear singly or in pairs in leaf axils on the same tree, as seen in the photo. The acorn is an ovoid nut 1-2 cm long, light brown, in a loose scaly cup covering the lower half. Florida-Texas and north into New York-Michigan-Oklahoma.

FAGACEAE
(Beech Family)
Quercus nigra L. **Water Oak**

This round crowned oak, to 24 m high, is more useful for fuel than timber because of its many close branches. The usually dark bark has rough, wide, scaly ridges. Its leaves, to 5 cm wide and 10 cm long, unlobed to 3-lobed at the tip, are somewhat variable but mostly spatulate, being wider at the tips and wedge-shaped to the base. Female "flowers" are borne in leaf axils on the same branches as the 5-8 cm long staminate catkins. It is generally an inhabitant of bottom-lands, along with willow oak, Q. *phellos,* whose leaves taper at both tip and base. Both of these oaks have small acorns and often are erroneously called "pin oak." The under 1-cm long acorns are good duck food in river valleys. The tree is not usually found in permanent watery swamps. Florida-Texas and north into Delaware-Kentucky.

ULMACEAE
(Elm Family)
Ulmus rubra Muhl. **Slippery Elm**

This tree grows 15-20 m high with a trunk 30-75 cm in diameter, rather widely branching. The alternate leaves are the largest of our elms, being 12-17 cm long by 5-7.5 cm wide. They are ovate-obovate or broadly elliptical with tapering tips and unequal rounded bases. The margins are coarsely toothed with teeth in pairs. Short petioles are about 8 mm long. The surface of the leaf is rough to the touch. Perfect tiny flowers have no petals, a bell-shaped 5-lobed calyx cup bears 5-6 stamens and a flattened pistil with 2 hairy stigma lobes. The pistil enlarges to an oval broad-winged dry fruit (samara) 1.8-2 cm long, slightly notched at the tip and glabrous. These hang in clusters from short flower stalks which appear before the leaves. Flowers February-March in rich soils of wooded slopes and alluvial woodlands; Florida-Texas and north into Canada.

Quercus falcata

ercus marilandica

Quercus nigra

s rubra

ULMACEAE
(Elm Family)

Ulmus crassifolia Nutt. **Cedar Elm**

This 15-20 m high, round-crowned tree with drooping crooked branches is widespread in our area but is not common. The heavily buttressed base of the trunk is characteristic and rather cedar-like. The alternate leaves are small, 2.5-5 cm long by 1.2-2.5 cm wide, elliptic-ovate, somewhat evergreen, thick and lustrous dark green. Leaf stalks are quite wooly and just under 1 cm long. Stems often have corky wings. Bark has thin, brittle, loose plates without fissures. Unusual for elms, flowers appear in late summer, followed by 1.3 cm oblong winged fruits ripening September-November. Flowers are perfect, without petals, and appear 3-5 per cluster in leaf axils. Found in plains, dry clay ridges, and along streams with other flood plain hardwoods. Limited to north Mississippi and Louisiana to west Texas and north into west Tennessee and Arkansas.

ULMACEAE
(Elm Family)

Ulmus alata Michx. **Winged Elm**

This is the most common of the native elms of the area, reaching a height of 15-20 m. Twigs often have opposite corky wings. Its alternate leaves on short petioles are 5-10 cm long by 1.5-4 cm wide, smaller than both American and Slippery Elms. Leaves are somewhat pubescent above, more so below, with tufts of hairs in the axils of the main veins. They are ovate lanceolate, with tapering tips and toothed margins. Tiny flowers, in clusters, have a bell-shaped calyx of 5 united sepals, no petals, 5 stamens, and a pistil with 2 spreading stigmas. The winged fruit, 2-4 mm wide by 8-10 mm long is orange-red, flattened, 1-seeded, narrowly ovate, 2-toothed at the tip, and quite hair-fringed on the margins. Flowers before leaves in February-March, widely distributed over flood plains and lower ridges; Florida-Texas and north into Virginia-Kansas.

ULMACEAE
(Elm Family)

Ulmus americana L. **American or White Elm**

This common shade tree grows 25-38 m tall and has a massive trunk 0.6-1.3 m in diameter, often with a buttressed base. The alternate double-toothed leaves 10-15 cm long by 5-7.5 cm wide, tapering sharply at the tip, are very similar to those of slippery elm but are smaller and usually have a smooth upper surface. Flowers are similar as well, have no petals and the calyx cup bears the 5-6 stamens and pistil, but the fruits are different. Both have green winged fruits of similar size and ovate shape but the American elm fruit is prominently ciliate-hairy around the wing edges, not found on slippery elm. Both of these elms are important timber trees. Flowers February-March commonly in alluvial woods, swamp forest, and water edges; Florida-Texas and north into Canada.

MORACEAE
(Mulberry Family)

Morus rubra L. **Red Mulberry**

This small tree, usually having a spreading crown, grows in rich deciduous woodlands and is a common understory tree of the oak-hickory forest, but it may grow over 20 m tall. Its alternate, finely-toothed leaves may have 0-3 lobes, are taper pointed, ovate, 7-30 cm long; they are rough and glabrous above, very veiny and soft hairy beneath. Male and female flowers are in separate catkins on separate-sexed trees or on the same tree. Flowers have no petals and there are 4 sepals and 4 stamens in male catkins 5-8 cm long. The sepals enclose a low ovary in female catkins about 2.5 cm long. Each ovary becomes a small, red druplet of the whole "berry" as the catkin. It is thus a multiple fruit of many separate flower pistils. These ripen May-August and are readily eaten by birds and other wildlife. The trees are found in moist flats, slopes, and protected ridges; Florida-Texas and north into Canada.

Ulmus crassifolia

us americana

Ulmus alata

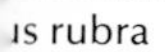

us rubra

ARISTOLOCHIACEAE
(Dutchman's-pipe Family)

Asarum canadense L. **Wild Ginger**

This deciduous plant has 7-13 cm wide, heart-shaped leaves with leaf stalks, stems, and calyx that are white-hairy. The related little brown jug has no such hairs. The plant runs by a creeping stem and a single flower rises between two terminal leaves. Flowers are made up of a brown-red calyx cup, 2 to 2.5 cm long enclosing 12 stamens and a 6-lobed pistil. There are no petals and reddish, triangular, pointed calyx lobes are about 1.2 cm long. Ginger spice is from an entirely different plant family. Flowers April-May on shady banks and woods; Alabama-Arkansas and north into Canada.

ARISTOLOCHIACEAE
(Dutchman's-pipe Family)

Hexastylis arifolia (Michx.) Small **Little Brown Jugs**

This genus is closely related to our *Asarum* or wild ginger. But since the ovary is partly superior instead of inferior and the stigma is bilobed rather than not lobed, it is not an *Asarum*. This is an evergreen trailing perennial with underground stems which give rise to flowers in the axils of the upright leaves. Leaves are trianglar with basal lobes, 5-15 cm long by 8-15 cm wide, sometimes variegated. Flowers are hidden from view by the leaves and humus. Flowers consist of a 1.5-2.5 cm long, 0.8-1 cm diameter, fleshy, urn-shaped brownish calyx tube with 3 spreading lobes; there are no petals; 12 stamens and a partially inferior ovary are within this "jug." Flowers April-May in woodlands; Florida-Louisiana and north into Virginia-Kentucky.

POLYGONACEAE
(Buckwheat Family)

Rumex crispus L. **Curly Dock, Yellow Dock**

This noxious biennial weed from Europe has extended its range through all of the U.S . and beyond. It commonly grows 60-130 cm tall and is seen in late summer and fall in a brown dry "dead" condition as fruits hang on. Its flowers are 6 tiny greenish-yellow sepals and its fruits are 3-winged, as the 3 outer sepals become 0.7 cm across and are heart-shaped. Leaves are 15-60 cm long by 2-7 cm wide, strongly puckered at their edges. Fruits are 3-sided, 1-seeded achene 4-6 mm broad, the wings are the surrounding 3 sepals. This is one of about 15 species of *Rumex* in our area. Flowers June-July in old fields, waste places, and roadsides.

POLYGONACEAE
(Buckwheat Family)

Rumex hastatulus Bald. ex. Ell **Wild Sorrel**

The sour taste of the leaves of this plant indicates its oxalic acid content and it has been called sour dock. The leaves 3-12 cm long, are point-lobed at the base of the somewhat arrowhead-shaped blade on a long, slightly winged leaf stalk. Mostly perennial, the plant grows 15-40 cm tall, most of which is branching stalks with whorls of flowers with no petals, 6 sepals, 6 stamens and a 3-angled ovary with a 3-parted style. The largest parts are the inner 3 reddish sepals, enlarging winglike, heart-shaped to 3-4 mm long, enclosing the 3-sided, 1-seeded reddish achene 1-2 mm long. Some flowers on the plant may have either stamens or pistil missing, called a polygamous condition. A similar smaller species *R. acetosella* has smaller leaves and wingless sepals around the achene. Flowers March-July in fields and roadsides; Florida-Texas and north into Massachusetts-Illinois-Kansas.

arum canadense

Rumex crispus

ex hastatulus

Hexastylis arifolia

POLYGONACEAE
(Buckwheat Family)
Polygonum coccineum Muhl. **Swamp Persecaria**

This water smartweed differs from *P. densiflorum* in that the stalk bears 1-3 spikes rather than several-many. The leaves are tapered only at the tip instead of tip and base. This species is in our northern range and beyond while *P. densiflorum* is mainly limited to the coastal plain. Both species are present at Reelfoot Lake in Tennessee. As in other species of *Polygonum*, there are no petals and 4-6 sepals are petallike. There are 3-9 stamens, the pistil is 1-celled with a 2-3 lobed stigma and the fruit is a triangular 1-seeded achene 2-3 mm long. Flowers July-September in wet prairies, shores or ponds, aquatic or terrestrial; Tennessee-east, north and west in the U.S.

POLYGONACEAE
(Buckwheat Family)
Polygonum densiflorum Meis. **Water Smartweed**

Smartweeds are also known as knotweeds, lady-fingers, *et al.* This member of the Buckwheat Family is found in low and watery places in woods, swamps, and shallow pools. Stems arise from a perennial rhizome and leaves 7-30 cm long by 1.5-4 cm wide taper at both ends. As in most members of the family, a thin sheath surrounds the stem at the node. Flowering spikes 2-10 cm long arise both terminally and in leaf axils. Flowers are tiny, have 3-6 petallike pinkish to white sepals but no petals. Nutlets are 3-sided and single seeded. Flowers June-October mostly along the coastal plain; Florida-Texas and north into New Jersey and into Missouri.

POLYGONACEAE
(Buckwheat Family)
Polygonum scandens L. **Climbing Buckwheat**

This species is one of the few viny members of this family. The twining (scandent) stem of this high climbing perennial has alternate cordate-ovate, long tapered leaves 5-13 cm long by 4-6 cm wide, without teeth, on short to long petioles sheathing the stem at their bases. Axillary flower clusters 5-20 cm long by 2-3 cm across have loosely spaced small yellowish-green perfect flowers on short stalks. There are 8 stamens, no petals and the 5-parted calyx has 3 white outer segments strongly winged, often crinkled, and 10-13 mm long in maturity. The superior 3-sided ovary without a style has a 3-lobed stigma above. Fruits are 3-sided black shiny achenes 4-6 mm long. Flowers August-November in damp thickets, wet bottoms, and openings; Florida-Texas and north into Canada.

CHENOPODIACEAE
(Goosefoot Family)
Salicornia virginica I. **Glasswort**

Plants in this family also have flowers with no petals and with perfect male and female flowers all on one plant. The glasswort is a 1.5-2 m tall marsh plant specially adapted for this habitat and it is found nowhere else. The leaves are only opposite scales at the nodes of the light green, much-branched, reclining-to-upright stems. The plant forms dense mats spreading by perennial rhizomes, branching at the nodes. Stems turn bright red in the fall. Flowers are produced 3 on each side at the nodes of 1.5-6 cm lengths of short jointed terminal and lateral branches. Flowers are only a calyx scale, with a tiny pistil and 1-2 stamens 1-2 mm long; the single seed is about 1 mm long. Flowers July-October around brackish marshlands of the outer coastal plain; Florida-Texas and north into Nova Scotia.

olygonum coccineum

Polygonum densiflorum

ygonum scandens

Salicornia virginica

BATACEAE
(Saltwort Family)

Batis maritima L. **Maritime Saltwort**

This is hardly a "wildflower," since there are no sepals or petals, and the flower spike is hardly more than a 1.2-cm tumorlike lump of tissue, bearing seeds. The plant is prostrate then upright, 50-150 cm high bearing 1.5-2.5 cm long opposite, yellow-green, thick, boat-shaped leaves which are flattened on top. The plant is a semiwoody, strong-scented marine shrub. It is often found in with another unusual beach plant, *Salicornia,* or glasswort, along sandy beaches, mud flats, and salt marshes; Florida-Texas and north into North Carolina.

AMARANTHACEAE
(Amaranth Family)

Alternanthera philoxeroides (Mart.) Griesb. **Alligator-weed**

This member of the Amaranth Family, to which the colorful *Celosia* (cocks-comb) belongs, grows in wet or aquatic habitats often frequented by alligators. These rather large, sprawling perennial plants have opposite, narrowly elliptic-oblanceolate leaves 3-10 cm long. Flower stalks, 1-7 cm long, arise from remote leaf axils and bear a 1.2-cm tall spike of small, greenish-white petalless flowers, producing a 1-seeded bladderlike fruit. This species probably originated in South America. Flowers April-October in ponds, marshes, and sluggish streams along the coastal plain; Florida-Texas.

PHYTOLACCACEAE
(Pokeweed Family)

Phytolacca americana L. **Pokeweed**

This perennial plant may grow to over 3 m tall, dying back to the ground each year. Leaves 8-30 cm long by 3-12 cm wide are elliptic-lanceolate, smooth, and without teeth. Stems and leaves are green with red areas on them. Axillary flowering racemes are 5-20 cm long. Small, greenish-white flowers, with 5 sepals but no petals, shortly give rise to 4-7 mm diameter shiny purple-black berries. There are 5-30 stamens and a superior ovary, compounded of several parts. Birds enjoy the berries, and man, the young leaves as "poke salet" cooked as "greens" in the south. "Poke" means root, formerly the source of a somewhat toxic drug used for rheumatism. Flowers July to frost in rich, low ground; Florida-Texas and north into Canada.

AIZOACEAE
(Carpetweed Family)

Mollugo verticillata L. **Carpetweed**

This prostrate, glabrous annual herb spreads radially over the ground in patches 25-50 cm across from a central root. Its 5-6 near-whorled or verticillate oblanceolate leaves are 12-25 mm long, narrowed to the base. The flowers arise near leaf axils on slender stalks and have no petals. There are 5 green sepals with white margins, 3-5 fertile stamens and 5 petal-like sterile stamens. The pistil has a superior ovary and a 3-lobed stigma. The 3-celled capsule produces several shiny red seeds. This is a common weed of fields and yards throughout most of the country, but it is more common southward.

olacca americana

Batis maritima

Alternanthera philoxeroides

Mollugo verticillata

PORTULACACEAE
(Purslane Family)
Portulaca oleracea L. **Purslane**

This prostrate purplish-stemmed annual, 1-45 cm across, branches freely from a deep central root. The very fleshy, sessile, mostly alternate leaves are clustered toward branch ends and are elliptic-obovate to wedge-shaped, 3-5 cm long by 1-1.5 cm wide. Flowers 5-8 mm across have 5 tiny yellow elliptic petals, 5 sepals and 7 or more stamens. They are open only in the morning. The pistil has 4-6 stigma lobes and a superior ovary producing a 6-10 mm long capsule. It is many-seeded and opens by "popping off a lid" at the top. Flowers May-November in open fields and waste places. Its origin is unknown and may be a European immigrant, or perhaps native to the southwest, spreading eastward and into Canada.

PORTULACACEAE
(Purslane Family)
Claytonia virginica L. **Spring Beauty**

When this herald of spring appears the season has definitely arrived. The flower has 5 stamens attached to the 5 pink-striped white petals 1-1.5 cm long, and only 2 sepals below, the latter a family characteristic. A pair of linear narrow leaves to 25 cm long arises from a vertical corm and the single stem 5 to 40 cm tall terminates in a 6-20 flowered, long-stalked raceme. The 1-celled compound pistil produces 3-6 seeds in a capsule 3-6 mm in diameter. Plants also reproduce by the corms and thus spread vegetatively into masses. Flowers March-May in rich woods, meadows, and clearings; Georgia-Texas and north into New England-Minnesota.

CARYOPHYLLACEAE
(Pink Family)
Stellaria media (L.) Cyrillo **Common Chickweed**

This weedy member of the Pink Family is quite a pest. Its rapidly spreading prostrate stems, with tiny 5-7 mm across, starlike flowers cover lawns and garden beds from winter into spring. The 5 white petals appear to be 10 but each is deeply cleft into 2 lobes. There are 3-10 stamens and a pistil which is 3-lobed, its ovary producing a 5-7 mm long ovoid capsule surrounded by a calyx of 5 sepals. The stem has a single line of hairs extending lengthwise and its ovate-elliptic 2.5-cm long leaves are opposite, as in most plants of the family. It is similar to another pest of the same family, the mouse-ear chickweed, *Cerastium,* which is quite hairy. Flowers January-May through most of the U.S.

CARYOPHYLLACEAE
(Pink Family)
Saponaria officinalis L. **Soapwort, Bouncing Bet**

This member of the Pink Family is devoid of hairs, is a perennial from a rhizome, and grows to 90 cm tall. The leaves are opposite, stalkless, toothless, elliptic-ovate and 3-veined; they are to 13 cm long by 5 cm wide. Flowers are white or pale pink, produced in branching terminal and axillary clusters. There are numerous bracts on the flower stalks. Flowers are 2.5 cm across and 2.5 cm long. The 5 petals are notched at the tips of the blade and the base of the blade narrows into a "claw" by which it is attached. At the top of the claw is a scalelike appendage. There are 10 stamens; a pistil bilobed at the top produces a 10-12 mm long capsule, 4-toothed at the top. Flowers May-October in fields and roadsides in most of the U.S.

Portulaca oleracea

aytonia virginica

Saponaria officinalis

laria media

CARYOPHYLLACEAE
(Pink Family)
Silene stellata (L.) Ait. f. **Starry Campion**

This erect short-lived perennial, 50-100 cm tall, has 4-6 whorled leaves at swollen nodes of the stem, though leaves may be opposite toward the base and top of the plant. The sessile simple, ovate-elliptic or lanceolate leaves are 3-10 cm long by 0.5-3 cm wide, rounded at the base and long tapered to the tip. Leaves become bracts at the top of the plant where axillary loosely branching flower stalks arise. Flowers have a 5-toothed bell-shaped calyx cup of 5 united sepals 1-1.5 cm high. The 5 white 1-2 cm long petals are narrowed into a "claw" at the base and fringed into narrow strips as they spread outward. There are 10 long stamens and a pistil with a 3-4 lobed stigma. A superior ovary produces a 1 or 3-celled capsule opening and splitting into 3-6 teeth at the tip. Flowers June-September in rich woodlands and clearings; Georgia-Texas and north into Massachusetts-Minnesota.

CARYOPHYLLACEAE
(Pink Family)
Silene virginica L. **Fire Pink, Catchfly**

This perennial, weak-stemmed plant may get 60 cm tall, with spatulate basal leaves and 2 to 4 pairs of opposite stem leaves. Stem leaves, to 13 cm long, are wider above the middle and taper downward from a width of 4 cm to the stem. Stems and sepals have sticky glandular hairs. The 2.5 cm long sepals are joined at their bases, making a tubular calyx; 5 separate crimson petals, 2-toothed at their tips, spread from narrow "claws" as long as the calyx to flowers 4 cm across. A pistil with 3-lobed stigma produces a 3-celled capsule 1.2-1.8 cm long. Flowers April-June in open woods and clearings; Georgia-Oklahoma and north into West Virginia-Minnesota.

NYMPHAEACEAE
(Water-lily Family)
Nuphar luteum (L.) Sibthorp & Smith **Spatter-dock, Yellow Pond-lily**

Leaves of this pond lily are 30-60 cm wide and cut into a heart-shaped base, otherwise rather circular. They arise from a thick submerged perennial rhizome by a long leaf stalk and float on the surface or become emergent. Sepals, 5-14, are petaloid, from outer green to inner yellow, cupping over the numerous small petals which grade into numerous stamens. The globular superior ovary with a stigmatic disk becomes a compound, many-celled berry-like fruit, 3-5 cm high. This and the American lotus are the more common water lilies of this area. Flowers May-October; Florida-Texas and north into New York-Wisconsin.

NYMPHAEACEAE
(Water-lily Family)
Nymphaea odorata Ait. **Fragrant Water-lily**

Nearly circular leaf blades 5-50 cm broad, except for a narrow triangular cut at the base, arise on long purplish-green petioles from a horizontal perennial rhizome anchored in mud of marshes or shallow ponds. The shining green floating leaves are purplish beneath. Strongly fragrant flowers 5-15 cm across are white-pink. The 4 ovate-lanceolate sepals are 3-8 cm long by 1-2.5 cm wide and many petals 5-10 cm long by 1-2.3 cm wide taper above to rounded tips. The inner petals grade into wide filament stamens but the inner stamens have filaments narrower than the anthers, many arising from the outer ovary wall. The pistil is compounded of 12-35 parts and is capped by as many radiating, linear stigmas. The fruit is globose, of many cells, 2-3 cm in diameter. Flowers June-September in ponds, swamps, and bogs; Florida-Louisiana and north into New Jersey.

Nuphar luteum

ymphaea odorata

Nymphaea odorata

lene stellata

Silene virginica

NELUMBONACEAE
(Lotus Family)

Nelumbo lutea (Willd.) Persoon **American Lotus**

This water-lily of the eastern U.S. has large, umbrellalike, circular aerial leaves 20-70 cm across attached at the center to 1-m or more long leaf stalk from a perennial rhizome below. Flowering stalks spread out into a flat, 4-5 cm wide flared top or receptacle into which are embedded many separate pistils, each maturing into a dry 1-2 cm long acornlike fruit. Numerous yellow stamens surround the flared, flat-topped receptacle and with many intergrading yellow petals and sepals 2-12 cm long produce a flower 12-25 cm across. Acres of these plants abound in ponds, lakes and sluggish streams; flowers June-September; Florida-Texas and north into Ontario-Minnesota.

CABOMBACEAE
(Water-shield Family)

Cabomba caroliniana Gray **Coon-tail, Fanwort**

This submerged pond weed is known more by its vegetative parts than by its flowers. The mostly opposite leaves are on a rhizomatous submerged stem 10-20 cm or more long. Submerged leaves are repeatedly divided into linear segments of a fan 2.5-5 cm across. Emergent alternate leaves may be lanceolate or parasol shape and small as seen in the photo. Flowers on axillary stalks have 6 similar white petaloid sepals/petals, 7-12 mm long, each with a pair of yellow spots at the base. There are 3-6 short stamens and a tiny 3-carpellate pistil producing 2-3 seeds. It may become an abundant pest in still ponds and lakes. Flowers May-September mostly in the Mississippi Valley and coastal states; Texas-Florida-New York.

RANUNCULACEAE
(Buttercup Family)

Aquilegia canadensis L. **Wild Columbine**

This is the only wild columbine of our area. Typical nodding flowers are two-toned, yellow shading into red, and the 5 petals are long-spurred near their bases. Five colored, nonspurred separate sepals alternate with the petals, and numerous stamens protrude around five separate pistils, each forming a dry, splitting follicle about 2 cm long. Leaves, mostly basal, are divided into three 3-lobed leaflets to 5 cm long on a somewhat branching, herbaceous perennial plant 30-60 cm high in rich rocky woods and ledges. Flowers April-June; Florida-Texas and north into Canada.

RANUNCULACEAE
(Buttercup Family)

Actaea pachypoda Ell. **White Bane-berry, Doll's-eyes**

This herbaceous perennial grows to a height of 80-100 cm from a rootstock. Its leaves are thrice-divided into groups of 3-5 leaflets 6-10 cm long which are sharply toothed and somewhat lobed. The small white flowers have 10-15 similar 3-5 mm long sepals and petals and numerous stamens. The flower cluster elongates from 1-2.5 cm to 15-20 cm in fruit. Rarely for this family, a single pistil in the flower becomes a single-seeded white berry at the tip of the thick elongating flower stalk which becomes red. The white fruits are the "doll's eyes" with black "pupils." The fruits are considered poisonous. Flowers April-May in rich woodlands; Florida-Mississippi and north into Canada.

elumbo lutea

Nelumbo lutea

Aquilegia canadensis

Cabomba caroliniana

Actaea pachypoda

Actaea pachypoda

RANUNCULACEAE
(Buttercup Family)

Cimicifuga racemosa Nutt. **Black Snakeroot, Black Cohosh**

This coarse, herbaceous, perennial to over 1-2.5 m high has pokerlike 25-40 cm long wands of tiny, fetid smelling nectariferous white flowers. There are no petals but 4-5 tiny 4 mm long sepals are petallike. Except for carrion types, insects seem to avoid these flowers. The white is due to the numerous stamens of each flower. *Cimicifuga* means "insect repeller" and bugbane is also a common name for this plant. A single pistil develops into a broad follicle about 8 mm long. Large ternately divided leaves resemble those of *Actea* except its leaflets are about 15 cm long. Flowers May-September in rich woods at higher elevations; Georgia-Tennessee and north into Massachusetts-Missouri.

RANUNCULACEAE
(Buttercup Family)

Clematis crispa L. **Leather Flower**

This southern viny member of the family has no petals but its 4 sepals are petallike, thick and "leathery." Margins of the sepals are ragged or "crisped," 2.5-5 cm long and turned back at the tips. Single bluish flowers are borne terminally on a stem and hang pendulous. "Seeds" are really 2-3 cm long achenes from many separate pistils in each flower, are flattened, long "tailed," and usually not hairy. Opposite leaves are pinnately compound, with 3-5 linear to ovate leaflets 2-10 cm long and are often tendrillike. Flowers April-August in low woods and marshes; Florida-Texas and north into Virginia-Illinois.

RANUNCULACEAE
(Buttercup Family)

Thalictrum thalictroides (L.) Boivin **Rue-Anemone, Windflower**

This fragile little perennial plant appears in early spring, growing to 10-30 cm high from tuberous roots. Like the meadow rue, its white to pinkish "petals" are sepals, as there are no petals. Sepals are elliptic-ovate, 5-18 mm long, and number 5-10 making a flower 1.5-2 cm across. Stamens are many and 5-15 separate pistils each produce a 3-4 mm long achene. Several flowers branch umbrella-like from the top of the plant. Leaflets are ternate, opposite or whorled below the flower cluster. Some botanists put this plant in the genus *Anemonella* in which this is the only species. Flowers March-June in open and sloping woodlands; Florida-Arkansas and north into Maine-Minnesota-Oklahoma.

RANUNCULACEAE
(Buttercup Family)

Thalictrum polygamum Muhl. **Tall Meadow Rue**

This perennial herbaceous plant grows to over 3 m high and is especially showy; its terminal, 30-40 cm long, sprays of tiny flowers tower over most other summer vegetation. Flowers are hardly 5 mm long or wide and may be staminate only, pistillate only, or stamens and pistils in the same flower all on the same plant. This is called polygamous, hence its species name. Flowers may be greenish-yellow, purplish, or white. Color is due to sepals and stamens as there are no petals. Leaves are 2-3 times compound, with leaflets mostly 3-lobed and 1.5-3.5 cm long, somewhat resembling those of columbine. Flowers June-August in meadows, swamps and thickets; Georgia-Mississippi-Tennessee and north into Canada.

Clematis crispa

icifuga racemosa

Thalictrum thalictroides

Thalictrum polygamum

RANUNCULACEAE
(Buttercup Family)

Ranunculus septentrionalis Poir. **Swamp Buttercup**

As in other true buttercups this one has 3-5 green to yellowish sepals, 5 or fewer petals, numerous stamens and always numerous pistils forming a cylindric or ovoid head. The pistils mature each into a dry, roundish 4-5 mm dry nonsplitting 1-seeded achene, 3-4.5 mm long, with a curved beak on top. This plant has yellow oblong petals 12-15 mm long and half as wide. Sepals are half as long and reflexed. Leaves are basal and on the 30-90 cm high branching stem, usually 3-parted (ternate) with leaflets ovate-rhombic, 3-13 cm long and variously lobed. Flowers April-August in wet meadows and bottom lands; West Virginia-Texas and north into Canada and Missouri.

RANUNCULACEAE
(Buttercup Family)

Ranunculus abortivus L. **Small-flowered Buttercup, Swamp Buttercup**

This weed-type erect, branching 12-85 cm tall buttercup is present through most of the eastern half of the U.S., found in low-lying yards, gardens, and waste places. Flowers are most noted as "seed heads," as yellow petals are only 1-4 mm long and few in number. Heads are globose to cylindric, about 7 mm long and half as wide. Achenes are nearly beakless and about 1.5 mm long. Leaves with long petioles are variable up the stem but basal ones are orbicular to kidney-shaped, with scalloped margins. Flowers March-August.

RANUNCULACEAE
(Buttercup Family)

Hepatica acutiloba DC. **Liverleaf, Hepatica**

This perennial favorite grows 10-25 cm high from a short rhizome, producing a cluster of a few leaves but no aerial stem. Its evergreen leaves are palmately 3-lobed with pointed or acute tip, thus its species name. Leaf petioles are 10-25 cm long, quite hairy, and tipped by a simple blade 4-7 cm wide by 3-6 cm long. White or purple flowers are borne singly on slender hairy stalks 10-15 cm long. Sepals and petals are alike, vary in number 6-10 just above 3 sepal-like green, ovate-lanceolate involucral bracts of similar length. Stamens are numerous and several separate pistils, each produces an ovoid achene 1.4-1.8 mm long. Flowers March-April in rich woodlands; Georgia-Alabama-Missouri and north into Canada.

RANUNCULACEAE
(Buttercup Family)

Anemone virginiana L. **Windflower, Thimbleweed**

Anemones differ from buttercups in that there are no petals, only sepals which may be few to many. This species is a herbaceous perennial 30-70 cm high, hairy, and branching from a persistent base. Long-petioled basal leaves about 8 cm long by 6 cm wide are 3-parted and prominently veiny as are the stem leaves above. One to three flower stalks arise from the whorl of stem leaves. Five white sepals are petallike, 8-20 mm long and hairy underneath. Numerous stamens surround a "head" of many separate hairy pistils, each pistil forming an achene in the cylindric "head" to 2.5 cm long. This is the "thimble" from which the common name comes. Flowers June-August on open or dry woods and slopes; Gerogia-Arkansas and north into Virginia-Kansas.

Ranunculus septentrionalis

nculus abortivus

Anemone virginiana

tica acutiloba

BERBERIDACEAE
(Barberry Family)

Jeffersonia diphylla (L.) Persoon **Twinleaf**

This harbinger of spring is a herbaceous perennial from an underground rhizome. It has no upright stems and from the rhizome several leaf stalks rise 15-30 cm high bearing bilobed or divided blades, 5-10 cm across. Leafless flower stalks rise from the rhizome and produce single flowers 2-3 cm across. Flowers have 4 petallike sepals that fall early, leaving 8 white 2-cm long petals. There are 8 stamens and a single pistil which becomes a 2.5-cm long seed capsule. Flowers March-May in moist rich woods; rare in Alabama and Tennessee and north in to Virginia-New York-Iowa.

BERBERIDACEAE
(Barberry Family)

Podophyllum peltatum L. **May-apple**

This herbaceous perennial sends up leaf stalks 30-45 cm high from a poisonous horizontal rhizome. Single leaves usually produce no flowers while 2-branched petioles produce a single flower between the two branches. Leaves are radially lobed and "peltate," having the leaf stalk attached near the center of the 20-30 cm broad, horizontal blade. On the single flower, 6 sepals fall early, leaving 6-9 waxy white petals 3-4 cm long. There are 12-18 stamens and an ovoid pistil with a short 2-lobed stigma. A greenish-yellow fleshy fruit (berry) 4-5 cm long matures in May and gives the name May-apple meaning. Flowers March-June in open woods and meadows; Florida-Texas and north into Canada.

MENISPERMACEAE
(Moonseed Family)

Cocculus carolinus (L.) DC. **Carolina Moonseed**

This perennial semiwoody vine climbs over other vegetation along fence rows, woodland and stream edges and thickets, but is not rampant. The 3-10 cm long, alternate non-toothed leaves vary from heart shape to nearly 3-lobed; there are no tendrils, the stem is twining. (The tendrils seen in the photo do not belong to this plant.) It is known especially for its clusters of bright red, 5-9 mm drupe fruits; *cocculus* means "little berry." Each drupe has a single flat seed the shape of a coiled snail shell. Flowers in 2.5-15 cm long clusters are 1-2 mm long, greenish yellow, have 6 each, sepals and petals on separate sexed plants. Flowers May-August with red drupes in September-November; Florida-Texas and north into North Carolina-Illinois-Missouri.

MAGNOLIACEAE
(Magnolia Family)

Liriodendron tulipifera L. **Tulip Tree, Yellow Poplar**

This is one of the most abundant and largest timber trees of the eastern U.S., but it is a magnolia as its flower structure indicates, not a poplar. It may grow over 60 m high. The large columnar trunk is usually limbless much of its height, gray to gray-brown bark with rounded ridges and deep furrows. Its alternate 8-20 cm long leaves have 2 apical and 2-4 basal lobes, and its 8-10 cm broad flowers resemble greenish-yellow tulips with orange centers. Each 4-6 cm long, erect petal is bicolored, ⅓ of the length at base is orange and the rest is greenish-yellow. The flowers have 3 sepals, 6 petals, and many stamens 3-4 cm long. Conelike clusters of dry 1-2 seeded elongate, woody, winged fruits 3-4.5 cm long ripen September-November, falling away later. The magnolia and buttercup families are among the most primitive of flowering plants. Flowers April-June in moist but well-drained soils; Florida-Louisiana and north into Vermont-Wisconsin.

dophyllum peltatum

Jeffersonia diphylla

dophyllum peltatum

odendron tulipifera

Cocculus carolinus

MAGNOLIACEAE
(Magnolia Family)

Magnolia virginiana L. **Sweetbay Magnolia**

This small tree grows 6-9 mm in height and has alternate, elliptic-oblong leaves 10-15 cm long by 3-8 cm wide. The short petioled leaves are toothless, bright green above, whitish below, and are shed in early spring farther south but in November farther north. Creamy-white 5-8 cm broad very fragrant flowers have 3 sepals, 9 or 12 petals, many stamens and many separate pistils, arranged spirally conelike. Fruits are dark red follicles containing a flattened red seed suspended by a thread when ripe. "Cones" are about 5 cm long by 2.5 cm wide. This plant is limited to the coastal plain and is found in low wet soils of swamps and ponds from Florida-east Texas and north, into New Jersey; it also reaches into west central Tennessee and south central Arkansas. Flowers May-June. This species is becoming rare and should be protected.

MAGNOLIACEAE
(Magnolia Family)

Magnolia grandiflora L. **Southern Magnolia**

This is our only native, completely evergreen magnolia and it may reach a height of 30 meters. The elliptic leaves are to 8x30 cm in size, with a waxy lustrous green upper surface, and rusty-hairy beneath. The fragrant flowers are the largest of the magnolias and may grow to 20 cm across. There are 3 sepals and 6, 9 or 12 creamy white petals. As it matures, the conelike aggregate of many pistils is colorful orange to red, about 10 cm long. When it is mature the aggregate turns brown and each pistil splits open, releasing 2 bright red seeds on the end of silken strands in September. Flowers May-June in rich bottom lands or slopes, aong with other hardwoods; Florida-Texas and north into North Carolina-Arkansas. This tree is commonly planted in gardens.

MAGNOLIACEAE
(Magnolia Family)

Magnolia tripetala L. **Umbrella Magnolia**

This small tree seldom reaches 12 meters in height and derives its common name from the close grouping of large leaves at the ends of bare branches. Deciduous leaves are obovate-elliptic, long tapering to the short petiole and may get 20 cm wide by 50 cm long. Large, cream-colored, ill-scented flowers have 3 broad petal-like reflexed sepals, and 6 or 9 petals, 8-12 cm long, narrowly taper to their bases. Rose colored cones are 8-12 cm long at maturity. Flowers April-May near streams and moist bottom lands; Georgia-Arkansas and north into Pennsylvania-Ohio-Missouri.

ANNONACEAE
(Custard Apple Family)

Asimina triloba (L.) Dunal. **Common Pawpaw**

This small understory tree is usually found in clusters or thickets in our low wet woods and may reach 9 meters in height. Its alternate leaves, 20-25 cm long, are smooth margined, obovate and long-tapered to a short petiole, usually appearing after the flowers. Flowers are 4-5 cm across, composed of 3 green sepals, falling early, and 6 reflexed maroon petals. Delicious (similar in flavor to papaya) fleshy fruits, 7-13 cm long, cylindric-oblong and yellowish, mature in late summer. There are several dark brown flat seeds 1.5-2 cm long. Flowers April; Florida-Texas and north into New York-Nebraska.

;nolia virginiana

Magnolia grandiflora

nolia grandiflora

Magnolia grandiflora

Magnolia tripetala

Asimina triloba

CALYCANTHACEAE
(Calycanthus Family)

Calycanthus floridus L. **Sweet-shrub**

This is a much-branched perennial shrub 0.3-3 m high with opposite, elliptic-ovate, pubescent leaves usually tapered at both ends, 5-18 cm long by 2-8 cm wide, on short petioles. The receptacle, or calyx cup bearing flower parts ("Calycanthus"), is deeply cup-shaped, figlike, and from the rim projects similar sepals and petals. These 25-35 segments are linear-oblanceloate, blunt-tipped, maroon colored, and 1.5-2.2 cm long. The plant is also called strawberry-shrub as crushed sepals have a strawberry odor. Many stamens line the receptacle cup around many small pistils, each producing an achene. The ovoid matured leathery structure, 3-7 cm long, is an accessory fruit with the stem its covering. Flowers April-August in rich woods, hillsides, and stream banks; Florida-Mississippi and north into Virginia-Tennessee.

LAURACEAE
(Laurel Family)

Sassafras albidum (Nuttall) Nees. **Sassafras**

This is one of the best known of eastern trees. Its aromatic oils from the bark of roots has been used as a spring tonic in sassafras tea, also for flavoring and perfumes. Scrape a young twig to get the oil odor. Its alternate leaves of 3 shapes, ovate unlobed, bilobed "mittens," and trilobed, are known by every scout. The small yellowish flowers, hardly a cm across, appear at the same time as the leaf buds become obvious in March-April. Those with stamens are on separate trees from those with single pistils which produce blue-black 1 cm drupes as fleshy fruits. There are no petals but there are 6 3-5 mm long, yellow-green sepals; there are 9 stamens in the male flowers (photo). Mostly in dry sandy soils; Florida-Texas and north into Maine-Iowa.

PAPAVERACEAE
(Poppy Family)

Sanguinaria canadensis L. **Bloodroot**

This member of the Poppy Family has a single leaf and single flower rising from each node of a perennial underground rhizome. Leaves grow 10-14 cm high and the circular 5-9 lobed, palmately-veined blade is 8-16 cm broad. Milky or colored juice is a characteristic of the family and this species has orange-red juice in all its parts, hence its names, both generic and common. Flowers have 2 sepals and 8-12 white to bluish petals about 2.5 cm long. Stamens are about twice the number of petals. A single pistil with 2-lobed stigma produces a 2-celled dry, splitting capsule about 2.5 cm long. Flowers March-May in open woods and slopes; Florida-Texas and north into Canada.

PAPAVERACEAE
(Poppy Family)

Argemone albiflora Hornemann **Prickly Poppy**
A. mexicana L. **Mexican Prickly Poppy**

These two prickly annual poppies, rare in our area, are similar in most respects except for color and size. *A. albiflora* has larger and white flowers, 7-10 cm broad *vs.* 2.5-7 cm and yellow flowers for *A. Mexicana*. Plant size is larger, over a meter for the former *vs.* 0.5-0.75 m for the latter. The white form has clear, while the yellow form has yellow, sap. Flowers have 2-3 sepals, 4-6 petals and many stamens. Fruiting capsules are 2.5-4 cm long, quite spiny and produce many seeds as annual plants. The genus is mostly western with about 12 other species. Flowers April-August in usually dry, open areas; Florida-Texas and north into New Jersey-Tennessee-Missouri.

lycanthus floridus

Sassafras albidum

anguinaria canadensis

gemone albiflora

A. mexicana

PAPAVERACEAE
(Poppy Family)
Stylophorum diphyllum (Michx.) Nutt. **Celandine Poppy**

This is a bright yellow flowered perennial member of the poppy family, bristly-hairy but not prickly and has yellow latex. Its basal leaves, as the few stem leaves, are 5-7 pinnately cleft to compound, grayish on back and grow 10-45 cm long. There are 2 coarse-hairy sepals, falling early and leaving 4 obovate petals of a flower 2-3 cm across. The many stamens are characteristic of the family. The pistil is 4 carpellate, has a 2-4 lobed stigma and produces a bristly-hairy capsule splitting on 2-4 sides. Reaches into our area from the north and east extending into southeast Missouri-Kentucky and Tennessee. Flowers March-May in rich woods, slopes and ravines.

FUMARIACEAE
(Bleeding Heart Family)
Dicentra cucullaria (L.) Bernh. **Dutchman's-breeches**

Members of this family are often included in the poppy family, but there are some differences. Flowers 12-15 mm long are flattened vertically, and have two different size petals, 2 larger and 2 smaller. Two petals are spurred or saclike, 7-9 mm long at the base (pantaloons), and there are 2 small scalelike sepals. Stamens are 6 in two sets of 3 each. Superior pistils are bicarpellate, have a bilobed but 1-celled stigma and produce a capsule splitting on 2 sides. Flowering scapes bear 4-10 pendulous flowers. Leaves and leafless flower stalks rise 12-25 cm high from a perennial bulblet-bearing rhizome. Leaves are divided into narrow fanlike segments. Flowers March-June in moist woods, shady slopes, and ledges; Georgia-Arkansas and north into Virginia-Kansas.

FUMARIACEAE
(Bleeding Heart Family)
Corydalis flavula (Raf.) DC. **Pale Corydalis**

This gray-green annual, 10-40 cm high has erect to reclining stems with its leaves finely dissected into linear-elliptic, arranged like an open fan. Flower racemes are as long as the leaves, have flowers with 2 sepals, and a bilateral corolla of 4 separate clear-yellow petals. The upper lip petal, 7-9 mm long is concave above, raised, and has a rounded spur 1-2 mm long at the rear. The other petals curve over the single 2-carpellate, 1-celled pistil. Two groups of 3 united stamens in each are on opposite sides of the pistil. Upon maturing, the brown capsules (seen in photo) become cylindrical point-tipped, 1.5-2 cm long, splitting on 2 sides. Flowers March-June in deciduous rocky woodlands and flood plains; Georgia-Louisiana and north into New York-Minnesota.

BRASSICACEAE
(Mustard Family)
Lepidium virginicum L. **Wild Peppergrass**

This common weedy annual plant is found throughout most of the country. We should recognize our pests too. Seeds sprout in winter and produce basal rosettes of spatulate blades, 2-10 cm long by 1-2 cm wide, variously dissected near the bases. Mature plants 50-100 cm high are quite branched. Upper leaves are reduced and clasping. Numerous tiny, 2-mm broad, white flowers with 4 sepals, 4 petals, and only 2 stamens scatter along a raceme 2-5 cm long. Flowers are followed by 3-4 mm circular flat 2-celled, 2-seeded pods, notched at their tips. They taste hot and peppery. Flowers May-November in fields and waste places; over most of the eastern half of the U.S.

ɩhorum diphyllum

Dicentra cucullaria

ium virginicum

Corydalis flavula

BRASSICACEAE
(Mustard Family)
Capsella bursa-pastoris (L.) Medicus. **Shepherd's Purse**

As a winter annual, the seeds of this plant sprout and produce leaves during winter, completing the cycle the next season. From the rosette of leaves 4-10 cm long by 1-3 cm wide, lobed and divided, the much-branched stem grows 10-60 cm high. Upper leaves are reduced, lanceolate-triangulate, and clasping the stem. Flowers are produced in elongating racemes and have 4 2-4 mm long petals, longer than the 4 sepals. The 6 stamens are of 2 lengths and the pistil grows into a flat, triangular, base-upward capsule, 5-10 mm long as the pedicel elongates to 1.5-2 cm. The capsule is fancied as the shepherd's purse. This is apparently a naturalized weed over much of the United States; flowers March-June in fields and waste places.

BRASSICACEAE
(Mustard Family)
Erysimum arkansanum Nutt. **Western Wallflower**

This member of the mustard family has made its appearance within our western range and will likely spread. Its leaves are narrowly lance-shaped, tapering to the mostly single stem, remotely toothed, 1-2 cm wide and 5-15 cm long. The plant grows 30-50 cm or more tall, has branched hairs on the stem and showy yellow-orange flowers. Petals are about 2.5 cm long, 0.7-1.2 cm wide, the lower half being a narrowed "claw"; 4 sepals, 4 petals, 6 stamens (4 long and 2 short), are typical of the family. Elongate, 4-sided upright pods are 2-celled, 8-10 cm long. Flowers May-July in dry or prairie type soils and dry bluffs; northward from central Arkansas-Missouri-Illinois and westward. This species has been considered a form of *E. capitatum* along with *E. asperum* by various specialists.

BRASSICACEAE
(Mustard Family)
Cardamine bulbosa (Shreb.) BSP **Spring Cress**

Although there are many members of this family all over the country, this and the following species are quite common, especially *C. hirsuta*. Spring cress is found in low wet places with few upper branches, rising to 50-70 cm from a perennial bulbous base. Basal leaves are broadly ovate and long-stalked while stem leaves are large-toothed, lanceolate, and sessile. There are 4 greenish sepals with white margins and 4 white petals, 7-16 mm long. Beaked slender seed pods are 1.5-3 cm long, plus tip beak. Flowers March-May in marshes and open wet woodlands; Florida-Texas and north into Canada.

BRASSICACEAE
(Mustard Family)
Cardamine hirsuta L. **Bitter Cress**

This very common mustard is a nuisance in yards and waste places in very early spring, along with the henbit seen in the photo. It is an annual and produces an abundance of seeds. The typical mustard flowers are only 4-6 mm across but produce over an extended time, with pods 1.5-2.5 cm long releasing seeds every day. Leaves are pinnately compound 3-8 cm long, mostly in a basal rosette. Although named "hirsuta" one must look hard to find the hairs on petioles. Flowering racemes terminate the branching stems which reach 10-40 cm in height. It is apparently a European import. Flowers February-May throughout most of eastern U.S.

ella bursa-pastoris

Erysimum arkansanum

amine bulbosa

Cardamine hirsuta

BRASSICACEAE
(Mustard Family)
Dentaria laciniata Muhl. **Toothwort**

Toothworts have been placed in the genus *Cardamine* by some authorities, but the palmately 3-5 cleft or divided (laciniate) leaves of *C. concatenata* (Michx.) Ahles are different from the basal pinnately compound leaves of the cardamines. None of the leaves are basal in the toothworts. Stems, 20-40 cm high, rise from an edible perennial rhizome of linked joints (catenate) and usually have the laciniate leaves along the stem, the upper two opposite. Leaf segments 1-3 cm wide are usually large-toothed or "dentate." Several rather large white to purplish flowers are produced in terminal clusters. Petals are 1.5-2.5 cm long, sepals 6-9 mm long, 6 stamens of 2 lengths, and the pistil becomes a slender, 2-celled, long-beaked pod 3-5 cm long. Flowers March-May in rich low woodlands, thickets and meadows; Florida-Louisiana and north into Canada.

BRASSICACEAE
(Mustard Family)
Arabis laevigata (Muhl. ex Willd.) Poiret **Smooth Rock-Cress**

This smooth biennial from a basal rosette grows 30-90 cm tall and usually branches above but not below. First-year basal leaves are spatulate in shape, 3-8 cm long, on petioles, and coarsely few-toothed. Second-year leaves on the stem are sessile, lobed and clasping at the base, are lanceolate-oblanceolate, toothed and 3-15 cm long by 1-2.5 cm wide, ascending (as in photo) or spreading. Terminal racemes to 30 cm long have stalked 4-petaled flowers, 5-10 mm high, twice the length of the 4 sepals, 6 stamens (4+2) and a typical mustard pod, upright and curving 7-10 cm long by 1-2 mm wide. Flowers April-September in rocky woodlands and shaded ledges; Georgia-Alabama-Oklahoma and north into Virginia-Colorado.

SARRACENIACEAE
(Pitcher-plant Family)
Sarracenia psittacina Michx. **Parrot-bill Pitcher-plant**

Several species of pitcher plants are found in our area, perhaps the most colorful being *S. flava* with 0.7-1.25 meter tall and 10-12 cm diameter bright yellow leaf "trumpets." Parrot-bill has nodding, 5-6 cm broad, solitary flowers on leafless, 20-40 cm tall stalks. There are 3 small red bracts, 5 2-2.5 cm long greenish-red sepals and 5 3-4 cm long, drooping, dark red petals. (Petals and stamens have shed from the flowers on the taller stalks in the photo). The pistil flares into an upside down "umbrella" 2.5-3 cm across (note taller stalks) under which many stamens are produced. Leaves, in a basal rosette, are 10-15 cm long, with a narrow tube and a broad wing. The leaf closes at the tip, presenting only a small lateral opening to the inside. Flowers April-June only along the lower coastal pinelands, roadside ditches, and bogs; Florida-Georgia-Louisiana. This plant is on the threatened species list and must be protected.

SARRACENIACEAE
(Pitcher-Plant Family)
Sarracenia alata Wood **Yellow Pitcher-plant**

The yellowish-green tubular trumpet leaves of this rather rare plant are purple veined, and strongly winged their 60-80 cm length. The green to yellow hood abruptly arches over the leaf cavity. The nodding flowers are 8-10 cm across, with bright yellow 6-7 cm long drooping fiddle-shaped petals, shed from those shown here. There are small red bracts and green to yellow sepals. The greenish pistil is as described for parrot-bill. As in leaves of most pitcher plants, water accumulates and hairs often lining in the leaf point downward, making insect escape difficult. As insects decay or are digested the lining cells apparently absorb the organic materials, especially amino acids. Flowers March-April in lower wet coastal lands; Alabama-Texas.

is laevigata

Dentaria laciniata

Sarracenia psittacina

Sarracenia alata

CRASSULACEAE
(Stonecrop or Orpine Family)
Sedum pulchellum Michx. **Widow's-cross, Rock-moss**

Members of this genus are fleshy or succulent leafed plants of dry, rocky outcrops. They have trailing or erect stems with closely spaced, glabrous, alternate or whorled leaves on mostly perennial stems terminating in branching flower clusters. In this winter annual, seeds sprout in winter and bloom next season. Upright flower branches branch again into 4 to 7, commonly 4, forming a horizontal cross of many small flowers. Leaves are sessile, linear-terete, 1-2.5 cm long and blunt tipped. Small pink to white flowers are 1-1.4 cm across with 4 or 5 linear sepals 2-2.5 mm long and 4 or 5 petals 4-8 mm long, and have 8-10 stamens. Four or five small separate pistils per flower become 5-6 mm long follicle pods splitting down one side. Flowers April-July on rocky outcrops; Georgia-Texas and north into Virginia-Kansas.

SAXIFRAGACEAE
(Saxifrage Family)
Itea virginica L. **Virginia Willow**

The saxifrages are a family of mostly perennial herbs and shrubs, with basal or alternate or opposite leaves. The calyx is usually 5-lobed or parted and petals are 4 or 5, rarely none. Stamens are as many or twice as many as the sepals. Fruits are a capsule or follicle. This perennial, a deciduous arching shrub 1-3 meters high is quite attractive in May or June because of its terminal 5-15 cm long flowering racemes. The 5-8 cm long alternate leaves are on short petioles, finely toothed, and taper at both ends. The small flowers have 5 white, linear, 3-5 mm long petals, with 5 stamens of the same length. Sepals are united into a 5-lobed calyx cup 1 mm long. The shrub is found in low wet woods and swamps around the coastal plain; Florida-Texas and north into New Jersey-Illinois.

SAXIFRAGACEAE
(Saxifrage Family)
Hydrangea quercifolia Bartr. **Oak-leaf Hydrangea**

This shrub may grow to 2 meters high and has opposite, prominently pointed-lobed, denitculate deciduous leaves 15-20 cm long. In shape, the leaves resemble those of the black oak *(Quercus)* group, thus the names. Hydrangeas may have both inner fertile and outer sterile flowers in 10-30 cm broad terminal clusters, as seen here, but either only fertile or rarely only sterile flowers appear. The showy white maturing to rose-purple, 2-4 cm petallike parts are 4 sepals of the sterile flowers; the fertile flowers have 5 petals only 2 mm long, and 5 sepals slightly larger. Flower heads remain into fall and are used in dry bouquets. Flowers May-July in moist rich soils of shaded slopes and ravines; Florida-Georgia-Louisiana and north into Tennessee and Kentucky in a very limited range.

SAXIFRAGACEAE
(Saxifrage Family)
Hydrangea arborescens L. **Wild Hydrangea**

This deciduous shrub may grow to 2 m high and has opposite, ovate taper-tipped, unlobed, toothed, 10-15 cm long leaves. The flower cluster, 5-15 cm across, tends to have a flat top and is not elongated as in the above. There are many fertile flowers and few showy sepals around the edge of the cluster. Showy sepals here are smaller, only 1 cm long, rather than the 2-3 cm long sepals of oak leaf hydrangea. Flowers 2-3 mm long have 5 tiny white petals, 8-10 stamens, and a 3-carpel ovary producing a tiny ovate capsule about 1 mm long. This species has a wide range; Georgia-Louisiana and north into New York and Iowa. Flowers June to July on moist or dry lowlands and rocky hillsides to over 6,000 feet elevation.

m pulchellum

Itea virginica

Hydrangea quercifolia

Hydrangea arborescens

SAXIFRAGACEAE
(Saxifrage Family)

Parnassia asarifolia Vent. **Grass-of-Parnassus**

This plant is not a grass; its 5 sepals, 5 petals and 5 fertile stamens plus 5 more (each divided into 3) sterile stamens, and other traits place it in this family. Sterile stamens "appear" to be 15 and are shorter than the 5 fertile ones. *Asarifolia* means "gingerlike leaf," which it resembles. Flowering stalks, with single flowers, grow 10-15 cm tall and have a circular leaf around the stalk above a basal rosette of 5-7 cm, circular notched, long petioled leaves. Flowers, 2-2.5 cm across have white, rounded, clawed petals with 11-15 green veins. Flowers late August-October in bogs and wet woods; Georgia-Alabama and north into Virginia and West Virginia. The species *P. grandifolia* also has been reported as far west from Florida as east Texas and is likely to be found in our area. *P. asarifolia* is a threatened species to be protected.

SAXIFRAGACEAE
(Saxifrage Family)

Tiarella cordifolia L. **Foamflower**

This woodland perennial grows to 30 cm tall from a rhizome. Its basal, heart-shaped leaf blades *(cordifolia)* are 3-5 cm long, 3-7 shallow lobed and toothed on long petioles from ends of the rhizome. Numerous 8-10 mm broad white flowers are scattered along the upper 10-15 cm of the leafless, hairy, nonbranching flower stalk. Flowers are white, both the 5 calyx lobes and 5 petals narrowed (clawed) to these bases. There are 10 stamens with long filaments and orange-red anthers. Alum-root *(Heuchera americana* L.) might be mistaken for foamflower, but the former has bluish-pink flowers with 5 stamens and branched flower stalks. They occupy similar habitats and distribution. Flowers April-June in rich wooded slopes of mountains and foot-hills; Georgia-Mississippi and north into Nova Scotia and Minnesota.

SAXIFRAGACEAE
(Saxifrage Family)

Saxifraga virginiensis Michx. **Early Saxifrage**

This is a perennial from a short rhizome and in winter produces a basal rosette of ovate-spatulate leaves tapering to a long petiole. Leaves are scallop-toothed, to 5 cm long and are often purple tinted beneath; one to several flower stems may rise 10-50 cm high, producing a branching flower cluster. Flowers have 5 usually erect sepals, 5 narrow white petals and 10 stamens. The entire plant is usually glandular hairy. Flowers March-June in open woodlands and rocky shaded slopes; Georgia-Mississippi and north into Canada.

HAMAMELIDACEAE
(Witch-hazel Family)

Liquidambar styraciflua L. **Sweetgum**

This large, to 50 m high, deciduous tree is in a family which has several "aromatic resin" producing members, the scientific name indicating this trait. The wood is used in veneering, trim, and furniture, sold as "satin walnut" to substitute for the dwindling supply of real walnut. Sweetgum is among the ecological dominants of our eastern deciduous forests. Alternate, star-shaped leaves 15-18 cm across, with palmate veins and lobing are typical. "Sweetgum balls" come from pendant globular heads of numerous female flowers of calyx scales and 2-carpel pistils (note the bilobed stigmas) as they mature. Male flowers, hardly more than numerous stamens, appear in 20-30 "balls" on upright branching flower stalks, falling after maturity. The 2.5-3 cm spiny dry balls release seeds in the fall. Flowers April-May in low rich woods in most of eastern U.S.

Tiarella cordifolia

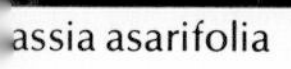

assia asarifolia

Saxifraga virginiensis

Liquidambar styraciflua

PLATANACEAE
(Plane-tree Family)

Platanus occidentalis L. **Sycamore**

Rather closely related to the sweetgum is this sycamore, also a deciduous tree to 50 m or more high. It has alternate, maplelike, palmately 3-5 lobed or large-toothed leaves, 10-20 cm or more across. Flowers are tiny and in tight globose heads, 1.2-1.7 cm in diameter, containing many male or female flowers, with petal-sepal scales, appearing with the leaves, on the same tree. Female heads are terminal on stems and disintegrate in winter, releasing achenes as 1-seeded fruits. Male heads (shown here) appear in leaf axils and fall early upon releasing pollen. Bark of upper branches is smooth and white, older bark becomes darker and furrowed. Wood is used for crates, butcher blocks, and furniture. Flowers April-June in low wet woods and along stream beds; Florida-Texas and north into Maine-Nebraska.

ROSACEAE
(Rose Family)

Duchesnea indica (Andr.) Focke **Indian Strawberry**

Is it a strawberry? Does it taste like one? No, to both questions. Its separate pistils on a conical stem (receptacle) are red achenes or dry 1-seeded fruits. Those pistils in true strawberries are brown, dry specks while the red is the fleshy conical stem, the juicy, tasty part of the edible "fruit." Indian or mock strawberry is edible but has no flavor. Many separate pistils to a set of 5 sepals, 5 petals, and many stamens are traits of the Rose Family. Fruits, however, are of several different kinds, follicles as in *Spiraea,* achenes as here, drupes as in raspberries and plums, and pomes as in rose hips and apple. *Fragaria* is the genus of true strawberry and has white flowers, while *Duchesnea* has yellow flowers. Both have trifoliate compound leaves and stolons. Flowers April-July in lower waste places; Florida-Texas and north into Oklahoma-Iowa-New York.

ROSACEAE
(Rose Family)

Potentilla simplex Michx. **Common Five-finger, Cinquefoil**

When this five-finger flowers in April-May the stems are about 15 cm long, becoming decumbent to creeping, and reach 45 cm long by July. The palmately compound leaves usually have 5 oblanceolate to oblong-elliptic leaflets 5-6 cm long and about a third as wide. Leaflets have toothed margins nearly to their wedge-shaped bases, are nearly glabrous above and silky appressed-pubescent beneath. The stems, petioles, and flower peduncles are also appressed-pubescent. The yellow 5-petaled flowers are about 1.5 cm broad, having their broad petals notched or obcordate at their tips. There are 5 narrowly lanceolate bractlets beneath the 5 slightly broader clayx lobes, all of nearly the same length. Flowers May-July in open or often shaded dry soil; Georgia-Texas and northeastward into Canada. A similar species, *P. canadensis,* has broad oval yellow-orange petals, 5-foliate leaves with shorter, broader wedge-shaped leaflets without teeth on the margins toward the base. This species reaches into our area and usually flowers earlier than the above.

ROSACEAE
(Rose Family)

Potentilla recta L. **Cinquefoil, Silver-weed**

This erect quite leafy perennial may grow to over 0.7 m high and has alternate, palmately compound leaves with 5-9 (rarely 5), coarse toothed leaflets. The plant is quite bristly-hairy which gives its common name, silver-weed. There are ovate-lanceolate stipules on either side of the petiole base. Terminal clusters of flowers have white to pale yellow, broad petals, notched at their tips, about 20 yellow stamens, and numerous pistils. Pistils become rough, brown dry achenes about 1.2 mm long. Of about 35 species in eastern U.S. 2 or 3 reach into our area; most are at higher, cooler elevations. Flowers June-August in dry fields and roadsides; Florida-Texas and north into Canada.

tanus occidentalis

Duchesnea indica

entilla simplex

Potentilla recta

ROSACEAE
(Rose Family)
Rubus trivialis Michx. **Southern Dewberry**

Many and confusing species of *Rubus* may be found in our area, blackberries, raspberries, and dewberries. In this species first year stems produce no flowers, become trailing and flower-producing the second year. There are then leaves with 3 leaflets rather than 5 of the first year. Hairs and stout prickles cover the stems. Single flowers are produced on long, upright stems, are 3-4 cm across, and have 5 sepals, 5 white overlapping petals narrowed at the base, and many stamens. In the center are many separate pistils, each one becoming a small drupe (like a cherry) with a single hard "seed" in it. Collectively, these make up the "berry," 1-1.5 cm broad by 1.5-2 cm long. Flowers March-April on sandy soils; Florida-Texas and north into Maryland-Oklahoma.

ROSACEAE
(Rose Family)
Geum canadense Jacq. **White Avens**

This finely pubescent perennial branches at the base into a few erect stems 20-120 cm high. The alternate leaves are long-petioled at the base with 3 pubescent, broadly ovate-rhombic leaflets. Middles leaves are smaller, only 3-lobed, and short petioled. Upper leaves are simple, ovate-lanceolate at nodes of widely branching, remote flower stalks. Leaves and leaflets are variously toothed in sets of 4-6 teeth around the margins. The 5 oblong white petals are 5-9 mm long by 2-4 mm wide. Reflexed calyx lobes 5-9 mm long are lanceolate and separated by 5 tiny ovate bractlets. The 1-2 cm broad head has over 60 hairy achenes, long-tailed and kinked at the end, each from a separate pistil. Flowers June-August in thickets and woodland edges; Georgia-Texas and north into New York-North Dakota.

ROSACEAE
(Rose Family)
Rosa palustris Marshall **Swamp Rose**

This rhizomatous perennial grows to 2 m tall and has pinnately compound leaves with 5-9 mostly glabrous leaflets, finely toothed and minutely pubescent below, 2-6 cm long by 1-3 cm wide. Stipules at petiole bases are 1.3 cm long with only 2-6 mm of free tips ciliate on their margins. Thorns are flat, curved and broad based, 2-8 mm long. There are 5 lanceolate, long-tapered sepals 2-3 cm long from the top of the calyx which surrounds numerous separate pistils. This becomes the red ovoid rose hip 1-1.5 cm long. Flowers June-August in swamps and wet thickets; Florida-Arkansas and north into Quebec-Minnesota. Cypress trees and stumps form a perch as high as 3-5 m above the water for this abundant rose at Reelfoot Lake in northwest Tennessee.

ROSACEAE
(Rose Family)
Crataegus marshallii Eggl. **Parsley Hawthorn**

There are about 100 species (?) of hawthorn or haw in the South and hybridization makes their separation difficult, even for experts. Alternate simple leaves are mostly ovate to obovate and unlobed to shallowly 3-5 lobed to deep-cut lobed as seen here. No other species of hawthorn has such deep-cut leaves. Leaf edges are always toothed, often scarcely so at their bases. Sometimes this species is thornless but rarely are there none or few thorns. Few-many-flowered, terminal or axillary clusters bear mostly white flowers with 1-2 inferior ovaries in a calyx cup. Here, 1-1.5 cm wide flowers have 10 red-tipped stamens. Elongate, bright red, succulent fruit is 4-8 mm by 5-9 mm long and usually is 2-seeded. At the tip may be seen a tiny star of 5 sepals, as on an apple; holly berries have only a tiny black speck. Flowers April in coastal plains, open woods and hillsides; Florida-Texas and north into Virginia and up the Mississippi Valley to Missouri and Oklahoma.

Rubus trivialis

a palustris

:aegus marshallii

Geum canadense

ROSACEAE
(Rose Family)
Amelanchier arborea (Michx.) Fern. **Serviceberry**

This small tree, 10-15 m high, is found in a wide range of habitats in most of eastern U.S. It appears to hybridize readily and it is difficult to separate species. About 15 white to pink flowers in terminal clusters appear before or with leaves. There are 5 petals, 1-1.7 cm long and wedge to strap-shaped at the base. There are 20 stamens and the fruit is a purplish rose-hip-like, dry 1-1.3 cm pome from a bell-shaped calyx. Leaves are alternate, simple, deciduous, ovate-lanceolate 2.5-5 cm wide to 5-10 cm long, finely toothed and may be reddish in the spring. Flowers May-June in dry or moist rocky woods, sandy hillsides, river banks, and even swamps; Florida-Oklahoma and north into New Hampshire-Iowa.

ROSACEAE
(Rose Family)
Prunus americana Marsh. **Wild Red Plum**

This is one of the common, more desired of wild plums. The plant forms thickets but may grow to over 10 m when isolated. Showy white flowers, 2-3 cm across, appear on spur branches in clusters of 3-5 before the leaves appear. There are about 20 stamens and a single pistil as long as the stamens. Fruits are yellow to red and 2-3 cm in diameter. Alternate leaves are ovate-obovate, sharply tapered, often double serrate, reaching 5 cm wide by 10 cm long. Flowers March-May along fence rows, woods edges, along stream banks and in bottom lands; Florida-New Mexico and north into Massachusetts-Minnesota.

FABACEAE
(Legume Family)
Albizzia julibrissin Durazzini **Mimosa**

This often spreading, flat-topped tree to 10 m tall is naturalized from Asia, frequently cultivated and is found along roadsides and woodland edges. The 2-4 cm long compound leaves are twice divided into 8-16 pinna pairs which are again divided into 25-35 leaflet pairs, each leaflet 8-15 mm long. Red and white pompomlike heads of 15-25 plumose flowers are 5-6 cm across. The peripheral flowers are staminate, the central ones perfect. There are 5 united, threadlike petals 5-10 mm long and stamens 2-3 cm long, united below. Indehiscent seed pods are 2-3 cm broad and 10-18 cm long. Flowers May-August through most of the U.S. Native to Asia, it is widely escaped from cultivation here.

FABACEAE
(Legume Family)
Schrankia microphylla (Dryand) Macbride **Senstive Brier**

Stems of this perennial plant are prostrate and covered with recurved spines. Twice divided deciduous leaves are sensitive to touch and their 2-8 mm long leaflets fold up when touched, or are in darkness. Flower heads, similar to mimosa, rise on slender stalks from leaf axils and are about 2 cm across. Both petals and stamens are deep pink, the 10 stamens are hardly united and are 8-10 mm long. Four-sided, prickly, taper-pointed pods from the head are 3-5 mm wide and 5-10 cm long. Flowers June-September in dry sandy or gravelly openings; Florida-Texas and north into Virginia-Kentucky.

nelanchier arborea

Prunus americana

Albizzia julibrissin

Schrankia microphylla

FABACEAE
(Legume Family)
Cercis canadensis L. **Redbud, Judas Tree**

Spring has arrived when this 5-10 m tall tree blooms before its leaves appear. Its flowers are more typical of the Legume Family than are those of the preceding mimosa type. These flowers are of the papilionaceous type (butterflylike) with 5 petals, a standard, 2 wings and a keel of 2 united petals. Clusters of 2-6 white to deep pink flowers appear on short stalks on large or small branches of the tree. These are followed by flat pods up to 10 cm long. Simple, alternate cordate leaves with prominent palmate venation have an entire margin, are to 10 cm long and 15 cm wide, on petioles 5-12 cm long. Flowers March-May in rich woods, slopes or bottom lands; Florida-Texas and north into New Jersey-Minnesota.

FABACEAE
(Legume Family)
Cassia fasciculata Michx. **Partridge Pea**

This attractive annual plant grows 15-60 cm high and has once-pinnate compound leaves 5-6 cm long. There are 12-36 narrow leaflets 1.5-2.5 cm long and they are somewhat sensitive to touch. Flowers are not papilionaceous, but have 5 separate, subequal bright yellow petals of a flower 2-2.5 cm across. Often a purple spot is at the base of the petals. Ten stamens are of unequal length, 6 are yellow and 4 are purple. Flowers are borne in clusters (fascicles) of 2-6 in leaf axils and they are larger than most species of *Cassia*. The straight, flat, dehiscent seed pod is 5-7 cm long and 5-7 mm broad and has ciliate-hairy edges. Flowers July-September in fields, roadsides, and woodland edges; Florida-Texas and north into Canada.

FABACEAE
(Legume Family)
Baptisia leucantha T.&G. **Wild False Indigo**

This plant is another prairie species found in our area and has reached into the St. Marks Wildlife Refuge in western Florida. The plant, as a herbaceous perennial, may grow to 2 m high and has 3 leaflets, 3-7 cm long, tapered to the tip and to the petiole about 1.3 cm long. Smooth, purplish stems with a white coating branch widely. Slender stipules at the petioles fall early. Stout, terminal racemes may be 60 cm long and have 2-3 cm long, white pealike flowers with gray calyx cups on pedicels 2-3 cm long, and widely scattered along the stem. Drooping, beak-tipped pods 2-3 cm long and 1.3-1.8 cm thick become black in maturity. Flowers May-July; western Florida-Texas and north into Ohio-Minnesota.

FABACEAE
(Legume Family)
Baptisia leucophaea Nutt. **Cream Wild Indigo**

This prairie plant reaches into our area from north and west. This false indigo, 20-80 cm high and spreading, has sessile compound leaves of 3 elliptic-oblanceolate leaflets 5-10 cm long and with entire margins. A pair of ovate-lanceolate stipules 2.5-4.5 cm long persist at each leaf base. Flowering stalks have terminal racemes to 20 cm long, with cream colored papilionaceous flowers 2.5-3 cm long on 1-3.5 cm long pedicels. A persistent lanceolate leafy bract 1-3.5 cm long appears at the base of each flower. Flowering stalks recline to nearly on the ground, unusual for the genus. Pubescent tapered pods are 3-5 cm long and 1.5-2 cm in diameter. Flowers April-June in sandy areas and open woods; Louisiana-Texas and north into Michigan-Minnesota. A similar species *B. bracteata* is nearly inseparable but has 1-1.5 cm long petioles and pedicels under 1.5 cm long, and is found Alabama-Georgia-South Carolina.

Cercis canadensis

Cassia fasciculata

aptisia leucophaea

Baptisia leucantha

Baptisia leucophaea

FABACEAE
(Legume Family)
Baptisia alba (L.) R.Br. **White Wild Indigo**

This is a widely branching perennial 35-100 cm tall, glabrous throughout, and has alternate 3-leafleted leaves. Leaflets are oblong-oblanceolate, toothless, 2.5-4 cm long by 8-12 mm wide, tapering to a slender petiole 8-20 mm long. A pair of minute stipules at the petiole base falls early. Flowering branches are 15-25 cm long and have white 1.2-1.8 cm long pealike flowers on slender stalks, 1-3 cm long. The bell-shaped calyx is 5-toothed, the 10 stamens are separate and the pistil produces an erect cylindric pod 2-3.5 cm long, 0.5-1 cm thick, darkening but not black upon drying. Flowers May-July in dry open woods and clearings. Usually limited to the southeastern states, Florida-Virginia and Tennessee, but this plant was photographed near Brinkley, Monroe County, in east central Arkansas.

FABACEAE
(Legume Family)
Thermopsis villosa (Walt.) Fern. & Schub. **Bush Pea**

This plant enters our area from the mountainous region to the northeast. This tall perennial plant to 1.3 m tall has yellow, pealike flowers 2.5 cm long on a flowering stalk to 50 cm long. Leaves are similar to those of *Baptisia* in having 3 leaflets, 3-10 cm long, but on petioles as long as the leaflets, and 2 broad, ovate stipules to 5 cm long, nearly clasping the stem at the petiole. *Villosa* refers to the long, hairy surface of the petioles, lower leaf surfaces, and the 5-cm long seed pod. Upon drying, the plant does not turn black as does *Baptisia*. The seed pod is closely appressed to the stem in maturing. Flowers May-June in upland woods, open places, and along river banks; Georgia-Alabama and north into North Carolina-Tennessee. Listed as an endangered species by Southern U.S. Forest Service.

FABACEAE
(Legume Family)
Lupinus villosus Willd. **Lady Lupine**

This, and *L. diffusus* (not shown here) in our area are exceptional lupines in that they do not have palmately compound leaves. Leaves here are 1-foliate or simple and appear as single, long-stalked, rather ovate-elliptic, shaggy-hairy gray, 15-25 cm long leaves. Most lupines or blue-bonnets, like our *L. perennis,* have palmately compound leaves with 5-15 leaflets. Lady lupine has 15 cm long flower racemes with numerous 1.5-2 cm long flowers with pink petals, the uppermost, or standard, having a large reddish-purple spot in it. Flowers April-June on sand hills, dry pine lands, and open woods along the coastal plain; Florida-Louisiana and north into North Carolina.

FABACEAE
(Legume Family)
Lupinus perennis L. **Wild Lupine**

This is the most widely distributed of the eastern lupines. *Perennis* refers to the creeping perennial rhizomes from which upright stems grow 60-70 cm high. Leaves are palmately compound, 2-5 cm across and have 7-11 leaflets at the end of a long petiole. Leaflets are oblanceolate, 2-5 cm long and 1-1.5 cm wide. Flowers, 1.5-2 cm long, are blue-purple to roseate, rarely white, terminating 30 cm of the stems. Flattish, hairy seed pods are 3.5-5 cm long. Flowers April-July in dry open woods and sand hills; Florida-Mississippi and north into Maine-Minnesota.

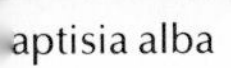

aptisia alba

Lupinus villosus

Thermopsis villosa

Lupinus perennis

FABACEAE
(Legume Family)
Trifolium incarnatum L. **Crimson Clover**

This annual clover, a European import, grows 30-45 cm high and has tall, columnar, 4-7 cm long heads or spikes of dark red flowers 1.2-1.8 cm long, rarely white, terminating the stems. There are 3 obovate-wedge shaped, denticulate leaflets, 1.5-2.5 cm long on the end of short or long petioles. Broad, membranous, toothed stipules nearly ensheathe the stem at the petiole. There are no tendrils in the clovers, those in the photo are on vetch leaves. This plant has been used on highway edges for erosion control and beautification. Widely cultivated to enrich soils with nitrogen. Flowers April-June in fields, roadsides, and waste places over much of the contiguous United States. A cultivated Eurasian species widely escaped in the South.

FABACEAE
(Legume Family)
Trifolium pratense L. **Red Clover**

This is a perennial clover, growing 30-60 cm or more high, quite pubescent, and having pink to light red or purple flowers. Flowering heads are ovoid to globose, 2.5 cm across, and usually subtended by a pair of opposite leaves. Leaflets are nearly sessile, 1.5-5 cm long, elliptic-ovate, short to long petioled and have 2 winglike, awn-pointed stipules clasping the stem. Leaflets commonly have a yellowish to white v-shaped zone near the center. Stipules are common in the legumes, becoming spines in black locust, leaflike in English peas, while others are tiny and drop off early. This common planted clover has become widely dispersed from cultivation. Flowers May-September throughout most of the contiguous U.S.

FABACEAE
(Legume Family)
Melilotus officinalis (L.) Lam. **Yellow Sweet Clover**
Melilotus alba Desr. **White Sweet Clover**

Yellow sweet clover may be seen along most roadsides across the country, growing to 2 m high. Its spikes of very fragrant yellow flowers are both sweet and colorful. Pealike blossoms are about 7 mm long and not densely crowded on the stem. Leaves are composed of 3 leaflets which are elliptic-ovate, round tipped, finely toothed, and have tapered bases. The flower standard is near the same length as the wings. White clover differs from yellow clover in that the plants grow taller, to nearly 3 meters; the standard is a bit longer than the wings, and the leaflets are nearly parallel-sided and squared or blunt at tips and bases. Flowers April-October in fields and waste places throughout most of the contiguous United States.

FABACEAE
(Legume Family)
Amorpha fruticosa L. **False Indigo, Indigo-bush**

This shrub (fruticose) may grow 2-6 m high, is considerably branched and has alternate, pinnately compound leaves, 15-40 cm long, with alternating, elliptic to oblong, 2.5-5 cm long leaflets abruptly short-pointed at their tips. Spikes of purple flowers with golden stamens appear singly or in clusters of 2-several, each spike 15-20 cm long. *Amorpha,* without form, refers to having only one petal, the standard, rather than 5 petals expected. It is about 0.7 cm long and folded around 10 purple stamens with golden anthers. There are several varieties and the plant has been propagated for landscaping. Flowers May-June along stream banks and thickets; Florida-Louisiana and north into Pennsylvania-Minnesota.

ifolium incarnatum

lelilotus officinalis

morpha fruticosa

Melilotus alba

Trifolium pratense

FABACEAE
(Legume Family)

Stylosanthes biflora (L.) BSP. **Pencil Flower**

This perennial, often bristly-hairy, prostrate to erect, herb grows to 50 cm tall and has 3-foliate alternate leaves. Toothless, ciliate hairy leaflets vary in width, mostly narrowly lanceolate to oblanceolate, 1.5-4 cm long, tapering to the base and to a tip with a short spine. A pair of stipules at the petiole base are 1-1.5 cm long. Upper leaves are crowded and bristly-hairy around the base of the terminal cluster of few flowers. The small pealike flowers with yellow petals are 7-10 mm long. The deciduous bell-shaped calyx 3-4 mm long is irregularly 4-5 toothed, and 10 stamens of 2 lengths are joined together by their filaments. The pistil produces an ovate 3-5 mm long pod. Flowers May-August in dry open woods and clearings; Florida-Texas and north into New York-Kansas.

FABACEAE
(Legume Family)

Robinia pseudoacacia L. **Black Locust**

This rapidly growing tree may reach over 30 m in height, and has pinnately compound leaves with 3-10 pairs of leaflets 2.5-5 cm long. Spines develop from stipules at leaf bases. Creamy-white, pealike flowers form drooping clusters to nearly 30 cm long. Flat, brown pods, 5-31 cm long, 12-15 mm wide may remain on trees for a year, as seen in the photo. Often cultivated for fence posts and wind-breaks, its sprouts and seedlings are too aggressive for landscaping a small area. Flowers May-June in almost any type of soil; Georgia-Louisiana and north into Pennsylvania-Indiana-Oklahoma.

FABACEAE
(Legume Family)

Vicia grandiflora Scop. **Large-flowered Vetch**

This annual vetch, to 60 cm high, naturalized from Europe, has 1-4, creamy-white to yellow, sessile flowers, 2.5-3.5 cm long in the axils of the upper leaves. The standard may be somewhat purplish and calyx teeth are ⅓-½ the length of the corolla tube. Pods mature black and are 3.5-5 cm long. The pinnately compound leaves have 3-6 pairs of linear-obovate leaflets terminated with a spiny tip. The 3 terminal leaflets are modified into a branching tendril. Flowers April-June, along roadsides, waste places, and open woods; Florida-Mississippi and north into Delaware-Missouri.

FABACEAE
(Legume Family)

Vicia dasycarpa Tenore **Smooth Vetch**

This annual or biennial vetch has pinnately compound leaves with 14-20 pairs of linear-oblong leaflets, the terminal 3-5 modified into tendrils. The flowering stalks, or peduncles, in leaf axils are nearly as long as the leaves. Blue-violet, or rarely white, flowers are 1 cm or more long, and the raceme is densely flowered. Flowers bend sharply downward in the raceme. The plants are slightly pubescent. *V. villosa* (Hairy Vetch) fits the same description given here but it has densely long-hairy stems and the calyx of the flower also has long hairs on it. Flowers May-October along roadsides, in fields, and waste places in most of the contiguous U.S.

ylosanthes biflora

Vicia grandiflora

cia dasycarpa

Robinia pseudoacacia

FABACEAE
(Legume Family)
Vicia caroliniana Walt. **Wood Vetch**

This slender trailing or climbing perennial vetch is another of the long-peduncled group but its mostly white flowers are in loose, 8-20 flowered racemes. Flowers may have a purple-tipped keel (the 2 united lower petals), and are 12-14 mm long. Pinnately compound leaves have 6-9 pairs of elliptic-elongate leaflets, 2.0-2.3 cm long except for 1-3 terminal leaflets which are tendrils. Flowers April-June in moist woodlands, thickets and along stream banks; Florida-Texas and north into New York-Minnesota.

FABACEAE
(Legume Family)
Erythrina herbacea L. **Coral Bean**

This interesting perennial plant of the coastal plain, herbaceous above ground, grows 1-1.5 m high. Its alternate, 7-10 cm long leaves are made up of three deltoid leaflets, each 4-8 cm long, sometimes prickly beneath. Near leafless stems are terminated by a 30-60 cm raceme of scarlet flowers 4-5 cm long, hardly opening to pealike bloom. Flowers appear closed because the standard enfolds the wings and keel. Mature pods are 7-15 cm long by 1.3-1.6 cm broad, constricted between bright red seeds that are considered poisonous. Most species of *Erythrina* are tropical. Flowers March-July; North Carolina to Florida-Texas and into Mexico.

FABACEAE
(Legume Family)
Lathyrus latifolius L. **Everlasting Pea**

This perennial pea, spreading to high climbing, has only its basal pair (of 4 or 5 pair) of leaflets leaflike, the others are sturdy tendrils. Stipules at petiole bases are 3-5 cm long and linear-lanceolate. The stem and petioles are broadly winged on opposite sides, adding to photosynthetic surface exposure. Flowers to 2.5 cm long are mostly pink to purple and borne 5-10 per cluster on peduncles 10-20 cm long. Mature pods grow 10 cm long. Flowers May-September along roadsides and in waste places; Georgia-Texas and north into New York-Wisconsin.

FABACEAE
(Legume Family)
Pueraria lobata (Willd.) Ohwi **Kudzu Vine**

This semiwoody perennial with 1-2.5 cm diameter stems grows rampant over all other vegetation as seen here. Leaves are killed back during frost. In place of erosion control, for which it was planted along highways, we now have a weed control problem. Compound leaves have 3 leaflets about 8 cm wide and 12 cm long, wide rhombic ovate, 0-3 lobed. Petioles, peduncles, and pods are densely hairy. Violet-purple, 2-2.5 cm long flowers have a yellow spot on the standard. Pods are bristly and 4-5 cm long. Flowering is infrequent in its northern range. Formerly introduced into southeastern U.S. for starchy roots and hay. Flowers July-October in woods, roadsides, and fields; Georgia-Texas and north into Maryland-Illinois-Missouri.

hyrus latifolius

Pueraria lobata

eraria lobata

Vicia caroliniana

Erythrina herbacea

OXALIDACEAE
(Wood-sorrel Family)

Oxalis montana Raf. **Common Wood-sorrel**

This species is usually found at higher elevations but is extending into the Ozark foothills in north-central Arkansas and the Cumberlands in Kentucky and Middle Tennessee. This plant is distinguished by its flowers with 1-1.5 cm long white petals with purplish veins and yellow basal spot. Petals are obovate and notched at their tips. Solitary flowers are borne on stalks only slightly longer than the long-petioled leaves with leaflets 1-2 cm long. The photo was made near Blanchard Springs in Stone County, Arkansas, 5 July 1966. Flowers May-August mostly at higher elevations in damp woods; Georgia-Tennessee-Arkansas and north into Quebec-Minnesota.

OXALIDACEAE
(Wood-sorrel Family)

Oxalis violacea L. **Violet Wood-sorrel**

This stemless perennial herb from a bulbous base produces 3-leafleted basal leaves 6-12 cm long with 6-13 mm long, heart-shaped leaflets purple-blotched above and mostly purple beneath. Hairless flower stalks 12-25 cm tall are several flowered. There are 5 separate sepals, often orange-tipped, 4-7 mm long, 5 violet petals, joined at their bases, 1-2 cm long, and usually 10 stamens of 2 lengths, united by their filaments at the base. A compound pistil of 5 carpels and 5 separate stigmas produces a globose capsule 4-6 mm long. Flowers April-July on alluvial or upland wooded slopes; Florida-New Mexico and north into New York-Minnesota.

OXALIDACEAE
(Wood-sorrel Family)

Oxalis stricta L. **Yellow Wood-sorrel**

A single genus represents this family in most of the contiguous United States. Leaves are palmately compound, 3-foliate obcordate; leaflets and sap contain oxalic acid, sour to the taste. Flowers have 5 sepals, 5 petals (yellow in most species) and 10-15 stamens united at their bases. Five pistils are united into 5-carpel, 5 parted style, developing into a 5-celled capsule. In this species, yellow flowers are 0.7-1 cm long and produced 1-4 per branching peduncle. Leaflets are 1-2 cm wide and appressed stiffly-hairy, as are the stems and branches. Flowers May-October in dry, open woodlands, fields, and waste places; Florida-Texas and beyond and north into Canada.

GERANIACEAE
(Geranium Family)

Geranium maculatum L. **Wild Geranium**

This family has flowers with 5 regular, separate petals, 10 stamens, a pistil of 5 carpels, and 5 awn-tipped sepals. Capsules with long beaks of 5 sections split by breaking at base and coiling upward to the apex. All of the genus have palmately lobed or dissected simple leaves. This perennial plant grows 20-50 cm high and has 7-15 cm broad leaves deeply 5 to 7-lobed large toothed segments. Long peduncles are 2-several flowered, each 5-cm broad flower rose-pink, rarely white. Mature capsules have a small globular base with a beak 1.8-2.5 cm long. Flowers April-June in woods and meadows; Georgia-Arkansas and north into Canada.

alis montana

Oxalis violacea

Oxalis stricta

ranium maculatum

Geranium maculatum

GERANIACEAE
(Geranium Family)
Geranium carolinianum L. **Carolina Cranesbill**

This "weedy" wild geranium is an annual from a taproot with branching stems to 50 cm high, densely hairy, and has deeply 5-lobed, 2.5-7 cm broad leaves which are again divided into narrow segments. Flowering stalks bear 2-several pale-pink to white flowers 1-1.4 cm across. These are followed by a "crane's bill" capsule to 2.5 cm long. Flowers May-June in dry sandy or rocky waste places; in all the contiguous U.S. and beyond.

GERANIACEAE
(Geranium Family)
Geranium dissectum L. **Cut-leaved Cranesbill**

This geranium is very similar to *G. carolinianum* but has narrower upper leaf segments and has red flowers in pairs at ends of shorter peduncles. Also, leaves are smaller, to 3.5-4 cm across. Flowers April-July in habitats similar to *G. carolinianum,* rather uncommon in our area, more abundant northward. This European introduction has spread from the Northeast.

ZYGOPHYLLACEAE
(Caltrop Family)
Tribulus cistoides L. **Puncture-weed, Goat-head**

This creeping herbaceous plant has opposite pinnately compound leaves at each node, one with 5-7 pairs of leaflets, the other with 12-18 pairs. *Zygo* means "yoked together"; *phyll* means "leaf." "Caltrop" is an old military term for a steel ball of spikes. Yellow flowers, 4.5-5 cm across have 5 petals, 10 stamens and a 5-carpel pistil which separates into 3-5 "goat heads" with 2 hard spines which can penetrate golf balls, tires, and rubber-soled shoes. Members of this family are mostly tropical; creosote bush of our Southwestern deserts is one. A more common species in our area is *Tribulus terrestris* which has much smaller flowers and is a pest for puncturing. Flowers March-September along coastal plain, Florida-Texas. *T. terrestris* ranges northward and farther west.

POLYGALACEAE
(Milkwort Family)
Polygala mariana Miller **Maryland Milkwort**

This erect annual, without milky juice, is 15-40 cm tall with slender upper branches ending in rose-purple ovoid-globose flowering spikes. There are no basal leaves and stem leaves are linear, 1.5-2.3 cm long by 2-4 mm wide. The many partially overlapping flowers are bilateral and have 5 sepals, the 2 lateral ones large colored petallike, the others smaller. They are keeled and referred to as wings. There are 3 petals united tubelike. The 6-8 stamens are somewhat united. Perfect flowers are 3-5 mm long and a capsule is about 2 mm broad. Spikes are 1-1.5 cm tall and flowers shed early from the axis, exposing a tiny bract below each flower. Flowers June-October, mainly around the coastal plain in dry to moist open places; Florida-Texas and north into New Jersey and Kentucky.

Geranium carolinianum

nium dissectum

Polygala mariana

lus cistoides

POLYGALACEAE
(Milkwort Family)

Polygala cruciata L. **Rosy Milkwort**

Milkworts may have leaves alternate, opposite, or in whorls, as does this species. Leaves are mostly in whorls of 4 on a square stem to 30 cm high, linear-oblanceolate to 5 cm long and 0.7 cm wide. Flowering racemes spikelike to 3.5 cm long and 1.5 cm diameter have flowers with pink to greenish petallike sepals with acutely pointed "wings." Inconspicuous petals are smaller and form a beaklike column around the 3-8 stamens. There are several other species in our area that are less conspicuous and have less compact racemes. Flowers June-October in wet sandy pinelands and bogs of the coastal plain and northern wetlands; Florida-Texas and north into Maine-Minnesota.

POLYGALACEAE
(Milkwort Family)

Polygala lutea L. **Yellow Milkwort**

These are not to be confused with milkweeds which have a milky sap; these do not. It was thought if cows ate milkwort they would give more milk. In this annual milkwort, 15-20 cm tall, flowers are produced in spikelike clusters 0.8-2.5 cm long and 2 cm broad. Flowers have 5 orange, drying to yellow, sepals, 2 larger. The 3 (basically 5, some missing) petals are not conspicuous and attached to them are 6-8 stamens. Spatulate, succulent, 5 cm long leaves form a basal rosette from which flowering stems with scattered 1.5-2 cm long elliptic-oblanceolate leaves may be found. Flowers April-October in wet, often sandy soils of the coastal plain; Florida-Louisiana and north into New York.

EUPHORBIACEAE
(Spurge Family)

Cnidoscolus stimulosus (Michx.) Engelm. & Gray **Spurge-Nettle**

Most of the members of this family are tropical. Of these, wild poinsettia, snow-on-the-mountain and spurge-nettle are more showy. Flowers are of separate sexes on one plant (monoecious) or separate sexes, male and female, on separate plants (dioecious). Flowers in this species are showy because of colorful leaflike bracts. These flowers have no petals, the 5 united sepals are 2.3-4 cm across in a 5-lobed calyx cupule. Female flowers are central or terminal in a cluster and male flowers are lower or lateral. There are stinging hairs on 60-cm long stems and on the palmately lobed alternate leaves. Flowers March-September in dry, sandy woods, and waste lands; Florida-Texas and north into Virginia along the coastal plain.

EUPHORBIACEAE
(Spurge Family)

Euphorbia heterophylla L. **Summer Poinsettia, Painted-leaf**

Growing to 1 m tall, this annual plant has variously shaped leaves, lobed and nonlobed, mostly alternate. Upper leaves become red-splashed bracts surrounding the rather inconspicuous calyx cupules. These are typical for the genus except the cups have only 1 or 2 yellow glands and have no white, petallike bracts as other species shown. The maturing, 3-lobed ovaries on elongated stalks from the cupule are seen at margins of the whole cluster of cups. These are similar to the structures in the Christmas poinsettia, *E. pulcherrima (Poinsettia pulcherrima)* of Mexico and Central America. Flowers August-September in damp, sandy soils, open or wooded; Florida-Texas and north into Virginia-South Dakota.

Polygala lutea

scolus stimulosus

rbia heterophylla

Polygala cruciata

EUPHORBIACEAE
(Spurge Family)

Euphorbia marginata Pursh. **Snow-on-the-mountain**

This 50-70 cm tall, annual plant, with milky sap, is a garden escape, locally abundant. Simple, alternate, ovate-oblong leaves 7-9 cm long, become nearly whorled, white margined, and smaller at the top. The much-branched top becomes a complex of small 5-7 mm wide cups with 5 broad, petallike white bracts, each with a nectar gland. From the base of each cup, the stalk of a single 3-lobed pistil elongates into the female flower, producing a 3-lobed capsule 5-6 mm long. Around the pistil and lining the cup are 2-many stamens, each a male flower. This represents the flower structure of the genus of this family, which is the only one with milky juice. Flowers June-frost in dry waste places; Georgia-Texas and north into Virginia-Minnesota.

EUPHORBIACEAE
(Spurge Family)

Euphorbia corollata L. **Flowering Spurge**

Leaves of this perennial plant are alternate, linear-elliptic, 2-7 cm long on 1-several stems to 1 m tall from a perennial root. Toward the branching rebranching top leaves are smaller and whorled. The milky sap is considered poisonous. The cuplike flower cluster (called a cyathium) with 5 white petallike bracts is 7-10 mm broad and fits the detailed description previously given for *E. marginata*. Flowers May-October in dry fields and open woodlands; Florida-Texas and north into New York-Minnesota.

ANACARDIACEAE
(Cashew Family)

Rhus radicans L. **Poison Ivy**

This perennial shrub may have a variety of form from simply erect to a stout climbing vine with many clinging roots from the stem. Its alternate, compound leaves have 3 leaflets, the terminal one longer and acute to acuminate, but variously sparsely toothed or lobed. All parts of the plant contain a poisonous oily sap. Small, greenish-white flowers with 5 petals, 5 stamens, and 5-lobed calyx appear in axillary clusters, followed by small whitish drupelike dry fruits. Seeds of fruits eaten by birds are not digested, spreading seeds over wide areas. This may be confused with poison oak *(R. toxicodendron)*, a nonclimbing shrub with 3 round-lobed leaflets. Flowers April-May in woodlands and fence rows over most of the eastern United States.

ANACARDIACEAE
(Cashew Family)

Rhus copallina L. **Dwarf or Winged Sumac**

The sumacs are spreading, flat-topped shrubs to 10 m or more in height and this nonpoisonous one may reach 7 m, usually 2-3 m. The alternate, pinnately compound leaves have 4-5, often more, pairs of 4-10 cm long entire leaflets which become fiery red in fall. The rachis of the leaf is winged between the leaflet pairs, a diagnostic trait. Small, greenish yellow male or female flowers appear on same or separate plants, have 5 sepals, petals, and stamens, produced in dense terminal clusters 10-30 cm long. Some flowers are also perfect, having both stamens and pistils. Red, densely fuzzy, 1-seeded dry fruits, 3-4 mm diameter follow July-September flowering in woodlands, fence rows, old fields and thickets; Florida-Texas and north into Canada.

orbia marginata

Euphorbia corollata

Rhus radicans

Rhus copallina

ANACARDIACEAE
(Cashew Family)
Rhus glabra L. **Smooth Sumac**

This sumac with alternate leaves has 7-9 pairs of leaflets 5-15 cm long, with toothed edges; the rachis is not winged. Young branches are smooth or glabrous, rather than hirsute-hairy. Smooth and staghorn sumac *(R. typhina)* are difficult to distinguish. If the new branches are densely covered with stiff hairs, it is staghorn, if not, but otherwise conforms, it is smooth sumac. Fruits of smooth sumac have appressed hairs while those of staghorn have stiff, spreading hairs. If the sumac is over 5 m high, it is probably staghorn, but if flowering stalks are in leaf axils and only 4-5 leaflet pairs, leave it alone, it is poison sumac. Flowers May-July in woodland borders, fence rows and thickets; Florida-Texas and north into New Mexico-West Virginia.

AQUIFOLIACEAE
(Holly Family)
Ilex decidua Walt. **Deciduous Holly**

This plant may reach a height of nearly 10 m, usually in lowland drainage systems. Its 4-7 cm long leaves are 2-3 cm wide, usually fine toothed, and elliptic-obovate, tapering to a short petiole. As the name implies, its leaves are shed in the fall. Tiny yellowish-green, usually separate-sexed flowers, with 4-6 petals and stamens appear in clusters on short branches April to May. Some solitary flowers bear only pistils and many 4-8 mm red fruits stand out in contrast during fall and winter, furnishing food for many birds. This is often called "possumhaw" but it is not a hawthorn, which is in the Rose Family; see *Crataegus marshallii* for contrast. Mostly in swampy woodlands and fence rows; Florida-Texas and north Maryland-Missouri.

AQUIFOLIACEAE
(Holly Family)
Ilex vomitoria Aiton. **Yaupon Holly**

This evergreen holly is a large, widely branching, thicket-forming shrub, but alone can become a tree. Elliptic-lanceolate, leathery leaves vary in size 2-4.5 cm long, have round shallow teeth, and are dark lustrous green. Small yellow-green flowers have parts in 4s, with sexes separate or both on one plant. Several staminate flowers are produced in clusters, while 1-3 nearly sessile, pistillate flowers are borne in leaf axils. Bright red berries, 4-6 mm in diameter, appear in abundance and remain through winter. They act both as an emetic and a purgative if eaten by man; birds enjoy them for food. Flowers March-May in sandy woodlands, clearings and bottom lands; Florida-Texas and north into Virginia-Arkansas-Oklahoma.

CELASTRACEAE
(Bittersweet Family)
Euonymus americanus L. **Strawberry-bush**

This 0.7-2.5 m high shrub is first noticed in late summer because of its striking red, 3-5 lobed capsules splitting and holding out 3-5 orange-red seeds on short "strings." The pods are 1-2 cm across and have tubercles on them, thus "strawberry bush," (but so is *Calycanthus*, note it). This is also called "Hearts-a-bustin." The 4-angled stems have 4-7 cm long, ovate, pointed, opposite, firm, green, fine-toothed leaves. The 1-1.5 cm wide, yellow-purple-tinged, 5-petaled flowers are axillary, on 2-2.5 cm long, 1-3 flowered peduncles. Flowers May-June in rich, moist woodlands; Florida-Texas and north into New York-Illinois-Missouri.

Rhus glabra

ɔmitoria

Ilex decidua

ymus americanus

Euonymus americanus

ACERACEAE
(Maple Family)

Acer rubrum L. **Red Maple**

This medium-sized maple, 12-15 m high, is one of the more common trees of the lowlands of the area, although it may grow on higher ground. It is often used as a shade tree, otherwise it has little commercial value. The leaves are shallowly 3-5 palmately lobed, and have various sized teeth. The opposite leaves, to 15 cm long, have blades longer than wide, and are paler below. Both sugar and silver maple blades are wider than long. Leaf stalks are 5-10 cm long and usually red, as are flowers and their stalks. Perfect and separate sexed flowers, their parts in 5s, appear on the same tree before or with the leaves in January-March, followed shortly by 2-2.5 cm winged fruits in pairs; Florida-Texas and north into New York-Minnesota.

HIPPOCASTANACEAE
(Buckeye Family)

Aesculus pavia L. **Red Buckeye**

This large, treelike deciduous shrub, 2-3 m high, has opposite, palmately compound leaves. The 5-7 large obovate-lanceolate leaflets are attached to the tip of the 5-15 cm long petiole. Leaflets are 4-6 cm wide, up to 17 cm long and are finely toothed. Terminal flowering stalks, to 20 cm long, bear few-many 2.5-3 cm long red flowers with 5-8 exserted stamens. The red tubular calyx is 1-1.5 cm long, and the upper 2 of 4 petals are longer than the lower 2. Both staminate and perfect flowers are present in the terminal flower cluster. A large, smooth, tan, leathery 4-5 cm diameter capsule contains 2-3 brown seeds (buckeyes) maturing in fall. Flowers in low woodlands and along streams, April-May; Florida-Texas and north into Virginia-Missouri.

SAPINDACEAE
(Soapberry Family)

Cardiospermum halicacabum L. **Balloon Vine**

This woody at the base, herbaceous vine is related to soapberry and golden rain tree, both uncommon in our area. This is mainly a family of tropical plants. Alternate leaves are bi-pinnately compound, divided into 3 sets of 3-pointed, serrate-lanceolate leaflets, 2-4 cm long and 1-2 cm wide. Small white flowers, 0.5-1 cm across, have 4 sepals and 4 ovate petals, 2 larger, 8 unequal length stamens and 3 stigma lobes. In September-October inflated balloon-like capsules ripen reddish-brown and contain black seeds with a light heart-shaped scar, *cardio* meaning "heart" and *spermum* "seed." "Heart-seed" is a common name. Flowers July-September in moist thickets and waste places; Florida-Texas and north into New Jersey-Missouri.

BALSAMINACEAE
(Jewelweed Family)

Impatiens capensis Meerb. **Jewelweed**

Jewelweed or spotted touch-me-not grows abundantly in low open wooded areas. It may reach 1.5-2 m in height, has alternate, elliptic to blunt-pointed, thin leaves with widely spaced teeth, appearing nearly scalloped. The orange, 2.5 cm long flowers have red-brown spots on their petals and the upper colored petal-like spurred sepal. The tip of the spur bends downward then forward. Of the 5 petals, the 2 lateral ones on each side are joined together appearing as only 2 rather than 4; the lower petal is free. Two upper lateral sepals are small and greenish, while the 2 lower ones are much reduced or missing, the spur is the 5th sepal. One to 3 flowers are produced at leaf axils, each suspended horizontally by its pedicel. Flowering is May to frost, Florida-Louisiana and north into South Carolina-Arkansas. *Impatiens pallida* Nuttal (yellow jewelweed) is a smaller flowered species with shorter spur, bent only downward. This plant is seen usually at higher elevations and is uncommon in our area.

Acer rubrum

Aesculus pavia

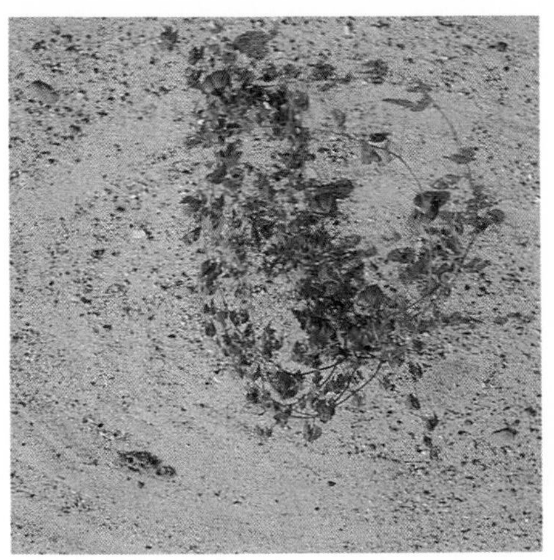

Cardiospermum halicacabum

npatiens capensis

Impatiens pallida

RHAMNACEAE
(Buckthorn Family)

Ceanothus americanus L. **New Jersey Tea**

This low shrub, to 1 m tall, grows in clumps in dry open woods and gravelly roadsides. It is conspicuous in June to July when it is flowering because of its numerous, thick, 5-15 cm long clusters of tiny white flowers on 5-25 cm long, axillary peduncles. Alternate deciduous leaves on short petioles are ovate-lanceolate, 5-10 cm long, and finely toothed. There are 3 conspicuous veins on the lower side of the leaf which is also gray pubescent. This is a plant of dryer habitats, there being more species farther westward. Flowers May-July; Florida-Texas and north into Canada.

RHAMNACEAE
(Buckthorn Family)

Rhamnus caroliniana Walt. **Carolina Buckthorn**

This shrub or small tree to 10 m high has a spreading crown of thornless branches with deciduous leaves alternate, broadly elliptical, tapered at the tip and tapered to rounded at the bases, 7-13 cm long by 2.5-4 cm broad. Margins are obscurely toothed or entire and there are 7-10 prominent pairs of veins. Several whitish flowers are clustered on short stalks at the leaf axils; they have a 5-point lobed calyx cup 3-4 mm long and 5 ovate petals notched at the tip, shorter than the calyx. There are 5 short stamens and a 3-celled ovary producing a 3-seeded, fleshy, red turning to black, leathery ovoid drupe 5-7 mm diameter. Flowers May-June in swamps to open rocky woodlands; Florida-Texas and north into West Virginia-Ohio-Nebraska.

VITACEAE
(Grape Family)

Ampelopsis arborea (L). Koehne **Pepper-vine**

This high-climbing perennial vine, in the family with grape and Virginia creeper, competes quite well in low swampy woods in our area. Its alternate, deciduous, 15-20 cm long leaves are twice, sometimes 3 times, divided into leaflets 1-4 cm long, rhombic-ovate, and with large teeth to deep lobes. There are 3-5 leaflets together in the final dividing of the leaves. Inconspicuous flowers, 2-4 mm across, are greenish-yellow and perfect or separate sexed, produced in dichotomous branching racemes 2.5-4 cm across, in which some tendrils might appear. Fruits are black, shiny 13-seeded inedible berries 0.8-1 cm in diameter appearing in late summer. Flowers June-August mainly in swampy wooded areas and along streams; Florida-Texas and north into Virginia-Missouri.

MALVACEAE
(Mallow Family)

Hibiscus moscheutos L. **Marsh Mallow**

This perennial plant grows to 2 m high. Cotton and okra are different genera of the same family. The leaves are ovate-elliptic to lanceolate, 8-25 cm long and 3-9 cm wide, rounded-cordate at base, with acute-acuminate tips, and have toothed margins. There are 10-15 linear bracts, shorter than and just below the 5 sepals. Sepals are united by their bases, as are the 5 petals, 7-10 cm long, white with purple bases. Also, the many stamen filaments are united into a long tube surrounding the 6-7 cm long, 5-carpel pistil, which is terminated by a 5-branched stigma. Union of parts indicates more recent innovations in plants. Flowers July-September in low wet marshes and roadside ditches; Florida-Louisiana and north into West Virginia-southern Illinois.

mpelopsis arborea

Rhamnus caroliniana

eanothus americanus

Hibiscus moscheutos

THEACEAE
(Tea Family)

Gordonia lasianthus (L.) Ellis **Loblolly-bay Gordonia**

This rather rare species and two species of *Stewartia* are our southern representatives of this family. The latter are quite rare camellialike deciduous shrubs. Evergreen leaves of *Gordonia* are oblanceolate, nearly sessile, 7.5-15 cm long and 2.5-5 cm wide, and have finely serrated margins. Trees grow 14-22 m high and have white, camellialike flowers clustered at the ends of branches. Flowers have 5 7-9 mm wide ovate sepals and a corolla 5-7 cm wide of 5 obovate petals with crimped margins. Many yellow stamens are united by their lower filaments into 5 groups, one group at the base of each petal. Flowers July-September in low, wet woodlands, around the coastal plain; Florida-Mississippi and north into North Carolina.

HYPERICACEAE
(St. John's-wort Family)

Hypericum stans (Michx.) P.A. & R. **St. Peter's-wort**

Most of the *Hypericums* have 5 petals, but this and a few others have only 4 and were placed in a separate genus, *Ascyrum*, by most previous authorities, and were called St. Peter's-worts. This 30-60 cm high plant grows erect with a few branches and has ovate-elliptic, opposite leaves 2-3 cm long and 1.2-1.5 cm wide clasping the somewhat winged stem. Terminal flowers have 2 outer, broad cordate, opposite sepals enclosing mature pistils, with 2 inner narrow opposite sepals at the edges of the flattened enclosure which is 9-13 mm long. Petals are obovate, orange-yellow, 10-18 mm long and 4 in number. Stamens are numerous and have long filaments. Fruit is an ovoid capsule about 6 mm long. Flowers May-October in dry sandy open areas and woodlands; Florida-Texas and north into New Jersey-Kentucky.

HYPERICACEAE
(St. John's-wort Family)

Hypericum fasciculatum Lam. **St. John's-wort**

This evergreen, much-branched, shrubby *Hypericum* may reach a height of 1-6 m in wet, sandy pinelands, and cypress swamps along the coastal plain. Narrow, linear 2.5 cm long, leather leaf blades without petioles have axillary branchlets bearing close clusters (fascicles) of leaves along the woody branches. Flowers may be terminal or axillary, solitary or in clusters. There are 5 linear sepals 3-7 mm long resembling the leaves; 5 petals are obovate and 6-9 mm long, about as long as the many stamens. Flowers May-September along the lower coastal plain; Florida-Texas and north into North Carolina.

HYPERICACEAE
(St. John's-wort Family)

Hypericum punctatum Lam. **Spotted St. John's-wort**

This *Hypericum* is a tough perennial to a meter high. It has opposite elliptic-oblong, 4-6 cm long leaves. Upon close observation, or with a lens, one may see tiny black spots and also scattered translucent spots on the lower side. The term *punctatum* refers to these characteristic spots. Branching flower clusters are borne terminally on the erect few-branched plant. Sepals, 1.5-3.2 mm long are black spotted as are the 5, 4-6 mm long yellow petals, the corolla being 1.5-2 cm across. Flowers June-September in fields and ditches and along roadsides; Florida-Texas and north into Canada.

rdonia lasianthus

Hypericum stans

ypericum fasciculatum

Hypericum punctatum

VIOLACEAE
(Violet Family)
Viola pedata L.
Bird's-foot Violet

This violet gets its name from the 2.5-5 cm long, palmately dissected (pedate) leaf blades with 5-11 narrow segments. The underground stem or rhizome is short and upright; leaves and flowers in abundance arise directly from it, hence it is called a stemless violet. The conspicuous flowers are 3.5-4.5 cm across with orange-yellow stamens protruding from the center. Petals of violets are of unequal sizes, making a bilaterally symmetrical flower, an advanced trait. Upper petals are reflexed, the lower ones protruding, presenting a horizontal flower. A scarce variety of this species has dark blue upper petals. Petals of this species are not bearded at the throat. Flowers March-May on rocky-sandy open slopes and woodlands; Florida-Texas north into North Carolina and Minnesota.

VIOLACEAE
(Violet Family)
Viola papilionacea Pursh.
Common Blue Violet

This, too, is a stemless violet without spreading stolons. Large, to 12 cm wide, leaves are ovate-cordate, are hairless glossy-green, have small teeth, and are on long petioles. The flowers, 2-2.5 cm across, are purplish with darker veins and with a white or yellowish throat. When petals are darker blue, veins do not stand out as seer here. The 2 lateral petals have conspicuous hairs (bearded) in the throat. Seed capsules become much longer, 12-14 mm, than the surrounding sepals. A completely white variety, *albiflora,* has been cultivated. This species is one of the most common in our area. Flowers in damp woods, meadows and roadsides; Florida-Texas and north into Canada.

VIOLACEAE
(Violet Family
Viola primulifolia L.
Primrose-leaf Violet

This, too, is a stemless violet with small rhizome, but it does produce stolons above ground. The leaves are similar to those of primrose. They are very much spoon-shaped or spatulate and on long petioles. Leaves may reach 18 cm long and have blades to 8 cm wide with scallop-toothed margins, which usually taper winglike into the long petiole. The small 1-2 cm broad white flowers have purple veins on the lower (1 or 3) petal which is also short round-spurred at its base. The flowering scape is often longer than the leaves. Flowers March-June in wet meadows, open woodlands, and along stream beds; Florida-Texas and north into Canada.

VIOLACEAE
(Violet Family)
Viola eriocarpa Schwein.
Smooth Yellow Violet

This long-stemmed yellow violet branches from the rhizome into 2-4 leafy ascending stems, 40-50 cm tall which are glabrous to slightly pubescent. Ovate-cordate basal leaves, when present, are longer petioled and deeper notched than the smaller stem leaves. They all have pronounced veins, are round-toothed margined and scarcely pubescent. Flowers arise in leaf axils to just above the leaves in most, have yellow petals, the lower and 2 lateral ones are purple veined. Flowers are 1.5-2.5 cm broad and the sepals have ciliate margins. Capsules are 7-11 mm long, and, if ovary or capsule is hairy it is var. *eriocarpa,* if both are glabrous, it is var. *leiocarpa.* Flowers March-May in rich woodlands, slopes and alluvial soils; Georgia-Texas and north to Canada.

·la pedata

Viola papilionacea

ɔla primulifolia

Viola eriocarpa

VIOLACEAE
(Violet Family)

Viola rafinesquii Greene **Wild Pansy**

This glabrous annual violet produces few branches at its base and grows 7-25 cm high. The upper leaves to 3 cm long are spatulate-obovate tapering into a long petiole. The 2 stipules at the base of the petiole are deeply divided into several linear segments and are more prominent than the blades, which are only 8-10 mm long. The flowers, 7-10 mm long, on 15-mm long flower branches range from white to blue and white, with a yellow "eye" and purple veins. Sepals are lanceolate and half the length of the petals. This violet is also called "Johnny-jump-up," and appears abundantly in early spring with bluets and spring beauty. Lawns, meadows, and open woodlands; Georgia-Texas and north into New York-Nebraska; also reported farther west in several other states.

PASSIFLORACEAE
(Passion-flower Family)

Passiflora incarnata L. **May-pops, Passion-flower**

The passion-flowers belong to a largely tropical family and only 2 species are represented in our area. Both are herbaceous, perennial, slightly pubescent vines, climbing with tendrils arising from the axils of the alternate leaves. Also at these nodes arise 1-2 flowering peduncles and often a lateral stem bud.

This species grows 2-3 m long and has simple palmately, deeply 3-lobed (rarely 5) leaves 8-10 cm long, and about as wide, on 1-3 cm long petioles. There are 5 sepals, 2.5-3 cm long, linear-oblong, blunt spine-tipped, green on the outside and and purple within. The 5 petals are 3-4 cm long, 0.4-0.7 cm wide and bluish white. Arising above the petals is a corona or crown of numerous fringelike segments as long as the petals, white and banded with purple. Arising in the center is a 3-lobed pistil, the styles horizontal and the stigmas bent downward. Surrounding the pistil, 5 stamens are united into a tube, then separate into 5 anther-bearing horizontal lobes. Upon maturity, a globose-oblong, many-seeded yellowish berry, 4-10 cm long, becomes the edible "maypop." Flowers May-July in fence rows, thickets and roadsides; Florida-Texas and north into Pennsylvania-Illinois.

PASSIFLORACEAE
(Passion-flower Family)

Passilfora lutea L. **Yellow Passion-flower**

The structures of this flower are similar to the above, but smaller. The greenish-yellow flower is 2-2.5 cm across and the purple-black berry is 0.8-1.2 cm in diameter. Leaf blades are shallowly palmately 3-lobed to 7 cm long and 8.5-9 cm wide, on 4-5 cm long petioles. The vine climbs or trails over 3.5 meters long. Flowers June-September; Florida-Texas and north into Illinois-Kansas.

LYTHRACEAE
(Loosestrife Family)

Decodon verticillatus (L) Ell. **Swamp Loosestrife, Water-willow**

This aquatic emergent perennial shrub to 3 m high has a square stem and opposite or whorled (verticillate) leaves. It spreads by forming roots and new plants where arching branches reach water or mud. Leaves, tapered at both ends, are up to 20 cm long and 5 cm wide on short petioles. Flowers, 1.5-2 cm long, resemble crape myrtle of the same family. There are 5 separate, 1-1.2 cm long, pink-purple, lanceolate petals, tapered at their bases, attached to the calyx tube. Short-pediceled flowers are clustered in the leaf axils. The 10 stamens are of 2 lengths. Globose seed capsules are 4-7 mm in diameter. Flowers July to September in swamps and marshes; Florida-Louisiana and north into Maryland-Minnesota.

ola rafinesquii

ecodon verticillatus

Passiflora incarnata

Passiflora incarnata

Passiflora lutea

MELASTOMATACEAE
(Meadow-beauty Family)

Rhexia mariana L. **Meadow-beauty**

This opposite-leafed, herbaceous perennial is one of several species, but the only genus of this mostly tropical family represented in our area. It spreads by stolons sending up branched or nonbranched plants to 80 cm tall. Stems, leaf margins and calyx tubes have scattered, bristly hairs. Leaves have 3 prominent nerves, finely toothed-ciliate margins, and are elliptic-lanceolate to 6.5 cm long by 2 cm wide. There are 4 pink-purple to white rounded petals 1.2-5 cm long from the tip of a constricted-necked, urn-shaped calyx tube 7-10 mm long. There are 8 stamens with horn-shaped horizontal anthers opening by a terminal pore. The pistil style bends sharply downward, then upward. Flowers June-September along wet ditches, meadows, and marshes; Florida-Texas and north into Massachusetts-Kentucky-Oklahoma.

ONAGRACEAE
(Evening Primrose Family)

Ludwigia peploides (Kunt.) Shinners **Primrose-willow**

This semiaquatic member of the family inhabits shorelines of lakes, streams, and marshes, growing in mud or water. Reddish stems are usually creeping or floating, upright at the ends, and reach a meter in length. Alternate elliptic-obovate leaves are 8 cm long and 3.5 cm wide. Most plants of this family have floral parts in 4s; this is an exception as they are in 5s, with 10 stamens. A family trait is the inferior ovary, often found far below the sepal lobes. Yellow-orange flowers are 2-3 cm across and have 5 broad petals and 5 broad-lanceolate sepals 7-10 mm long. Below the sepals is developed a cylindric capsule 2.5-4 cm long. Flowers May-September; Florida-Texas and north into New Jersey-Kansas, uncommon.

ONAGRACEAE
(Evening Primrose Family)

Oenothera drummondii Hooker **Beach Evening Primrose**

This rather uncommon perennial trailing or decumbent plant to 60 cm long has large yellow flowers 6-7 cm across, produced singly in the leaf axils. Most of the plant is abundantly covered with appressed hairs. The leaves are about 5 cm long, on no or very short petioles, somewhat variable obovate-elliptic, have entire margins, and are alternate on the stem. The sepals become reflexed, are narrow and over ¾ the length of the 4-5 cm calyx tube attached to the inferior, 2-4 cm long, upward-curving seed pod. Flowers April-June or later, along the sandy coast; Georgia-Louisiana-east Texas.

ONAGRACEAE
(Evening Primrose Family)

Oenothera laciniata Hill **Cut-leaf Evening Primrose**

Oenotheras have 4 sepals, usually reflexed; 4 petals, yellow, pink or white; 8 stamens and a pistil with a 4-branched stigma, and a long style (to 4.5 cm long) to an inferior ovary which develops into a cylindric, often curved capsule 1-4 cm long. Alternate leaves may be simple to deeply pinnately lobed (laciniate). Stems are usually branched pubescent biennials or perennials. This species is pubescent, biennial, and has basal decumbent branches to 70 cm long, with variously lobed to pinnatifid leaves 2-10 cm long. The calyx tube is 2-2.5 cm long with lobes 6-12 mm long; yellow to reddish petals are 8-25 mm long; the capsule 2.5-4 cm long. Flowers May-Ocotber in fields and waste places over most of the eastern United States.

xia mariana

Ludwigia peploides

Oenothera drummondii

Oenothera laciniata

ONAGRACEAE
(Evening Primrose Family)

Oenothera speciosa Nuttall **Showy Evening Primrose**

This evening primrose is usually under 60 cm tall, spreading from a perennial rootstock. The leaves are to 8 cm long by 3 cm wide, unlobed, and variously lobed to pinnatifid. Flowers are white to pink 5-7 cm across, with obcordate petals, and are produced singly to several on branching peduncles in the axils of the leaves. Buds are nodding before flowering. Calyx lobes are 1.5-3 cm long and long-tapered on a calyx tube 1-2 cm long above a maturing, 4-angled or 4-winged, obovate capsule, 1.5-2 cm long. Flowers May-August in fields, waste places, and especially along roadsides as a showy spectacle; Florida-Texas and north in prairies and plains to Virginia-Kansas.

ONAGRACEAE
(Evening Primrose Family)

Oenothera pilosella Raf. **Sundrops**

This evening primrose may grow decumbent, spreading to 60 cm high from a perennial rhizome and have flowers 6 cm across, few in number at branch tips. Flowers are axillary on only slightly reduced upper leaves. The petals are obcordate or heart-shaped, with the notch at the tips, and are noticeably veiny. The unopened calyx has 4 free tips, 2-3 mm long and is somewhat hairy. Pilose refers to the presence of hairs on the stems and flower buds, but they are scarce on older leaves. The blunt-tipped leaves are ovate to lanceolate, sparsely minute-toothed, and to 13 cm long and 1-4 cm broad. It is a thrill to see these flowers open in just a few seconds at dusk. Flowers May-July in meadows, prairies, and open woodlands; West Virginia-Arkansas and north into Michigan-Iowa.

HALORAGACEAE
(Water-milfoil Family)

Myriophyllum brasiliense Camb. **Parrot-feather**

This aquatic flowering plant imported from South America is a common aquarium plant. It exists and is apparently spreading through most of the states from Florida to Mississippi and northward to New York, but it seldom flowers. Submerged, often purplish, and emergent leaves are in whorls of 3-6 all similar, pectinate or finely pinnate, 3-6 cm long leaves. Leaf segments number 10-18 on a stout stem. When flowers are produced, they are tiny and have 4 sepals, no or 4 petals, and 8 stamens. Other myriophyllums are distinguished by having emergent leaves simple (not divided) and finely divided submerged leaves. Found in ponds, lakes, and roadside ditches mostly around the coastal plain.

ARALIACEAE
(Ginseng Family)

Aralia spinosa L. **Devil's Walkingstick**

This shrub or small tree may reach 8 m high, with a flat-topped crown and have quite large clusters of small round clumps of minute, white, 5-petaled flowers. The alternate, deciduous leaves are twice pinnately compound and may reach 1 m or more long and 0.6-1 m wide. There are 5-6 pairs of lateral leaflets and 1 terminal; they are ovate-elliptic, to 7 cm wide and 13 cm long, dark green above, paler below, and finely toothed. Spines are prominent on stout twigs and less prominent on leaf stalks. Black, berrylike 5-seeded pulpy fruits, 4-6 mm in diameter are enjoyed by wild-life; it is occasionally used medicinally. Flowers July-September in woods, thickets, and stream edges; Florida-Texas and north into New York-Iowa.

enothera pilosella

yriophyllum brasiliense

ralia spinosa

Oenothera speciosa

Aralia spinosa

APIACEAE
(Parsley Family)
Hydrocotyle umbellata L. **Water-Pennywort**

The Parsley Family has also been called the Umbelliferae (to bear little umbrellas), and contains carrot, hemlock, and other plants with umbels of flowers. Leaves of this plant resemble those of nasturtium in being peltate. The leaves have circular blades with the petiole attached at their center. Blades are 1-4 cm wide, on petioles to 15 cm or more long. The umbels of tiny, whitish, 5-petaled flowers are 1.5-3 cm across. Two similar species in the same range are *H. verticillata,* with successive whorls of flowers on the stem axis, and *H. bonariensis,* with a larger, multibranched umbel. Flowers April-September in shallow water or moist places in open woodlands and roadside places; especially along the coastal plain-Texas and north into Massachusetts-Michigan.

APIACEAE
(Parsley Family)
Hydrocotyle sibthorpioides Lam. **Lawn Water-Pennywort**

This creeping lawn weed makes near full coverage in shady areas but has such tiny flowers they go unnoticed. The plant has round scalloped leaves to 1 cm across on slender petioles, arising from prostrate stems rooting at their nodes. Leaf blades are deeply notched at their bases. There are 3-10 flowers in an umbel only 2-4 mm across. Flowers have 5 stamens and 5 purple-tinged petals, followed by tiny greenish fruits only 1-1.5 mm in length. Flowers March-September in lawns and roadsides; Virginia-Alabama-southwest Tennessee northward into Delaware-Indiana. This plant is apparently introduced from Asia and Africa.

APIACEAE
(Parsley Family)
Eryngium yuccifolium Michx. **Button Snakeroot**

This perennial plant is coarse-leaved, with spine-toothed edges and parallel veins, resembling those of yucca, but it is not a monocot plant. Lower leaves, clasping the stem at their bases, are about 4 cm wide and may get nearly 1 m long on a plant reaching to 1.5 m tall. Its flowers grow in compact spherical heads, as umbels, at branching stem tips and leaf axils. The heads of tiny white flowers are 1.5-2.5 cm in diameter and have several short bracts at their bases. Flowers July-August. This is essentially a prairie type of plant found in dry or wet open woods or fields; Florida-Texas and north into New Jersey-Minnesota.

APIACEAE
(Parsley Family)
Daucus carota L. **Queen Anne's-lace**

This biennial grows from a taproot "carrot" its second year, to a height of nearly 2 m and is familiar over most of the country. Its leaves are 2-3 times compounded, the segments being narrower toward the top. The stems usually branch widely, terminating in umbels of small 5-petaled white flowers, the umbels to 10 cm across. Umbels are flat to round-topped in flowering, but the "ribs" curl inward, presenting a depressed center with numerous brownish, bristly, 3-5 mm long fruits upon maturing. Also in our area, a smaller, mostly unbranched plant with smaller umbels is *D. pusillus.* Flowers May-September in open prairies, fields, and roadsides. This is probably a naturalized European import.

Hydrocotyle sibthorpioides

Hydrocotyle umbellata

Daucus carota

Eryngium yuccifolium

Daucus carota

APIACEAE
(Parsley Family)

Osmorhiza longistylis (Tor.) DC. **Sweet Cicely, Sweet Chervil**

This mostly glabrous perennial grows to 100 cm tall from thick aromatic roots and the scent of anise emerges from the crushed leaves. Larger leaves have 3-forked petioles forming 3 main divisions, again pinnately divided; the final leaf segments are 2-9 cm long by 1-4 cm wide. The branching and rebranching flower cluster finally ends in 3-6 small umbels of tiny white flowers on 1-2 mm long pedicels, elongating to 1-1.5 cm in fruit. Petals are 1.5-2.5 mm long, both perfect and male flowers are present in the clusters. There are 5 long stamens and a slender beaked pistil 3-5 mm long, longer than the petals, which elongates into a 1.2-1.5 cm fruit tapering at at both ends, with a short bilobed beak at the tip. Flowers May-June in rich, mostly alluvial, woodlands and thickets; Georgia-New Mexico and north into Canada.

APIACEAE
(Parsley Family)

Zizia aurea (L.) Koch. **Golden Alexander**

This member of the family grows to a meter high from a fleshy taproot, has brilliant yellow tiny flowers in flat-topped clusters of still smaller umbels. It has also been called golden meadow parsnip. The umbels rise, widely spreading, as 3-20 "ribs" of the umbrella at the tips of branching ribs. Leaves are pinnate with three leaflets, some of which may be similarly ternately divided. The leaflets are lanceolate, 2-7 cm long and 1-3 cm wide, sharply toothed on the margins. As in other members of the family, the small flowers have 5 sepals, 5 petals, and an inferior ovary that becomes a 2-celled pair of 1-seeded structures. Flowers April-June in low alluvial meadows and woodlands; Florida-Texas and north into Canada.

NYSSACEAE
(Tupelo Family)

Nyssa sylvatica Marshall **Black Gum, Sour Gum**

Nyssa was a Greek water nymph and *sylvatica* refers to woodlands. This interesting tree grows in swampy, low woodlands throughout our area. Its glossy green leaves become fiery orange-red in fall, evoking comment. The moderately large tree grows to 10 m or more high and has a diameter to 1.3 m. The base of the tree is not buttressed, as in the water tupelo. Leaves are alternate, deciduous, 5-10 cm long by 3-7 cm wide, and oval-obovate with mostly an entire margin. Trees may be of separate sexes or have separate sex flowers on one tree. Female flowers are borne 2-several per cluster and have 5 sepals and 0-10 greenish-yellow minute petals, falling early. The southern variety, shown here, has flowers mostly in 2s and the leaves appear before the flowers. Also, the fruit pit has more prominent ridges than those of the northern form. In both, the fruit is dark blue and plumlike, 1.2-1.4 cm long. Flowers April-June in acid woods and swamps; Florida-Texas and north to Maine-Wisconsin.

NYSSACEAE
(Tupelo Family)

Nyssa aquatica L. **Water Tupelo**

The water tupelo has leaves twice the size of the sour gum, to 20 cm long and 10 cm wide; has female flowers borne singly and fruits 2.5 cm long on slender 7-10 cm long stalks in the fall. The tree grows in deep swamps mostly standing in water mixed with cypress trees. The trunk is strongly buttressed, flaring outward 1-2 m above the water. Found Florida-Texas and north into Virginia along the coast and to Illinois up the Mississippi River and its tributaries.

Zizia aurea

sa sylvatica

Osmorhiza longistylis

sa aquatica

CORNACEAE
(Dogwood Family)

Cornus florida L. **Flowering Dogwood**

Although it is called flowering dogwood, the flowers are really inconspicuous in the center of the 4 showy bracts. Flowers are perfect with both pistils and stamens. Each flower is 3-4 mm across, with 4 sepals, 4 straplike yellow petals and 4 stamens arising from the top of an inferior ovary, the latter becoming a red drupelike fruit.

Among other dogwoods in our area are the roughleaf dogwood, *C. asperifolia, aspera* meaning "rough." It has opposite leaves with harsh hairs on the upper surface. Small white flowers are in a loose branching flare-topped cluster followed by 3 mm diameter globose white fruits. *C. alternifolia,* the alternate-leaf dogwood, bears smooth-surfaced alternate leaves and rather dense flat-topped clusters of small white flowers followed by blue-black fruits 8-10 mm in diameter. The alternate-leaf dogwood is found in uplands while the roughleaf dogwood prefers low wet woodlands.

ERICACEAE
(Heath Family)

Monotropa uniflora L. **Indian Pipe**

This unusual, perennial, nongreen plant is also one of the most widespread in its distribution through most of North America. It has no chlorophyll and cannot make its own food; it apparently absorbs organic foods from decaying forest litter. The single stem, 10-20 cm high, has scalelike leaves about 1.5 cm long. Whole plants are mostly waxy white but may be pale yellow to pinkish. Flowers of most of the family have united petals, but *Monotropa* has 4-5 separate, 1-1.5 cm long petals, 0-5 sepals, and 10 stamens. The terminal flower is nodding in bloom, becoming erect as the capsule matures. The pistil is disk-shaped at the top and the 2-cm long capsule has 5 chambers. Plants are widely spread, usually in clumps but sometimes singly, in mixed hardwood and pine forests. Flowers in our area June-October.

ERICACEAE
(Heath Family)

Monotropa hypopithys L. **Pinesap**

This plant is also very widespread in its distribution, but is usually yellowish to purplish and has several flowers along its single waxy stem. The terminal flower has 5 petals 0.8-1.5 cm long, while there are only 4 on the lateral ones. Here too, the capsule becomes erect upon maturing, as seen in the photo. *Monotropa* probably refers to the single feeding (trop or troph) stem and *hypopithys* means under pine in Greek. Both species have been placed in the Pyrolaceae or Wintergreen Family by some specialists.

ERICACEAE
(Heath Family)

Rhododendron calendulaceum (Michx.) Torr. **Flame Azalea**

Azaleas have deciduous leaves and 5-10 stamens, while rhododendrons have evergreen leaves and 10-20 stamens. Both belong to the genus *Rhododendron.* The petals are united into a funnel form, 2-lipped, yellow-orange to red corolla 1.5-2.5 cm long with 5 lobes. The 5 long stamens and pistil are twice the length of the corolla tube. Slightly fragrant flowers appear before or along with the leaves. Obovate-elliptic, 5-8 cm long, alternate, deciduous leaves are hairy beneath, mostly smooth above, and have finely toothed ciliate margins. The shrubs grow to a height of 2-5 m in dry, mixed deciduous forest; flowers May-July; Georgia-Mississippi and north into Pennsylvania-Ohio.

Cornus florida

Monotropa uniflora

notropa hypopithys

Rhododendron calendulaceum

ERICACEAE
(Heath Family)
Rhododendron canescens (Michx.) Sweet **Wild Azalea**

Although this shrub, 2-3 m high, is called a wild honeysuckle, it is not of the genus *Lonicera* of the Honeysuckle Family; perhaps it is because of the similar pungent fragrance of the flowers. The elliptic-obovate alternate leaves are deciduous, so azalea is correctly applied here. Canescent means gray pubescent and leaves, corolla tubes, and even the stamen filaments are quite hairy. The corolla tube is 1.5-2.5 cm long, flaring into reflexed lobes, pink tinged or white. Stamens are twice the length of the corolla tube and the pistil longer. Pubescence on the calyx and the corolla tube is glandular hairy. Flowers before the leaves emerge in April-early May in dry woodlands, wooded swamps, and stream beds; Florida-Texas and north Maine-Missouri.

ERICACEAE
(Heath Family)
Kalmia latifolia L. **Mountain Laurel**

This 3-5 m high treelike shrub is commonly found in the mountains but it occurs less frequently in coastal plain sandy, swampy woods, and rocky areas. It is evergreen with alternate, leathery, elliptical leaves 5-21 cm long and 2-5 cm wide. Saucer-shaped flowers, 2-3 cm across, are produced in clusters at ends of branches. Buds are pink-white and open flowers have 10 stamens and 10 purple sunken pockets, 2 to each of the united petals. The pockets are where there are hornlike projections noted on the Japanese lanternlike buds. Spherical capsules, about 1 cm across, have 5 lobes and a long style making up the dry fruit. Flowers March-July; Florida-Louisiana and north into New York-Indiana.

ERICACEAE
(Heath Family)
Lyonia lucida (Lam.) K. Koch. **Fetter-bush**

This evergreen shrub may reach 2 m in height in low, wet acid woods and thickets along the coastal plain from Virginia to Florida and Louisiana. The leathery dark-green, elliptical leaves are 3-8 cm long by 1-4.5 cm wide and have their margins rolled under. Flowers are pink to red, seldom white, urn-shaped and hang in clusters from leaf axils. The 5 calyx lobes are 3-5 mm long and the 6-8 mm long corolla is constricted at the top with 5 reflexed lobes. The 10 stamens are shorter than the corolla. A 5-cavity ovoid 3.5-5 mm capsule produces many club-shaped 1 mm long seeds. Flowers April-May.

ERICACEAE
(Heath Family)
Oxydendrum arboreum (L.) DC. **Sourwood**

This small tree may get over 17 m high and has 15 cm long elliptic-lanceolate, alternate, deciduous leaves with fine teeth, on 1-2.5 cm petioles. The white, 0.8-1 cm long, urn-shaped flowers are produced on one-sided branching terminal racemes 15-30 cm long. *Oxydendrum* means "sour tree;" the leaves are quite acid and have been used as a diuretic. The glandular flowers produce nectar used by bees in making honey, a much sought-after delicacy. Leaves in the fall turn from a bronze-green to bright red. The tree is often used in landscaping. Flowers June-August on well-drained rich slopes and woodlands; Florida-Mississippi and north into New England-Ohio.

mia latifolia

Rhododendron canescens

Lyonia lucida

Oxydendrum arboreum

ERICACEAE
(Heath Family)
Epigaea repens L. **Trailing Arbutus**

This trailing evergreen is really a woody perennial plant, 5-8 cm high. It was among the first very fragrant plants noted by the Pilgrims and was called "Mayflower." Pink fading to white flowers appear in terminal or axillary clusters. The 6-10 mm long corolla tube spreads widely to a 2-cm wide, 5-lobed corolla which is densely pubescent within. The 10 stamens are about the length of the corolla tube. The elliptic-ovate leaves to 4 cm wide and 8 cm long, rounded at the base, are not toothed. The leaves are stiffly hairy on the surfaces, as are the 1-5 cm long petioles. Flowers March-May in sandy or rocky woodlands; Florida-Mississippi and north into New England-Ohio.

ERICACEAE
(Heath Family)
Vaccinium stamineum L. **Deerberry**

Blueberries and others are included in the many species of Vaccinium. One common member is this shrub to 3 m high. Its elliptic-oblanceolate leaves are deciduous, to 10 cm long and 4.5 cm wide, and covered with minute hairs as are the twigs and sepals. Flowers appear in hanging axillary clusters, 1-5 cm long, among leaflike bracts usually smaller than the leaves. Saucer-shaped flowers are greenish white to pink, with 5 flared lobes to 1.5 cm across, and the 10 stamens extend to twice the length of the corolla. Pistils have an inferior ovary, which becomes a pubescent yellowish to purplish many-seeded berry to 1.5 cm long. Flowers April-June in dry woods and thickets; Florida-Louisiana and north into New York-Missouri.

ERICACEAE
(Heath Family)
Vaccinium vacillans Torr. **Low Blueberry**

This low growing shrub is about 1 m high, and has deciduous leaves that are elliptic-ovate to 5 cm long, 3.5 cm wide and whitish beneath. Flowers from terminal and axillary clusters have greenish-yellowish to pinkish urn-shaped corollas to 5-8 mm long and somewhat constricted at their tip. There are 8-10 stamens shorter than the corolla tube. Flowers appear before or with the leaves in March-April, followed in June or later by very sweet, dark blue berries to 1 cm long, covered with a whitish bloom. Plants are found in dry, open woodlands, rocky ledges, and thickets; Georgia-Alabama-Tennessee and north into New Hampshire-Michigan.

PRIMULACEAE
(Primrose Family)
Dodecatheon meadia L. **Shooting-star**

This perennial rosette-leaved plant belongs to the Primrose Family, not to be confused with the Evening Primrose Family, *Onagraceae.* In this family, the ovary is superior, the calyx not being attached to the ovary. Flower parts are in 5s, the petals united by their bases, their lobes 1.5-2.5 cm long and strongly reflexed in flower. Flowers may be purple, pink or white. There are 5 stamens, opposite and attached by their short filaments to the short corolla tube. The longer anthers converge closely, beaklike, around the pistil. Flowers appear, 12-14 in an umbel, atop the leafless 20-60 cm stem or scape. The basal, spatulate or oblanceolate leaves can be 10 cm wide and 30 cm long. Narrowly ovoid capsules 1.5-2 cm long split in 5 parts at maturity. Flowers April-June in prairies, open woodlands, and slopes; Georgia-Texas and north into Pennsylvania-Wisconsin.

Epigaea repens

Vaccinium stamineum

Vaccinium vacillans

Dodecatheon meadia

PRIMULACEAE
(Primrose Family)

Lysimachia ciliata L. **Fringed Loosestrife**

These perennial plants from spreading rhizomes grow to 1 m or more tall and have 5-20 cm long, ovate-lanceolate leaves with 1-6 cm long petioles with small *ciliate* hairs along their margins. Yellow flowers, 1.7-2.7 cm across, have their corolla lobe tips *fringed* with several teeth. Thus is seen the origin of both species and common names. Petals are united and widely spreading into a rotate corolla with 5 lobes. Flowers on long slender stalks are mostly whorled in the axils of the opposite leaves. Globose capsules are 3-6 mm long at maturity. Flowers June-August in low wet woodlands, thickets, and swamps; Florida-Louisiana and north into Pennsylvania-Wisconsin.

PRIMULACEAE
(Primrose Family)

Anagallis arvensis L. **Scarlet Pimpernel**

This small-flowered annual is the only species of the genus in North America and is found throughout most of the country. Flowers are more often orange than scarlet and may even be blue. Flowers are 0.5-1.5 cm across, with 5 round petals spreading from a short corolla tube. There are 5 stamens, united by their bases and attached to the corolla tube. Flowers appear singly on long slender stalks in the axils of the opposite 1-3 cm long, non-toothed stalkless leaves. The plant is much-branched with low spreading 10-30 cm long stems to a height of only a few centimeters. Flowers April-August in lawns, fields, and waste places. *Arvensis* means "of the cultivated fields." This is a naturalized European import.

STYRACACEAE
(Storax Family)

Halesia carolina L. **Carolina Silverbell**

This tree with alternate, deciduous, ovate pointed leaves may reach 12 m in height. The leaves are dark green above and pale green below with stellate hairs. The calyx of united sepals adheres to the whole ovary, making it inferior. The petals are united below into a 4-lobed white to pinkish bell-shaped corolla. The flowers are 2-2.5 cm long, borne 2-5 per cluster on drooping stalks 1.5-2 cm long. Stamens are 8-16, united by their bases and to the corolla tube. Fruits, 3-4.5 cm long, are dry, 4-winged longitudinally and tipped by 4 tiny calyx teeth and the dry style of the pistil. Flowers with appearance of the leaves, March-May, in rich, well-drained soils; Florida-Texas and north into Virginia-Illinois-Oklahoma.

STYRACACEAE
(Storax Family)

Halesia diptera Ellis **Silverbell, Snowdrop-tree**

This tree to 10 m high is closely related to the Carolina silverbell, differing mainly in having 2 broad wings on the fruit rather than 4 narrower ones. The 4 lobes of the corolla are more pubescent, cut a little deeper and are more pointed than the other species. The stamens are longer, as long as the pistil rather than shorter. Leaf bases in this species are less tapered than are those of *H. carolina* and the leaf tips are less tapered. Flowers February-May in sandy moist soils and stream beds, even brackish; mainly along the coast Georgia-Texas and north into South Carolina-Arkansas-Oklahoma.

allis arvensis

Lysimachia ciliata

Halesia carolina

Halesia diptera

OLEACEAE
(Olive Family)

Fraxinus americana L. **White Ash**

This common and important timber tree is especially used for tool and implement handles. Its 20-30 cm long opposite leaves are pinnately compound, with 5-9, usually 7 leaflets, each 8-12 cm long, dark green above and paler below. Leaflets are ovate-lanceolate, with smooth or slightly toothed edges. Trees are of separate sexes. Stamens are produced, 2 per flower, in clusters on branchlets above leaf scars before leaves appear. Anthers are purplish and short beaked at the tip. Pistils with long, purple styles end in a bilobed stigma. Dry, winged fruits 2.5-5 cm long, of which ⅔ is the flat terminal wing, 4-7 mm broad, are produced in long, hanging clusters through summer. In dry, rich, low woodlands; Florida-Texas and north into Canada.

OLEACEAE
(Olive Family)

Chionanthus virginicus L. **Fringetree**

This fringetree, to 6 m tall with a 20-30 cm diameter trunk, is one of only two species known, the other grows in China. It has simple, deciduous leaves that are elliptic-obovate, 10-15 cm long by 2.5-7 cm wide, and taper into a short petiole. Flowers, mostly with 4 2-3 cm long, straplike petals barely united by their bases, hang in clusters 15-25 cm long, and appear April-May, with the leaves, from lateral buds. Flowers are often without stamens but when present, there are 4 stamens on very short filaments attached to the very short corolla tube. There are 4 sepals 1-2 mm long. The fruit is a blue-black olivelike drupe 1-1.5 cm long, 6-10 mm in diameter seen July-September. Grows in wet rich woods and thickets; Florida-Texas and north into Pennsylvania-Oklahoma.

LOGANIACEAE
(Logania Family)

Gelsemium sempervirens (L.) Ait. **Yellow Jasmine**

This species, along with the Indian-pink, is the most common representative of this more tropical family in our area. The beautiful evergreen, high-climbing vine reaches its northernmost range in Virginia, Tennessee, and Arkansas. Its opposite, short-petioled leaves, are elliptic-lanceolate, 3-7 cm long by 1-2.5 cm wide, have a rounded base, and a tapering tip. Bright, yellow waxy flowers have their petals united into a funnellike tube 2 cm long which flares into 5 regular lobes 0.8-1 cm long. The 5 stamens are attached to the corolla tube, opposite its 5 lobes. The stigma of the slender pistil is divided into 4 parts. The capsule is 1.5-2 cm long and 1 cm across, somewhat flattened, and contains 2 cavities. Flowers March-May in dry to wet woods, thickets, and fence rows; Florida-Louisiana and north into Virginia-Arkansas.

LOGANIACEAE
(Logania Family)

Spigelia marilandica L. **Indian-pink**

This striking herbaceous plant grows to 60 cm or higher, in clumps from perennial roots. Its 4-7 pairs of opposite lanceolate leaves have a very short leaf stalk, are entire, 5-12 cm long by 1.5-6 cm wide and have rounded bases. Flowers are produced 2-12 on terminal, one-sided spikes. The 3-4.5 cm long tubular flowers, red-maroon outside, yellow within, flare into 5 starlike 1-1.5 cm long lobes above. The 5 stamens are attached to the corolla tube and protrude from it, surrounding the longer pistil. The 5 sepals are 5-12 mm long, linear, and joined at their bases. The ovary matures into a bilobed capsule about 5 mm long and 10 broad. Flowers May-June in rich woodlands; Florida-Texas and north into Maryland-Missouri.

Fraxinus americana (male)

Fraxinus americana (female)

ianthus virginicus

Gelsemium sempervirens

Spigelia marilandica

GENTIANACEAE
(Gentian Family)

Sabatia angularis (L.) Pursh **Rose-pink Sabatia**

This annual herb with square, winged stems and opposite leaves has axillary branches at the leaf axils and grows 20-90 cm high, usually in pyramidal form. Spatulate basal leaves may not remain as the plant matures; the sessile, toothless stem leaves are cordate-ovate to lanceolate, clasping the stem and 1.8-5 cm long by 1-4 cm wide. Rose-pink (seldom white) flowers 2.5-3.5 cm across are single on slender axillary branches. The wide-spreading 1-2 cm long obovate corolla lobes are joined below and have a yellow-green "eye" usually outlined by a red star-shaped line. Stamens are usually 5, their anthers longer than the filaments. A long pistil with bilobed stigma produces a 2-celled capsule 6-10 mm long. Flowers July-August in open woods, marshes, and fields; Florida-Louisiana-Oklahoma and north into Virginia-Indiana.

GENTIANACEAE
(Gentian Family)

Gentiana villosa L. **Pale or Striped Gentian**

This is a rather uncommon but widely spread perennial with thick fleshy roots. It grows 15-50 cm high, has 5-12 pairs of opposite, elliptic-lanceolate, smooth-margined leaves, 5-8.5 cm long by 1-3 cm wide, and with no or a very short petiole. Stems are unbranched above. Stalkless flowers are produced 3-7 crowded at the stem tip with several leaves surrounding them. Both sepals and petals are united, the calyx 2-3.3 cm long, with 5 1-2 cm long lobes; the corolla 3-4.3 cm long, with 5 4.8 mm long lobes. This is a short tooth, off-center between the corolla lobes. Corollas are greenish-white, sometimes yellowish, purple-tinged, with green veins. Club-shaped, somewhat flattened 2-lobed capsules mature 1.7-2.5 cm long. Flowers August-October in mostly oak, oak-pine open woodlands; Florida-Louisiana and north into New Jersey-Indiana.

GENTIANACEAE
(Gentian Family)

Gentiana saponaria L. **Soapwort Gentian**

This opposite leaved perennial gentian somewhat resembles the soapwort (see *Saponaria officinalis*), hence its species name. The 30-90 cm tall, hairless plant has 7-15 pairs of narrowly oblanceolate-elliptic leaves 4-8 cm long and 2-4 cm wide. The corolla is deep blue to nearly white, with darker blue veins. The 3-5 cm long tubular corolla, slightly open at the top, has 5 4-10 mm long lobes, pleated and 1-2 toothed where they join. The calyx of 5 partially united sepals is 1.3-2.5 cm long, with oblong-lanceolate lobes 4-17 mm long. Flowers September-November in moist woodlands and boggy or swampy fields and woodlands; Florida-Texas and north into New York-Illinois-Oklahoma.

APOCYNACEAE
(Dogbane Family)

Amsonia tabernaemontana Walt. **Blue Star**

Members of this family and the next usually have milky juice which is true of this plant. The species name is in honor of a 16th century herbalist, and the generic name in honor of a German physician, Dr. Amson. This perennial, herbaceous, loosely branching plant (to 1 m high) has alternate 8-12 cm long by 1-6 cm wide and ovate to narrowly lanceolate leaves on short petioles. Corollas are blue, the 5 petals united into a narrow 6-8 mm long tube. The corollas are minutely hairy both inside and out. There are 5 short stamens attached to and within the tube. Unusually for plants, 2 separate pistils are united by their stigmas and give rise to a pair of very slender, 5-10 cm long, dry follicles splitting along one side. Flowers April-July in moist woodlands, slopes, and bottomlands; Florida-Texas and north into Massachusetts-Kansas.

Sabatia angularis

Gentiana villosa

Gentiana saponaria

Amsonia tabernaemontana

APOCYNACEAE
(Dogbane Family)
Amsonia rigida Shuttlw. **Blue Star**

This rather rare species is similar to *Amsonia tabernaemontana* but there are some differences. The leaves are more numerous, they are acute not long-tapered at their tips, and they are elliptic-lanceolate rather than ovate-oblanceolate. The corolla lobes are longer than the tube and are oblong-lanceolate, less straplike, and the corolla is glabrous, without hairs, on the outside. The stems and branchlets are reddish brown rather than green. Flowers March-June, usually in sandy soils of open pine woodlands; south Georgia-north Florida into south Alabama and Mississippi.

ASCLEPIADACEAE
(Milkweed Family)
Asclepias viridis Walt. **Spider Milkweed**

This milkweed is also called green-flowered milkweed by some, but so is *A. viridiflora*. The older generic name *Asclepiodora* was once used for this plant. This perennial plant with alternate, short-petioled, ovate-oblong to lanceolate leaves, 6-14 cm long by 1.5-4 cm wide, grows to a height of 30-60 cm and is erect to decumbent. Flowers are produced in single umbels, or several umbels combined into a 8-10 cm compound umbel. Flower parts are in 5s, the united green, 1-1.5 cm wide corolla being deeply 5-lobed but having a corona or crown derived from either the corolla tube or united bases of the stamens. This structure makes up the purple "spider," its ends spreading and curving upward. There are 5 stamens, mostly united, arising adjacent to the pistil and growing around it. The pistil is really 2, as in the Dogbane Family, united by their tips, separate below, each growing into a dry, smooth tapered follicle, 2 per flower, 5-8 cm long. Flowers May-July in open prairie type dry soils; Florida-Texas and north into South Carolina-Kansas.

ASCLEPIADACEAE
(Milkweed Family)
Asclepias incarnata L. **Swamp Milkweed**

This perennial grows to 1.5 m tall, freely branching, and has opposite elliptic-lanceolate leaves, 6-12 cm long by 2-3.5 cm wide, short petioled and pubescent beneath. Flowers are in several umbels per cluster with 5 rose-pink to purple, reflexed corolla lobes 4.5-5.5 mm long below. A corona of 5 parts each, a usually lighter hood, 2-4 mm long, turning upward with a longer hornlike beak arching over the pistil. Follicles opening on one side, 2 per flower, are 5-12 cm long and smooth. The above flower description is quite typical of most milkweeds. Flowers July-September in swampy areas; Florida-Texas and north into Nova Scotia-Minnesota.

ASCLEPIADACEAE
(Milkweed Family)
Asclepias tuberosa L. **Butterfly-weed**

This orange colored milkweed without milky juice is found in clusters of several hairy stems 20-70 cm high. Leaves are generally more numerous than in other milkweeds, more than 12 per stem. Leaves are alternate, variable from linear to elliptic-oblanceolate, 4-10 cm long by 3-25 mm wide and usually hairy, especially beneath. The base of the leaf may be rounded or cordate and with a short or no petiole. Small umbels, 3-many, are arranged on one side of stem ends. Flowers, red to yellow, are 12-15 mm tall, 5 petals strongly reflexed and the erect 5-lobed corona, spreading at the tips, each with a short horn over the pistil. Follicles are smooth, finely pubescent, and 8-15 cm long. Flowers May-September in prairie type dry fields; Florida-Texas and north into Maine-Minnesota.

pias viridis

Amsonia rigida

pias incarnata

Asclepias tuberosa

ASCLEPIADACEAE
(Milkweed Family)
Asclepias syriaca L. **Common Milkweed**

This large, usually single-stemmed, perennial herb may reach 2 m tall, producing 5-10 cm broad umbels of greenish, rose-purple flowers in the upper leaf axils. Leaves are elliptic to ovate elliptic, with blunt tips and rounded bases. They are 25 cm or more long by 5-11 cm wide on 10-14 mm long petioles. Stems are pubescent as are the underside of leaves. Fragrant flowers are 10-12 mm high, the corolla lobes reflexed and spreading outward, while the upright, shorter corona lobes or hoods are round-tipped, spreading, each with a small lateral tooth and a sharp median horn arching over the pistil. Follicles mature 8-12 cm long, have soft coarse "spines," and are densely pubescent. Young pods are often eaten after boiling twice, disposing of first water. Flowers May-August in fields, roadsides, and thickets; Georgia-Arkansas and north into Maine-Iowa. Not on the coastal plain.

ASCLEPIADACEAE
(Milkweed Family)
Asclepias variegata L. **White Milkweed**

This plant has single stems 30-90 cm high, pubescent above and glabrous below, bearing 2-6 pairs of opposite somewhat undulate margined leaves. Leaves are ovate to widely elliptic-lanceolate, 7-15 cm long by 3-6 cm wide, on petioles 1-2.5 cm long. Umbels, 1-4, are mostly terminal, densely flowered, globose and 3-6 cm across. Flowers (12-15 mm high) have reflexed ovate corolla lobes 6-8 mm long, and erect ovate corona lobes arising from a reddish purple base to 4-7 mm. (Perhaps this is how the term "variegata" originates.) Beaklike horns from the corona project over the pistil. Follicles are 10-14 cm long, 1.5-2 cm broad, somewhat downy, and long taper-pointed. Flowers May-July in dry, open, sandy woodlands and margins, Florida-Texas and north into New York-Illinois.

ASCLEPIADACEAE
(Milkweed Family)
Cynanchum laeve (Michx.) Persoon **Blue Vine, Sand Vine**

The genera *Cynanchum* and *Matelea* differ from *Asclepias* in being vines, no *Asclepias* are viny. This is a high climbing, 3-4 m vine with long tapered, heart-shaped, opposite leaves and milky juice. The leaves are 5-15 cm long by 3-12 cm wide, on petioles 8-10 mm long, with smooth margins and bluish-green color, hence the common name. Only the flower stalks are hairy, and *laeve* means "smooth." Flowers appear in umbellike clusters in leaf axils, not looking like those of milkweeds. Flowers have 5 calyx lobes and 5 corolla lobes, both lanceolate. A short, membranous crown from the corolla tube has 5 2-toothed, erect lobes. The whole flower is only 6 mm long and the calyx half as long. The pistil is bilobed at the stigma and it becomes a follicle 10-15 cm long, about 3 cm diameter, long-tapered, and glabrous. Flowers June-August in low thickets and fence-rows; Florida-Texas and north into Pennsylvania-Kansas.

ASCLEPIADACEAE
(Milkweed Family)
Matelea gonocarpa (Walt.) Shinn. **Large-leaved Angle-pod**

This perennial, twining vine has opposite, broad, heart-shaped to elliptic-oblong leaves, to 12-20 cm long by 4-15 cm wide. Umbels are 7-12 flowered in leaf axils. Buds are short and conical, quickly tapering to a point. Flowers are yellow to greenish-brown, with 5 petals, united at their bases, from which a short, 5-lobed crown arises around a short pistil. Corolla lobes are 7-10 mm long, gradually tapering to their blunt tips, glabrous, and somewhat recurving. Sepals are 1.5-2 mm long and short pointed. Stems and leaves are pubescent. Follicles are glabrous, prominently 5-angled, but not winged, 8-13 cm long by 2-3 cm diameter, and quickly tapering. Flowers June-July in woodlands, thickets, and bottomlands; Georgia-Texas and north into Virginia-Missouri.

epias variegata

Asclepias syriaca

ıanchum laeve

Matelea gonocarpa

ASCLEPIADACEAE
(Milkweed Family)

Matelea decipiens (Alex.) Woodson **Angle-pod**

This rather uncommon viny milkweed has opposite, ovate leaves, 8-15 cm long by 4-8 cm wide, rounded and notched at the base. Umbels with 12-24 flowers from conical-cylindric buds arise in leaf axils along the stem. Brownish-purple corollas have straplike lobes, 10-15 mm long by 3-4 mm wide, extending upward, rather than spreading and/or reflexed. A similar plant, *M. carolinensis*, has shorter and spreading or rotate corolla lobes, and short, ovate flower buds. Follicles of both species are similar, 9-12 cm long to 2.5 cm diameter, and have soft, short hornlike projections scattered over the surface. Flowers April-June in dry, open woodlands, thickets, and valleys along streams; Louisiana-Oklahoma and north into Maryland-Missouri. Apparently common in the Missouri Ozark Mountains.

CONVOLVULACEAE
(Morning-glory Family)

Cuscuta species **Dodder, Love-vine**

Dodder is an annual twining plant without leaves or chlorophyll, but containing golden carotenoid pigments. Lacking chlorophyll, the plant cannot produce its own food but parasitizes other plants by sending rootlike suckers into their tissues, usually stems, absorbing food from them. There are several species in our area but their flowers are so small good magnification is needed to identify them. Flowers average 2-2.5 mm long, with both the sepals and petals united and 5-lobed. The corolla tube is longer than the short rounded or pointed lobes. A corona of 5 united scales projects from near the base inside the tube, alternate with the corolla lobes, and above them 5 short stamens are attached to the tube. The pistil becomes a 2-cavity globose capsule, 5-8 mm long, producing 4 seeds. Flowers usually June to frost over most of the contiguous United States.

CONVOLVULACEAE
(Morning-glory Family)

Ipomoea sagittata Cav. **Arrow-leaf Morning-glory**

This perennial twining or trailing plant has leaves narrowly sagittate or arrow-shaped, one lobe pointed forward and 2 similar, somewhat shorter ones pointed backward. Blades from tip to tip of basal lobes are 5-10 cm long, on petioles 3-5 cm long. The rose-lavender flowers have 5 petals united into a funnel-form corolla, 5-7 cm long and 6-8 cm across, with 5 notches around the margin. Sepals are elliptic-oblong, 9-11 mm long. The 5 stamens are as long as the narrow corolla tube, as is the pistil. Capsules are globose to ovoid, 1-1.5 cm long. Flowers May-October along the coastal plain in wet, sandy roadsides and brackish marshes; Florida-Texas and north into North Carolina.

CONVOLVULACEAE
(Morning-glory Family)

Ipomoea lacunosa L. **Small-flowered White Morning-glory**

This annual, small-flowered morning-glory spreads 1-2 m or more long over other vegetation. Its alternate, slender-petioled, 3-9 cm long by 2-6 cm wide, leaves are variable from heart-shaped to long-triangular, with rounded basal lobes. Axillary flowers are generally white, point-lobed and hardly 1.5-2.3 cm long and about that wide. Stamens and the 2-lobe-tipped pistil are about the length of the corolla tube. Sepals are ovate-lanceolate, 9-11 mm long, bristle-tipped and pubescent on the margins. Capsules are globose, 7-10 mm in diameter, 2-4 seeded, pubescent on top and glabrous below. Flowers July-frost in low moist fields and marshes; Georgia-Texas and north into Pennsylvania-Ohio-Kansas.

Matelea decipiens

noea sagittata

Cuscuta sp.

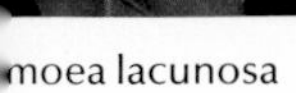

moea lacunosa

CONVOLVULACEAE
(Morning-glory Family)
Ipomoea pandurata (L.) Meyer **Wild Potato Vine**

This perennial vine, 2 m or more long, grows from a tuberous, 10-20 pound root, and entwines itself over other vegetation. Alternate leaves, ovate to fiddle-shaped, 4-8 cm long and broad, arise from a reddish-purple stem. White, trumpetlike flowers, to 8-10 cm broad, have a purple "eye" in the center. Stamens and the pistil are the length of the corolla tube. The calyx tube has oblong-elliptic, ridged, sepal lobes, 12-15 mm long, and glabrous. The mature capsule is ovoid-globose, 2-2.5 cm in diameter, glabrous, and produces 2-4 strongly pubescent seeds. Flowers May-September in dry open woodlands, thickets and roadsides; Florida-Texas and north into Connecticut-Michigan-Kansas.

CONVOLVULACEAE
(Morning-glory Family)
Dichondra carolinensis Michx. **Dichondra**

This creeping, branching, prostrate perennial has alternate, circular leaves, notched at the base, 1-3 cm across, sparsely pubescent below and on slender 1-4 cm long petioles. Axillary, greenish-yellow to white flowers are 5-7 mm across; both the 5 petals and 5 sepals are united below, the sepals longer than the petals. Sepals and petals are pubescent on the outer surface. Pistils are nearly divided into 2 and when both develop produce pairs of globular 1-seeded capsules only 1-2 mm in diameter. The plant can become a lawn pest, but some use it for a ground cover. Flowers March-June in low sandy pine-lands, clayey roadsides, and waste places; Florida-Texas and north into Virginia-Arkansas.

POLEMONIACEAE
(Phlox Family)
Phlox drummondii Hooker **Garden Phlox**

This herbaceous annual phlox has alternate leaves above, rather than opposite as in other phlox; the lower leaves are opposite. Stems, leaves, and flowers are glandular pubescent. Leaves are elliptic-oblong to lanceolate, and 4-8 cm long by 1-1.7 cm wide. Flowers borne on terminal clusters of branches are mostly red, but can be white or variegated. Corollas, 1.2-1.6 cm long and 2.5-3 cm across, are narrowly tubular with wide-spreading, obovate lobes. The 5 stamens of unequal lengths are attached to, and deep within the corolla tube. The calyx tube is 4-7 mm long as are the linear lobes. This phlox, apparently a native of Texas, is a garden escape elsewhere, the red-flowered form growing quite well uncultivated. Flowers March-July in open, dry, sandy areas, mostly coastal; Florida-Texas and north into South Carolina.

POLEMONIACEAE
(Phlox Family)
Phlox divaricata L. **Blue Phlox**

This phlox is a 30-45 cm tall, sticky pubescent perennial usually having 4 pairs of opposite, ovate-lanceolate leaves, 2-3.5 cm long and 5-12 mm wide. There are usually some decumbent or erect sterile branches around the base of the plant. Branches bearing flowers are loosely spreading, rather than being closely compacted. The calyx is glandular pubescent, 7-11 mm long, the narrow teeth longer than the tube. The lavendar to bluish glabrous corolla has a tube 11-17 mm long with lobes obovate to notched, 10-15 mm long. Stamens are attached to the tube and deep within it, as is the pistil which is deeply split at the top. Flowers March-June in dry to moist open woods and slopes; Florida-Texas and north into Canada.

noea pandurata

Phlox drummondii

x divaricata

Dichondra carolinensis

POLEMONIACEAE
(Phlox Family)

Phlox pilosa L. **Prairie Phlox, Downy Phlox**

This is a common phlox in our area, having erect stems 20-60 cm high with 6-12 pairs of opposite, narrow lanceolate leaves 3-10 cm long and 3-8 mm wide. Older, flowering plants become spindly and spreading. The lavender-pink to even white corolla usually has a pubescent tube 11-16 mm long with obovate lobes 8-12 mm long, abruptly pointed at the tip. The 5 stamens are deep in the corolla tube and attached to it. The pistil is tube length, split halfway by the 2-lobed stigma. The calyx is glandular pubescent 6-12 mm long, and has linear lobes longer than the calyx tube. In a similar species, *P. amoena,* the flower cluster is more compact and the sepal lobes are stiffly pointed. Flowers April-July in dry deciduous and sandy pinelands; Florida-Texas and north into Connecticut-Minnesota.

POLEMONIACEAE
(Phlox Family)

Polemonium reptans L. **Jacob's-ladder**

This clumpy, moist woodland perennial, 20-40 cm high with bell-shaped clustered flowers, gets its name from the pinnately compound leaves made up of leaflets or "rungs" of a ladder. Leaves are 5-10 cm long, with 5-21 elliptic-ovate to lanceolate leaflets 1.5-3.5 cm long by 5-16 mm wide. Flowering stalks, 20-40 cm tall, are loosely branching from leaf axils and bear pale to dark blue flowers with petals united at the lower half of the 1-1.8 cm long, bell-shaped corolla. The 5 stamens are attached to the base of the corolla tube. The pistil is 3-lobed at the top and the globose capsule produces a few seeds in its 3-celled fruit. Sepals enlarge and are persistent. Flowers April-June in rich woodlands and bottoms; inland Georgia-Mississippi-Oklahoma, and north into New York-Minnesota.

HYDROPHYLLACEAE
(Waterleaf Family)

Hydrolea ovata Nutt. **Ovate-leaved Hydrolea**

This is a perennial, herbaceous plant with simple, alternate leaves 3-8 cm long, with a sharp spine at most leaf-stem nodes. It usually branches and flowers at the top of the 60-75 cm tall stem. Dark blue, saucer-shaped flowers are 2.5-3 cm across with 5 petals united below, 5 stamens attached to the corolla tube, and a pistil with 2 stigma-style branches widely spreading from the top of the ovary. Long, lanceolate, long-pubescent sepals are joined by their bases into a short calyx tube. Stems and leaves are sparsely pubescent to stiff hairy and leaves may be short petioled or sessile. Flowers May-October in standing water or wet marshes, prairies, or pinelands; Georgia-Texas and north into Missouri.

HYDROPHYLLACEAE
(Waterleaf Family)

Hydrophyllum macrophyllum Nutt. **Largeleaf Waterleaf**

This villous pubescent herbaceous perennial, 30-90 cm tall, has alternate pinnately lobed to compound leaves, the lower ones 20-30 cm long, long petioled, and with 5-7 ovate leaflets. Upper leaves are shorter, with segments variously lobed and the marginal teeth obtuse or triangular, with a short pointed tip. Leaflets are 4-7 cm long and 2-3.5 cm wide. Flower stalks, arising in leaf axils, are longer than the petioles and have 2-3 branching clusters of white to greenish 8-12 mm long flowers. Petals are united basally with hardly spreading ovate lobes. The 5 stamens are attached on the tube between the corolla lobes and are ⅓ longer than the corolla lobes; there are longitudinal folds on the corolla tube between the stamens. The calyx lobes are narrow-pointed from a broad base and are bristly hairy. Flowers May-June in rich, moist woodlands; Florida-Alabama-Arkansas and north into Virginia-Illinois.

Polemonium reptans

olea ovata

Phlox pilosa

rophyllum macrophyllum

HYDROPHYLLACEAE
(Waterleaf Family)

Phacelia purshii Buckl. **Miami-mist**

This 15-45 cm tall annual with much-branched stems has alternate leaves 4-8 cm long, long-petioled below, and pinnately compound; upper leaves are 9-15 pinnate lobed, and sessile. Flower stalks have 10-25 flowers on one side of the curled stems, each on its own 1-2.5 cm long pedicel. The 1.3-1.6 cm broad corolla is saucer-shaped, its rounded lobes fringed, and is pale blue to white. The 5 stamens are attached to the base of the corolla between and longer than the lobes. The long pistil has a 2-lobed stigma and the ovary matures into a 2-celled globose capsule 4-5 mm in diameter. Most of the plant is pubescent. Flowers April-June in moist woodlands, thickets, and meadows; Georgia-Oklahoma and north into Pennsylvania-Illinois.

HYDROPHYLLACEAE
(Waterleaf Family)

Phacelia bipinnatifida Michx. **Phacelia**

The leaves of this biennial herbaceous plant, 25-60 cm tall, are petiolate and pinnately compound into 5-7 leaflets, the leaflets 1.5-4.5 cm long and further divided (bipinnate), or lobed. Stems and petioles are glandular pubescent and leaf surfaces are pubescent. Flowering stalks are only slightly curled, produce blue, saucer-shaped flowers 10-15 mm broad, with rounded lobes, and a white "eye." The 5 stamens are attached to the corolla tube at its base, between longitudinal ridges on the tube. Stamen filaments are hairy on the lower half. The ovary matures into a globose capsule 4-5 mm long, as the pedicel becomes recurved and hangs downward. The calyx has 5 linear-lanceolate pubescent teeth 5-8 mm long. Flowers March-June in rich woodlands and rocky slopes; Georgia-Alabama-Arkansas and north into Virginia-Iowa.

BORAGINACEAE
(Borage Family)

Heliotropium indicum L. **Indian Heliotrope, Turnsole**

This rather coarse, hairy, erect annual herb grows 20-70 cm tall and has alternate, non-toothed elliptic-ovate petioled leaves 5-10 cm long by 3-6 cm wide, moderately tapering to the tip. As in other species of this family, the flowers are on 1 side of the coiling spike, usually terminating the stem. The tiny numerous blue flowers have a short calyx tube with 5 linear teeth 1-2 mm long. The blue corolla has a slender tube 2.5-3 mm long, flaring widely to a saucerlike disk 3-3.5 mm broad, faintly 5-lobed. The 5 stamens are shorter than the corolla tube and are attached to it within. The tiny pistil produces a 2-lobed dry fruit separating into 2 tiny nutlets. Flowers June-November in dry exposures, swamp forests, and waste places; Florida-Texas and north into West Virginia-Illinois-Oklahoma.

BORAGINACEAE
(Borage Family)

Cynoglossum virginianum L. **Hound's-tongue**

This perennial, stiff hairy, herbaceous, single-stemmed plant 40-90 cm high has large, 15-30 cm long by 13 cm wide, spatulate leaves at its base, becoming ovate, smaller and clasping the stem above. The single stem branches above into 2-6 clusters of small drooping flowers. Corollas are 7-12 mm across, funnel-form with round lobes, blue to white; the tube is nearly closed at the top by 5 scalelike appendages of the corolla. The 5 stamens with short filaments are attached to and within the corolla tube. The short pistil has a deeply 4-lobed ovary, at maturity dividing into 4 spiny nutlets (a family trait), 5-7 mm long. Flowers April-June in open deciduous woodlands; Florida-Texas and north into New Jersey-Illinois.

ıcelia purshii

Heliotropium indicum

/noglossum virginianum

Phacelia bipinnatifida

BORAGINACEAE
(Borage Family)

Lithospermum canescens (Michx.) Lehm. **Hoary Puccoon, Gromwell**

This perennial, quite white-hairy plant grows 15-45 cm tall with simple or branched stems and has alternate, linear-oblong, blunt-tipped leaves, 1.5-4 cm long by 3-7 mm wide, shorter ones below, with no petiole. The terminal branching flower stalks have 1-3 curled, 1-sided, densely flowered clusters. Bright yellow-orange flowers are tubular, spreading into 5 round-pointed lobes at the top. Corollas are 1-1.5 cm long and as broad; the throat has 5 low-rounded scales surrounding the mouth of the tube. The 5 short stamens are attached midway in the tube. The ovary develops into 2-4 smooth nutlets, 2-3.5 mm long. Calyx teeth are 3-6 mm long and hairy. Flowers April-June in sandy, open woodlands and prairies; Georgia-Texas and north into New York-Montana.

BORAGINACEAE
(Borage Family)

Mertensia virginica (L.) Pers. **Virginia Bluebells**

This early spring, smooth herbaceous perennial grows, seldom branching, 30-70 cm high and has long-petioled basal, elliptic-ovate leaves to 20 cm long. Stem leaves have short or no petioles, are ovate-obovate, blunt tipped, and 5-15 cm long. The terminal, one-sided drooping flowering stalk bears blue, pink-in-bud, tubular-trumpet-shaped flowers 2-2.5 cm long. The corolla is hardly lobed and has no scales at the throat but is pubescent inside near the base of the tube. The 5 stamens are attached near the top of the corolla tube. The calyx is 5-toothed and about 8 mm long. The ovary is 4-lobed and produces 2-4 ovoid nutlets, wrinkling upon maturity. Flowers March-June in rich woodlands and moist meadows; Georgia-Alabama-Arkansas and north into New York-Minnesota.

VERBENACEAE
(Vervain Family)

Verbena simplex Lehm. **Narrow-leaved Verbena**

This nearly glabrous perennial grows from a rhizome 30-60 cm tall. It has a square stem and opposite leaves as in the Mint Family, but its flowers are not obviously bilabiate and the ovary is not deeply 4-lobed at the top. Leaves are linear-oblanceolate, 2.5-8 cm long by 3-10 mm wide and have toothed edges, especially toward the tip. A slender terminal spike (often 3) 5-20 mm long produces overlapping flowers 5-6 mm broad. Corollas are tubular with 5 nearly equal lobes, the upper 2 are smaller. The upper of 5 stamens is missing in *Verbena* and the 4 are of 2 lengths attached to the corolla tube. The ovary is not 4-lobed at the top but separates into 2-4 nutlets. Flowers May-September in dry open woods and fields; Georgia-Louisiana-Oklahoma and north into New Hampshire-Minnesota.

VERBENACEAE
(Vervain Family)

Verbena rigida Spreng. **Stiff Verbena**

This freely branching, erect to decumbent perennial has opposite, lanceolate-oblanceolate leaves, 4-11 cm long by 1-3 cm wide, with wide-apart teeth and sharp pointed tip. Leaves are stiffly oblique to the stem and clasp together around it with their bases. Terminal and axillary branching stems have stiffly erect flower spikes, each 1-6 cm long and 1.3 cm in diameter. Stems and leaves are rough-hairy and the bracts, calyx, and corolla tube are pubescent. Purple to violet, 8-12 mm broad corollas are tubular with 5 slightly irregular lobes. The ovary produces 2-4 nutlets about 2 mm long at maturity. See comparison with mints under *V. simplex*. Flowers April-September around the coastal plain; North Carolina-Florida-Texas.

ıospermum canescens

Mertensia virginica

ırbena simplex

Verbena rigida

VERBENACEAE
(Vervain Family)
Verbena canadensis (L.) Britt. **Rose Vervain**

This showy verbena produces erect and decumbent, usually pubescent, stems 10-40 cm long in clumps from perennial rhizomes. Opposite leaves are pinnately lobed to divided, triangular-ovate in outline, 1-7 cm long 1-3.5 cm wide, with petioles to 2.5 cm long. Flowering spikes 5-15 cm long and 2-5 cm in diameter produce many flowers, blooming successively from the base upward. A linear bract subtends each flower in the spike. Rose pink to white corollas are 2-2.5 cm long and 1.5-2.5 cm broad. The calyx tube with 5 linear teeth is half the length of the corolla tube and a little longer than the bract, both are pubescent. Flowers March-October in dry sandy-rocky soils; Florida-Texas and north into Virginia-Colorado.

VERBENACEAE
(Vervain Family)
Verbena tenuisecta Briq. **Moss Verbena**

This plant closely resembles *V. bipinnatifida,* but its leaf segments are much narrower, the bract below each flower is shorter than the calyx and the plant is less pubescent. Stems are 10-30 cm long, spreading decumbent, with opposite leaves finely, deeply dissected and broadly triangular in outline, 1-3 cm long by 1-4 cm wide on petioles 1-1.5 cm long. Single terminal spikes 1-10 cm long by 1-3.5 cm in diameter bear pink, lavender, or white flowers 1.4-1.8 cm long, the spike elongating as blooming progresses. The calyx and bract are pubescent, enclosing 2-4 grayish nutlets about 3 mm long. Flowers March-frost in sandy open woods and fields around the coastal plain; Florida-Texas and north into North Carolina.

VERBENACEAE
(Vervain Family)
Verbena bipinnatifida Nutt. **Small-flowered Verbena**

This is a much branched, upright rather than decumbent, plant wtih dissected, ovate in outline, leaf blades 2.5-3 cm long, tapering into short petioles. Blade segments are linear-oblong and lobes are often divided again. Most of the plant is bristly hairy. Single terminal spikes are short and densely flowered, reaching 5-10 cm long at maturity. Flowers are 13-20 mm long by 10-13 mm across, lilac-purple and slightly irregular with 5 notched lobes. The upper half of the 8-10 mm long calyx is 5 long narrow teeth. A single linear-lanceolate bract is usually longer than the calyx it subtends. Both have long, stiff hairs. This plant reaches into our area from the west. Flowers May-August in dry, open prairie type soils; Georgia-Arizona-Mexico and north into Missouri-South Dakota.

VERBENACEAE
(Vervain Family)
Lippia nodiflora (L.) Michx. **Fog-fruit**

This opposite-leaved, creeping perennial plant with some ascending branches is 30-90 cm long, rooting at the nodes where it may also send up 2.5-15 cm long flower stalks with compact spikes 12-25 mm long. Leaves are thickish, obovate-spatulate, rounded at the tip, 1.5-4.5 cm long by 0.7-2 cm wide and 3-7 teeth on each side. Stems are somewhat 4-sided and they and the leaves may become brownish purple as seen here. Flowers are purple-white with 2-lipped, 4-lobed corollas about 3 mm across, only a few opening each day. There are 4 stamens of 2 lengths within the tube. The ovary separates into 4 nutlets at maturity. Mainly tropical plants. Flowers May-frost; Florida-Texas north into Virginia-Oklahoma-Missouri and south into Mexico.

pia nodiflora

Verbena bipinnatifida

Verbena canadensis

Verbena tenuisecta

VERBENACEAE
(Vervain Family)

Callicarpa americana L. **French Mulberry**

This 1-2 m high perennial shrub is especially known for its many clustered, fleshy, purplish-violet drupes in late summer. The leaves are opposite, ovate-lanceolate with fine rounded-toothed margins. Many pink-bluish flowers appear on short stalks in the leaf axils. Flowers are about 1 cm long, tubular at the base, the upper third being 4 (or 5) equally lobed; 4 (or 5) long stamens arise from the corolla tube. The single ovary is a 2-celled globose drupe 3-5 mm in diameter, with 2-4 seeds. The round stems and leaves have pubescence of star-shaped hairs. *Callicarpa* means "beauty berry," another common name. Flowers June-August in rich woodlands and thickets; Florida-Texas and north into Maryland-Missouri-Oklahoma.

LAMIACEAE
(Mint Family)

Scutellaria integrifolia L. **Larger Skullcap**

While mints have square stems, opposite leaves bilabiate flowers and mintlike odor, skullcap is odorless. Its skullcap is the 2-lipped calyx covering the fruit, somewhat resembling a military or policeman's cap. Leaves are ovate-lanceolate to oblong, 2.5-5 cm long with smooth to slightly toothed margins and lower ones petioled. Stems and leaves are pubescent. Flowering stems are terminal, and have the corollas bent upward at the calyx. Corollas are densely pubescent on the outside, 1.5-2.3 cm long, blue violet, and usually white on the raised surface of the lower lip which is notched at its tip. The 4 stamens, 2 long, 2 short, are attached in the corolla tube. The pistil is deeply 4-lobed, separating into 4 nutlets. There are several species in the area, all bearing "skull caps." Flowers April-July in open woodlands and fields; Florida-Texas and north into Massachusetts-Arkansas, mostly along the coastal plain.

LAMIACEAE
(Mint Family)

Glechoma hederacea L. **Ground-ivy**

This herbaceous perennial, pubescent, opposite round-leafed plant is decumbent to creeping and roots at the stem nodes. Its 12-16 mm broad by 12-16 mm long leaves have toothlike scallops and long, hairy petioles. The 2-lipped, 1-2 cm long flowers appear singly in leaf axils. The upper corolla lobe arches over 2 long stamens, 2 lateral ones are short; the lower, middle lobe is notched, purple-mottled, and has coarse, club-shaped hairs rising from its surface. The nearly regular calyx is 4-8 mm long with 5 short, sharp-pointed teeth and is pubescent. The deeply 4-lobed ovary produces 2-4 nutlets, reddish-brown, 1.3-2 mm long at maturity. In most places considered a garden pest. Flowers March-July, Georgia-Louisiana and north into New England-Minnesota.

LAMIACEAE
(Mint Family)

Prunella vulgaris L. **Heal-all; Self-heal**

This perennial, square-stemmed herb may grow to 60 cm or higher and has opposite, toothed, ovate-lanceolate, 3-9 cm long by 1-4 cm wide, short to long petioled leaves. Stems may be erect or creeping and bear terminal compact flower spikes 2-8 cm long in the axils of broad, rounded, usually ciliate edged bracts. The 1-2 cm long corolla is widely bilobed with the upper, purple lobe arching over the 2 long and 2 short stamens; the lower, middle, white lobe is usually fringed or irregularly toothed at the tips. The 8-10 mm long calyx is bilobed, the upper 3-toothed, the lower with 2 narrower teeth. The 4-lobed ovary produces 2-4 dark brown nutlets, 1.8-2.2 mm long. Flowers April-frost in fields and clearings over most of the United States and into Canada. This plant is a European import, long naturalized.

carpa americana

Scutellaria integrifolia

Callicarpa americana

Prunella vulgaris

choma hederacea

LAMIACEAE
(Mint Family)

Dracocephalum virginianum L. **False Dragonhead, Obedient Plant**

This perennial from a slender rhizome has a square stem, opposite leaves, only 4 stamens, and a fruit breaking into 4 1-seeded nutlets. The flower could be mistaken for a *Pentstemon* but for the above traits. Stems are 0.5-1.5 m high, unbranched except within the flower cluster, and have opposite sharply-toothed lanceolate leaves 5-15 cm long by 1-4.5 cm wide. Bilabiate flowers are 1.5-3 cm long, pink or lavender to white with lavender spots. The upper lip is not lobed and is concave, the lower is 3-lobed. The 5 short sepal lobes of the calyx tube (separate in *Pentstemon*) are nearly equal. The 4 equal stamens arch upward under the upper lip and have widely divergent anther sacs. The bract subtending each flower is longer than the flower pedicel. Flowers July-October in low damp woods edges; Florida-Texas and north into New York-Minnesota. Recognized by some under the name *Physostegia virginiana*.

LAMIACEAE
(Mint Family)

Lamium amplexicaule L. **Henbit**

Lamium is the genus name from which the family name comes, given by Linnaeus in 1753. *Amplexicaule* means "clasping around the stem," as the upper leaves do. This low annual typifies the family, with square stems, bilabiate flowers and deeply lobed ovaries separating into nutlets. Round to ovate leaves are 1.2-3.5 cm broad, have round-toothed margins and have no to 3 cm long petioles. Stems are decumbent, erect in flowering, 15-45 cm long and sparsely pubescent. Bilabiate, reddish-purple flowers have slender corolla tubes 1.5-1.8 cm long, the pubescent upper lobe erect, concave and arching over 2 long and 2 short stamens. The lower lobe is notched and usually mottled; the 2 lateral ones are short and curve inward. The deeply lobed ovary bears 2-4 nutlets 2-2.5 mm long. Flowers from late winter to frost in open fields, lawns, and waste places throughout most of the United States. It is a completely naturalized Eurasian import.

LAMIACEAE
(Mint Family)

Salvia lyrata L. **Lyre-leaf Sage**

This perennial, pubescent herb, 30-80 cm high, is characterized by its basal rosette of variously lobed to pinnately compound, petiolate leaves 5-17 cm long, broader toward the tip, and by its close to distant whorls of blue flowers stretched along the nearly leafless branching stem tops. Basal rosettes of leaves may remain green through winter. Although called "lyre-leafed" the leaf is not that shape but as described above. Whorls of 3-10 blue flowers, 2-3 cm long, are above linear bracts longer than the bilobed, stiffly hairy calyx, the upper lip of 3 small teeth and the lower of 2 longer sharp teeth. The 2-3 cm long, pubescent corolla has a short upper lobe, 2 rounded lateral lobes and a long, broad lower lobe. There are just 2 fertile stamens, each with 2 anthers; 2 stamens are rudimentary or missing. Flowers April-July in low, moist open woodlands; Florida-Texas and north into New York-Illinois-Arkansas.

LAMIACEAE
(Mint Family)

Monarda fistulosa L. **Wild Bergamot**

This is a pubescent, usually branched, perennial to 1.5 m high, with opposite, toothed, triangulate to ovate-lanceolate, petioled leaves 5-11 cm long by 1.5-4 cm wide. The terminal flowering head is 5-8 cm broad, usually subtended by a few pink-tinged leaflike bracts. Lilac to pink, pubescent flowers are 2.5-2.8 cm long, wide-spreading bilabiate, the upper long-bearded at the tip, beyond which extend the 2 fertile stamens from the tube. The 2 lateral lobes are long, tipped by a notched, tonguelike lower lobe. The 8-10 mm long calyx is a nearly regular tube with 5 short bristle-tipped teeth, densely hairy within. Of the species treated here, *Salvia, Monarda* and *Blephilia* have only 2 fertile stamens, the others have 4. Flowers May-September in dry or moist openings, thickets, and edges; Georgia-Texas and north into Canada.

cocephalum virginianum

Lamium amplexicaule

alvia lyrata

Monarda fistulosa

alvia lyrata

LAMIACEAE
(Mint Family)

Monarda punctata L. **Horsemint**

This perennial mint with pubescent square stems branches from a tough rootstock at the ground to 60-90 cm tall and has opposite, 3-9 cm long by 5-17 mm wide, linear-lanceolate leaves with low-toothed margins. Terminating the stems are greenish-yellow to purplish linear-lanceolate bracts in whorls of 2-7, each bearing many yellow-green flowers in their axils. The flowers are very similar to those of bergamot in structure. The 5 sepals are united into a regular tube 6-8 mm long with 5 low triangular teeth. The yellow purple-spotted corolla, 1.5-2 cm long, is pubescent, the upper lip bearded at the tip with the 2 stamens extending beyond it. The typical deeply-lobed ovary produces 2-4 brown to black nutlets about 1.5 mm long in the base of the tubular calyx. Flowers in dry, sandy open woodlands and fields; Florida-Texas and north into Vermont-Minnesota.

LAMIACEAE
(Mint Family)

Blephilia ciliata (L.) Benth. **Wood-mint**

These perennial plants, 40-80 cm tall, resemble other mints but lack a minty odor. Their square stems are downy white as are the leaves beneath. The ovate-lanceolate leaves are quite veiny, 3-8 cm long by 0.7-3 cm wide, almost without petioles, and usually taper at tips and bases. Their margins are shallowly and remotely toothed. Flowers are in 2-6 dense whorls subtended by leaflike bracts, terminating the branches. The upper bracts have ciliate hairs around their margins. The corolla also has long cilialike hairs on the surface. The bilabiate calyx is stiffly hairy and has 2 long teeth above and 3 low triangular teeth below. The purple corolla is 1-1.3 cm long, bilabiate, the upper lip rounded and erect, the lower spreading and 3-lobed, the middle one tonguelike. There are 2 stamens growing from the corolla tube. Flowers June-August in dry open woods and thickets; Georgia-Texas and north into Canada.

LAMIACEAE
(Mint Family)

Pycnanthemum muticum (Michx.) Pers. **Mountain-Mint**

This mountain-mint is not limited to the mountains but is also found in low woods, meadows, and bogs. *Pycnanthemum* means "dense-headed flowers," referring to the 1-3 heads, 1-1.5 cm across at the end of the stems and axils of the upper pair of leaves. The plant is 30-75 cm high, much branched, and has short or no petioles on opposite ovate to lanceolate gray-green leaves 4-8 cm long by 1.5-4 cm wide. Flowers open only a few at a time in the dense heads. The calyx is nearly regular, with 5 short triangular teeth. The white, purple-speckled corolla is only 5-6 mm long, with a single, rounded upper lobe and 3 lower lobes, the middle one tonguelike. Flowers June-September; Georgia-Arkansas and north into Maine-Michigan.

LAMIACEAE
(Mint Family)

Pycnanthemum tenuifolium Shrader **Narrow-leaved Mountain-Mint**

This glabrous square-stemmed perennial, 40-100 cm tall, has opposite linear-lanceolate toothless leaves 2-5 cm long by 1-5 mm wide, sessile or nearly so. Stem branches are axillary and many small flowers form terminal compact clusters 5-10 mm across, with a pair of linear bracts just below. The pubescent calyx of united sepals 3-4.5 mm long is only slightly bilateral and has 5 short firm teeth. The white to pinkish mottled corolla is 6-7 mm long, bilabiate with 3 narrow lobes below and 2 ovate lobes above, somewhat pubescent. The 4 nearly equal long stamens are attached within the corolla tube. The deeply 4-lobed ovary produces 4 black nutlets about 1 mm long. Flowers July-September in thickets, meadows, and bogs; Georgia-Texas and north into New England-Minnesota.

ephilia ciliata

Monarda punctata

'cnanthemum tenuifolium

Pycnanthemum muticum

SOLANACEAE
(Potato Family)

Physalis angustifolia Nutt. **Narrow-leaf Ground-cherry**

This 15-30 cm high perennial from a creeping rhizome is scarcely stellate pubescent and has much-branched, angled, purple stems and petioles. The alternate, thickish, linear-oblanceolate leaves are 4-9 cm long by 4-10 mm wide, tapering into a short petiole. Only the mid-vein is prominent and the margin of the blade is smooth. Numerous, solitary, nodding yellow flowers are borne in leaf axils on erect, slender purple stalks 2-3 cm long, each bending downward at the top. The 5-7 mm long, purple-tinged tubular calyx is regular, has 5 short triangular teeth and has marginal stellate hairs. The calyx becomes ovoid and inflated, enclosing a yellowish tomatolike berry. The regular bell-shaped, united-petal corolla, about 2 cm long and broad, is purple-veined outside and has a purple center inside. The 5 similar stamens with yellow anthers are attached to the base of the corolla tube. Flowers May-August near the beaches along the coastal plain; Florida-Mississippi.

SOLANACEAE
(Potato Family)

Solanum rostratum Dunal. **Buffalo-bur, Prickly Nightshade**

This alternate-leaved, stickery, herbaceous annual to 60 cm tall has entered our area from the western plains, where it is a vicious weed. The leaves are pinnately lobed to compound and petioled, 5-31 cm long by 3-7 cm wide, and are densely pubescent beneath with stellate hairs. Yellow flowers, 15-25 mm across, have petals united into a star-shaped spreading corolla upon which 5 stamens are attached at its base. The lower stamen is larger than the other 4, is long-beaked and bent downward along with the slender style of the pistil. The calyx, nearly hidden by many long, yellow stickers, completely encloses the 10-12 mm diameter berry that makes up the bur. Flowers May-October in prairie type dry, sandy grasslands; Florida-New Mexico and north into New York-Wyoming.

SOLANACEAE
(Potato Family)

Solanum eleagnifolium Cav. **Silver-leaf Nightshade**

This perennial, almost shrubby, freely branched plant to 50 cm or more tall is densely silvery-white with stellate pubescence. Its alternate leaves are simple, wavy-margined, linear lanceolate to oblong and 3-10 cm long by 1-3 cm wide on petioles 1-2.5 cm long. The stems may or may not be armed with slender brownish prickles. Several-flowered branching clusters are nearly terminal on the stems. The star-shaped corollas, 2-2.5 cm across, are blue-violet with contrasting yellow stamens, all of equal size, attached at the corolla base. The 10-12 mm long calyx is puberulent and has 5 long, slender teeth. The white-hairy ovary develops into a globose yellow berry 8-12 mm in diameter. A prairie type plant flowering June-October in dry, open woodlands and fields; Florida-Arizona and north into Ohio-Kansas.

SOLANACEAE
(Potato Family)

Solanum carolinesne L. **Horse-nettle**

This weakly branching 30-90 cm tall perennial from a rhizome has rather coarse prickles on the back of leaf veins and sparsely scattered over the stem. The alternate, ovate-lanceolate, petioled leaves, 5-12 cm long by 3-8 cm wide have 3 pairs of lobes or large teeth and are covered with stellate hairs. Terminal 1-sided clusters of white-purple flowers with 5 pointed corolla lobes are 2.3-3 cm across, spreading or reflexed, and have 5 crowded stamens 7-9 mm long arising from the base of the corolla tube. Fruits are smooth, orange-yellow, tomato-like berries 1-1.5 cm in diameter. Flowers May-October in dry fields and waste places; Florida-Texas and north into Vermont-Nebraska.

Physalis angustifolia

um eleagnifolium

Solanum rostratum

um carolinense

SCROPHULARIACEAE
(Snapdragon Family)
Paulownia tomentosa (Thun.) Steud. **Empress-tree**

This garden-escape tree, introduced from Asia before 1900, closely resembles the *Catalpa* which has white flowers and a slender, cylindric capsule 25-50 cm long. *Paulownia* was named for the daughter of Czar Paul I of Russia. It grows 9-15 m high, is widely branching, and has opposite, petioled, heart-shaped leaves, smooth-margined, 15-35 cm, even to 60 cm long by 10-25 cm wide which are densely stellate hairy (tomentose). Terminal, upright, branching clusters are 25 cm long with olive-drab pedicels and calyx and bear many 6-cm long, snapdragonlike pale purple flowers. There are 2 long and 2 short stamens on the corolla tube. The mature seed capsule is 2-celled and 2.5-5 cm long. The somewhat similar *Catalpa* is in the Bignoniaceae. Flowers April-May in deep, rich, loose soils; Florida-Texas and north into New York-Kentucky-Arkansas.

SCROPHULARIACEAE
(Snapdragon Family)
Mimulus alatus Ait. **Monkey-flower**

Mimulus (little clown) *alatus* (winged) and *M. ringens* are the only 2 species represented in our area, most being western; both have lavender flowers. The "laughing face" of the flower gives its common name. This herbaceous, 5-15 cm high perennial has opposite, ovate-lanceolate, toothed-margined, petioled leaves 5-13 cm long by 2-4 cm wide. Solitary flowers are produced on pedicels shorter than the 1.5 cm long calyx. The lavender, bilabiate corolla is 2-2.4 cm long, shaded with yellow, closed and pubescent on the ridges of the lower lip; the tube is longer than the rounded lobes. In contrast *M. ringens* has no petioles, pedicels longer than the calyx and the stem angles are not alate or winged. Flowers June-frost in low wet woodlands, streams, and marshes; Florida-Texas and north into Connecticut-Nebraska.

SCROPHULARIACEAE
(Snapdragon Family)
Verbascum blattaria L. **Moth Mullein**

This is usually a biennial from a basal rosette of leaves or a simple to few-branched erect stem 60-120 cm tall with leaves alternate, glabrous, elliptic-lanceolate or triangular, wavy-toothed margined and 7-14 cm long by 2-5 cm wide. Flowers are in a loose raceme 30-60 cm long, with yellow, often white, short-tubed wide-spreading 2.5-3.5 cm broad corolla of 2 smaller upper and 3 larger lower round lobes. This is the only genus of this family in our area with all 5 stamens fertile; filaments of all 5 stamens have long purple hairs on them. All upper parts of the plant are glandular hairy. Globose capsules are 2-celled and 6-8 mm in diameter. Flowers June-October in fields and open areas throughout most of the contiguous United States.

SCROPHULARIACEAE
(Snapdragon Family)
Verbascum thapsus L. **Woolly Mullein**

This simple-stemmed erect biennial, 1-2 m high, rises from a basal rosette of very woolly elliptic-ovate velvety leaves 10-30 cm long by 4-12 cm wide. The stem elongates the second year, produces flowers and dies back, but remains standing through winter. Leaves along the stem continue winglike down it. A dense terminal spike of flowers is 30 cm or more long and 3-4 cm thick, only a few flowers opening at a time. Corollas 2-2.5 cm across have 5 nearly equal rounded lobes. The corolla tube is short and 5 stamens, 3 short upper hairy, and 2 longer nonhairy ones are attached to the tube. The ovary becomes an ovoid, 2-celled, many-seeded capsule 6-8 mm long, slightly longer than the woolly calyx. Flowers June-September in dry fields and waste places; Florida-Texas and north into Nova Scotia-South Dakota.

Mimulus alatus

ownia tomentosa

Verbascum blattaria

Verbascum blattaria

Verbascum thapsus

SCROPHULARIACEAE
(Snapdragon Family)
Chelone obliqua L. **Pink Turtlehead**

Chelone is Greek for "turtle," the flower resembling a turtle head with an open mouth. These perennials, 50-100 cm tall, have opposite, elliptic-lanceolate, smooth leaves 10-14 cm long by 2-5 cm wide, tapering to a petiole to 1.5 cm long, with toothed margins. The short terminal and axillary spikes of purple flowers are compact, not in 4 rows, and have 2 small ovate, pointed bracts arising below each flower. Bilabiate flowers are 2.5-3.2 cm long, have the upper lip closing downward over the lower 3-lobed lip which is bearded inside with yellowish hairs. Attached to the corolla tube are 5 bearded stamens, a sterile one without anthers is short and white; it is green in *C. glabra*. The 1-cm long ovoid capsule is 2-celled and many seeded. Flowers August-October in wet woodlands and swamps; Georgia-Mississippi-Arkansas and north into Maryland-Illinois-Minnesota.

SCROPHULARIACEAE
(Snapdragon Family)
Chelone glabra L. **White Turtlehead**

Both pink and white species of turtlehead are found in similar lowland habitats along the coastal plains and inland eastern United States. This white one is perhaps more widespread and reaches 1000 m elevation in the Adirondacks. This erect or spreading species is 60-150 cm tall, somewhat larger, and the leaves (10-18 cm long), somewhat longer than pink turtlehead. They are not so obviously petioled and bracts have whitish edges, in contrast to pink turtlehead. The corolla is white, sometimes pink tinged the outer third, and has a green sterile stamen. Flowers July-October. See also descriptions under *Chelone obliqua*.

SCROPHULARIACEAE
(Snapdragon Family)
Pentstemon digitalis Nutt. **White** or **Foxglove Beard-tongue**

The term "Pentstemon" refers to the 5th stamen, which is sterile but bearded with hairs at the top of the filament, tonguelike. The large flowers resemble those of the foxglove. *Digitalis*, in this family. This large perennial with opposite leaves rises over 1.5 m from a basal rosette of elliptic-oblanceolate leaves. The plant is mostly glabrous, with 5-7 pairs of stem leaves elliptic-lanceolate 7-21 cm long by 2-4.5 cm wide and toothed edges. The open branching terminal stalks bear many white bilabiate flowers 2-3 cm long. The corolla flares from a short narrow tube to a broad throat 1-1.5 cm wide which has a 2-lobed upper and 3-lobed lower lip. The sterile stamen has 2-mm long hairs at the top and the 4 fertile stamens have purple anthers. Flowers May-July in open woodlands and meadows; Florida-Texas and north into Maine-South Dakota.

SCROPHULARIACEAE
(Snapdragon Family)
Pentstemon laevigatus Ait. **Smooth Pentstemon**

This may be called smooth pentstemon because "laevigatus" means "not pubescent." This perennial is 40-100 cm tall and its opposite, glabrous, stem leaves are oblanceolate, 5-13 cm long by 1-3.5 cm wide and finely toothed. The flower cluster is very loosely branched with slender stems and linear bracts. Flowers are 1.5-2.3 cm long, with purplish corollas, often with darker lines inside and somewhat glandular pubescent outside. The corolla lobes are not wide spreading, the upper being somewhat reflexed. The tube is only 3 mm in diameter below, flaring rapidly to a throat 6-11 mm broad. Ovate-lanceolate sepals are 2-4 mm long and 4-8 mm long capsules are 2-celled. Flowers May-June in low meadows and bottom lands; Florida-Mississippi and north into New Jersey-Pennsylvania.

elone glabra

Chelone obliqua

'entstemon digitalis

Pentstemon laevigatus

SCROPHULARIACEAE
(Snapdragon Family)
Pentstemon cobaea Nutt. **Purple Pentstemon**

Flowers of this species, *P. cobaea,* may be purple, violet or white. The purple form shown here has been referred to as variety *purpureus* and appears to be more common than the other forms. Plants of the species grow 60-75 cm high and have deep purple 3.5-5 cm long flowers on them. It is entering our area from the prairie states and we have isolated islands of prairie vegetation in Mississippi, east Texas and eastern Arkansas. The stems are pubescent, and the opposite sparsely pubescent stem leaves are oblong-ovate, sharp-toothed, cordate or clasping the stem at the base. The rather short flower cluster is pubescent as is the 9-11 mm long calyx. The short corolla tube flares widely above the calyx to an inflated throat, hardly bilabiate, with 5 broad, rounded lobes. The sterile stamen of the five is sparingly bearded. The 2-celled ovoid, pubescent capsule is the length of the calyx at maturity. Flowers May-June in open grassy, mostly calcareous soils; Louisiana-Texas and north into Ohio-Nebraska. This is not an abundant plant and should be protected.

SCROPHULARIACEAE
(Snapdragon Family)
Collinsia violacea Nutt. **Blue-eyed Mary, Innocence**

This plant of quite limited range is entering our area from adjacent prairie habitats and has reached into north central Arkansas. The finely pubescent annual is somewhat branched, 5-20 cm high, with leaves opposite, mostly linear-lanceolate, upper ones sessile and the margin scarcely if at all toothed. The 1-cm long flowers are borne mostly singly in upper leaf axils. The upper 2-lobed lip is white, the lower 3-lobed lip is violet, not blue. The middle lower lobe is folded under and the lobes notched at their tips. The pedicels are not longer than the corolla and the calyx is finely pubescent. The stamens are 2 long, 2 shorter, and 1 sterile. The 2-celled capsule is 1-1.5 mm long and 2-6 seeded. Flowers April-June in rather open wooded and sandy open areas; east Texas-northward into Kansas-Illinois. Further findings in our area should be reported.

SCROPHULARIACEAE
(Snapdragon Family)
Linaria canadensis (L.) Dumont. **Toad flax**

This is a slender, glabrous annual or biennial from a basal rosette of leaves, 15-70 cm tall, with opposite or nearly so, linear leaves 5-20 mm long. It often spreads by horizontal sprouts from the base. Branches terminate in long, loose racemes, each flower subtended by a small bract. The bilabiate pale blue-white corolla is 5-10 mm long, including the 2-6 mm long spur at the base. There are 2 upper and 3 lower lobes of the corolla tube within which are 2 long and 2 short stamens, the 5th is missing. The globose capsules are 2-celled and 2.5-3 mm long. Flowers March-September in open sandy areas throughout most of the contiguous United States.

SCROPHULARIACEAE
(Snapdragon Family)
Linaria vulgaris Hill **Butter-and-eggs**

This perennial European garden escape is found throughout most of the country. It reaches a height of 1 m or more and has pale, alternate, linear leaves 1.5-4 cm long, narrowing at base and tip. The terminal flower cluster is closely crowded with 2.5-4 cm long, spurred upright flowers on short pedicels. The strongly 2-lipped yellow flowers have a darker yellow-orange, raised palate at the throat, nearly closing it. The spur projects downward and is about the length of the corolla tube. The 4 stamens, 2 long, 2 shorter are attached to and included within the corolla tube. Not found frequently in our area. Flowers May-October in dry fields and waste places.

ntstemon cobaea

Linaria canadensis

aria vulgaris

Collinsia violacea

SCROPHULARIACEAE
(Snapdragon Family)
Veronica persica Poiret **Birds-eye Speedwell**

This low-spreading pubescent annual has branches 10-30 cm long, with opposite, toothed, ovate, petioled leaves 7-20 mm long and 5-15 mm wide. In the leaf axils single flowers are borne on pedicels longer than the leaves. Corollas are saucer-shaped with 4 lobes of unequal sizes, the lower is the smallest. In the union of petals, one of the 5 is not evident; also in stamen reduction, only 2 remain. The flattened bright blue corolla has dark blue lines with a white center. There are 4 ovate sepals at the base of a bilobed, 2-celled pubescent capsule containing 15-25 seeds at maturity. Flowers March-September in lawns, fields, and waste places; over most of the United States and Canada.

SCROPHULARIACEAE
(Snapdragon Family)
Aureolaria pectinata (Nutt.) Penn. **Hairy False Foxglove**

Aureo means "golden," perhaps for its yellow flowers; *pectinata* refers to the pectinate or comblike teeth of the leaves. This genus has also been called *Gerardia*. This annual is much branched, has opposite, lanceolate, deeply pinnately lobed to compound leaves and is very glandular hairy throughout. The leaves are 2-6 cm long and 8-21 mm wide on plants 30-100 cm high. Solitary flowers, 3-4 cm long, about that broad, appear in leaf axils and are quite hairy in bud. The weakly 2-lipped corolla spreads widely to bell-shape, with 5 rounded and reflexed lobes. There are 2 short and 2 longer stamens with hairy anthers attached to and included within the corolla tube. The long pistil produces an ovoid, 2-celled capsule 8-10 mm long at maturity, the lower half enclosed by the hairy calyx with 5 linear lobes. Plants of this genus are apparently parasitic on roots of oak trees. Flowers July-October in dry, sandy, wooded areas; Florida-Louisiana and north into North Carolina-Missouri.

SCROPHULARIACEAE
(Snapdragon Family)
Agalinis purpurea (L.) Britt. **Purple Gerardia**

Agalinis was also placed in the genus *Gerardia* but that name has been dropped. *Agalinis* has rose purple flowers with purple spots within the corolla while those of *Aureolaria* are yellow and not spotted. Opposite leaves of *Agalinis* are linear. The several species in our area are quite similar, this one having a smooth stem without axillary leaf clusters while *A. fasciculata* has a rough stem with axillary clusters. This species is a much-branched annual 40-120 cm tall with linear leaves 1-4 cm long. Corollas 2-4 cm long are scarcely 2-lipped, with the upper of 2 and the lower of 3 rounded, ciliate-edged, lobes widely flared from a narrow tube. The purple corolla inside has 2 yellow lines and is nearly white with many purple spots, the upper throat is long-hairy, as are the filaments of the 2 long, 2 short stamens attached to the tube. Flowers August-frost in open woodlands and fields; Florida-Texas and north into Maine-Minnesota.

SCROPHULARIACEAE
(Snapdragon Family)
Agalinis fasciculata (Ell.) Raf. **Fascicled Gerardia**

This much-branched plant, 40-120 cm tall, has round rather than angled stems below as in the preceding species. Also, the leaves are rough rather than smooth. *Fasciculate* refers to leafy buds in axils of the opposite leaves giving a clustered appearance. The bracts at the flower bases are shorter than the 2-3.5 cm long flowers. The globose 2-celled capsule is 5-7 mm long, slightly longer than the calyx at maturity. The calyx teeth are much shorter than the broad space between them, not so obvious in *A. purpurea,* the smooth species. Both species have single flower stalks the length of the calyx or less. Most of the *Agalinis* seem to be parasitic or partially so on roots of other plant species. Flowers August-frost in wet or dry sandy soils and marshes; North Carolina-Florida-Texas and north into Arkansas-Missouri.

ica persica

Aureolaria pectinata

Agalinis purpurea

Agalinis fasciculata

SCROPHULARIACEAE
(Snapdragon Family)
Agalinis tenuifolia (Vahl.) Raf. **Slender Gerardia**

This glabrous annual, 20-80 cm high, is sparingly branched, has opposite linear leaves 2-5 cm long and 1-3.5 mm wide, with no axillary fascicles of leaves. Ends of branches have axillary flowers on slender pedicels 1-3 cm long and flowers 1.2-1.8 cm long. The light purple, rarely white, corolla is 2-lipped, the upper glabrous one arching flatly over the stamens and nearly closing the throat; the lower 3-lobed lip protrudes forward and upward. If the upper lobe is not flattened as above, the species is likely *A. setacea*. Stamens and capsules are as in other described species. Capsules are ⅓ longer than the calyx with 5 short, widely separated teeth. Flowers August-frost in dry woodlands, thickets, and fields; Florida-Texas and north into Maine-Minnesota.

SCROPHULARIACEAE
(Snapdragon Family)
Pedicularis canadensis L. **Wood Betony**

Pediculus means "louse" and a common name is lousewort, which by legend harbored lice. This perennial with a basal rosette of oblong-lanceolate, pinnately lobed leaves 5-15 cm long by 1.5-5 cm wide is quite hairy and has several leaves along its single stem, 15-45 cm high. The terminal flower spike is compact in flower but elongates 12-20 cm upon maturing. Strongly 2-lipped yellow-purple tinged, rarely white, corollas are 2-2.5 cm long. The upper lip is folded, vertically flattened and arched over the stamens and pistil; the lower 3-lobed lip is spreading and somewhat reflexed. The 4 stamens are sub-equal in length. The calyx is almost lobeless and toothless, bell-shaped but longer on the upper side. The compressed, 2-celled capsule, 12-16 mm long is about 3 times as long as the calyx. The genus is mostly northern, this is the only species found in our area. Flowers April-June in dry woodlands and thickets; Florida-Texas and north into Canada.

BIGNONIACEAE
(Bignonia Family)
Anisostichus capreolata (L.) Bur. **Cross-vine, Bignonia**

This family, in our area, differs from the Scrophulariaceae in these respects: (a) they are woody trees or vines, (b) viny members have compound leaves, (c) the details of capsule structure differ but remain 2-celled, and the seeds are flat-winged. A section across the stem reveals a cross of central tissue, hence its name. The high-climbing vine has opposite, pinnately compound leaves, the 2 lower leaflets firm, evergreen, oblong-lanceolate 5-15 cm long by 2-7 cm wide, with rounded bases while the other leaflets become 1-3 tendrils. Axillary flowers appear 2-5 per cluster on 1.5-5 cm long pedicels. Corollas, yellow on the inside, red-orange outside, are weakly 2-lipped, bell-shaped, 5-lobed and 4-5 cm long. The 2 long, 2 short stamens are hairy at the base and grow from the corolla tube. The calyx cup is toothless and the 2-celled flat capsule with large flat-winged seeds is 13-18 cm long by 2-2.5 cm wide. Flowers April-June in low woodlands; Florida-Texas and north into New Jersey-Ohio-Oklahoma.

BIGNONIACEAE
(Bignonia Family)
Campsis radicans (L.) See. **Trumpet-creeper**

This climbing or sprawling woody vine has deciduous, opposite compound leaves of 7-15 ovate, sharply-toothed leaflets 3-7 cm long by 1-3.5 cm wide. There are no tendrils but aerial roots may be seen. The narrowly funnel-form red-orange corolla, 6-8 cm long, is slightly 2-lipped with 5 round-spreading lobes. The 4 stamens of 2 lengths are glabrous. The capsule is 2-celled, rather podlike and stalked, 10-18 cm long by 2-3 cm diameter. Seeds are broadly flat-winged, rectangular, and about 1 cm long, in several rows on each side of the capsule partition. Flowers July-September in low woods, thickets and especially fence rows; Florida-Texas and north into New Jersey-Illinois-Oklahoma.

'inis tenuifolia

Pedicularis canadensis

ıpsis radicans

Anisostichus capreolata

BIGNONIACEAE
(Bignonia Family)

Catalpa bignonioides Walt. **Southern Catalpa**

This flowering tree to 15 m high has opposite, decidous, cordate-ovate, smooth-margined leaves to 30 cm long, abruptly pointed at their tips. Terminal flower clusters, 15-30 cm long have numerous 2.5-4 cm long by 2-3 cm broad white flowers, spotted yellow within, along with lines of tiny purple spots. There are usually only 2 fertile stamens, sometimes 4, often 1-3 are sterile stamens of the potential 5, attached to the corolla tube. The calyx is deeply 2-lipped and the mature capsule is 2-celled, cylindric, and 15-40 cm long by 8-12 mm diameter. The seeds are flat, about 2.5 cm long including wings with hair-tufted tips, and about 4 mm wide. The northern catalpa is similar but has fewer flowers in the clusters. Native to Georgia-Florida. Flowers May-July in lowland woods escaping into Texas and northward into other southeastern states.

OROBANCHACEAE
(Broom-rape Family)

Conopholis americana (L.) Wallr. **Squaw-root**

This unusual plant is parasitic on roots of various other plants, found especially in oak woodlands. Erect, stout stems 7-25 cm tall, usually clustered, have overlapping scalelike reduced leaves without chlorophyll and are yellowish in color. The upper half of the stem becomes a spike of erect flowers from leaf axils, each being tubular, 2-lipped white-yellow and 1.2-2 cm long. The upper lip forms a hood arching over the 4 stamens with pubescent anthers, attached to the corolla tube. The lower lip is short and 3-lobed. The ovoid capsule is 1-celled, 8-13 mm long and produces 1 mm long yellowish seeds. Flowers March-August in rich, dry woodlands; Florida-Louisiana and north into Maine-Michigan.

LENTIBULARIACEAE
(Bladderwort Family)

Pinguicula pumila Michx. **Dwarf Butterwort**

The Bladderwort Family includes the insectivorous butterworts and bladderworts which secrete digestive enzymes from their leaf surfaces. The leaves are "buttery" (from *pinguis,* meaning "grease"), viscid, rolling over at the edges, and digest captured insects. *Pumila* means "dwarf." This perennial is terrestrial and has a basal rosette of thick, yellow-green leaves 1-3 cm long by 6-10 mm wide, with 1-10 single-flowered glandular pubescent scapes 5-15 cm tall rising from its center. The white-purple united petals make up a 2-lipped corolla 1.4-2 cm long having 5-notched, nearly regular lobes and a spur 3-4.5 mm long. There are only 2 stamens on the corolla tube and the capsule is 1-celled. Flowers any time except late summer in low pinelands and grasslands; Florida-Texas and north into North Carolina.

LENTIBULARIACEAE
(Bladderwort Family)

Pinguicula caerulea Walt. **Violet Butterwort**

The overall size of this species is twice that of *P. pumila,* with leaves 2-6 cm long by 1-2 cm wide and 1-6 single-flowered, glandular pubescent scapes, long-hairy at the base, 10-30 cm tall. Flowers are blue-violet, with darker veins, 2.5-4 cm long, with lobes 1 cm long and a spur 4-10 mm long. The glandular pubescent calyx is scarcely 2-lipped, 5-7.5 mm long and with 4 or mostly 5 lobes 3-6 mm long. Capsules are 1-celled, 3-4.5 mm in diameter and produce many tiny brown seeds. Flowers February-May around the coastal plain in low pinelands and peaty marshlands; North Carolina-Florida-Mississippi. These plants are close to extinction and must be protected.

Catalpa bignonioides

ɔnopholis americana

Pinguicula caerulea

;uicula pumila

LENTIBULARIACEAE
(Bladderwort Family)
Utricularia gibba L. **Humped Bladderwort**

Utriculus means "little bladder." Members of this genus produce, as modified leaf parts, small bladders lined with enzyme secreting cells and an opening preventing escape of small aquatics which might swim in. *Gibbous* means "swollen or humped," the lower lip is raised on the surface, nearly closing the corolla throat. This species is one of the smaller ones, with creeping stems in mud or shallow water. From these arise alternate, hairlike branching leaves bearing scattered traps. Upright scapes, 2-9 cm high, bear 1-3 2-lipped yellow flowers only 6-8 mm broad by 6-12 mm long including a blunt spur 3.5-4.5 mm long. The upper lip is sub-triangular in shape and both lips project forward. Sepals are 2-3 mm long, about the length of the ovoid, 1-celled capsule. Flowers May-September in marshes and pools along the coastal plain and inland bogs; Florida-Texas and northward into Canada.

ACANTHACEAE
(Acanthus Family)
Ruellia humilis Nutt. **Hairy Ruellia**

Many of the characteristics of this family are common to the preceding several families, having 5 united petals, 5 united sepals, 2 or 4 stamens attached to the corolla tube, and a 2-celled capsule. This species is an erect to spreading, 18-60 cm tall, herbaceous perennial with opposite, ovate-lanceolate, smooth-margined leaves. Most parts have long spreading hairs. Stalkless leathery leaves are to 6 cm long by 3 cm wide and produce a few sessile flowers with blue corolla 3-4 cm long in their axils. The narrow corolla tube with its 4 attached stamens is longer than its flared throat with 5 nearly equal lobes. The calyx teeth are linear, 1.5-2.5 cm long, and bristly hairy. The pistil with the 2-lobed stigma exserted from the corolla tube produces a 2-celled capsule 12-15 mm long. Flowers May-September in dry open woodlands and prairies; Florida-Texas and north into Pennsylvania-Iowa.

ACANTHACEAE
(Acanthus Family)
Ruellia caroliniensis (Walt.) Steud. **Wild Petunia**

This opposite-leaved perennial, 10-80 cm in height, has short petioled leaves to 10 cm long by 4.5 cm wide, varying from ovate to lanceolate in shape. The erect simple to branched plant is pubescent in varying amounts, with internodes shorter toward the top of the plant than lower down. Lilac-blue, 2-5 cm long flowers, 1-4 each at upper nodes, are sessile or nearly so and have linear, bristly hairy calyx teeth 1.3-2.5 cm long. The 5 corolla lobes are nearly equal, the 4 stamens of near equal length are attached to the corolla tube and scarcely extend beyond it. The ovary is pubescent but the 1.2-1.6 cm long capsules are usually glabrous. This species has several varieties based upon differences in pubescence, length of the corolla tube and variable leaf shapes. Flowers April-August in dry sandy woodlands; Florida-Texas and north into Virginia-Kentucky.

ACANTHACEAE
(Acanthus Family)
Justicia americana (L.) Vahl. **Water-willow**

This perennial herbaceous plant rises 30-80 cm high from a spreading rhizome. Its opposite simple leaves 8-20 cm long by 0.5-2 cm wide are lanceolate-oblanceolate, long tapered, and without teeth. Close spikes of strongly bilabiate flowers are borne on axillary stalks about 10 cm long. The 5 calyx lobes are linear-lanceolate and 4-8 mm long. The united petal, bilabiate corolla has a notched recurved upper lip and a 3-lobed, wide-spreading lower lip. The corolla tube is 4-5 mm long and the lobes 6-8 mm long, violet to near white with purple mottling. The 2 stamens are attached below the upper lip, the pistil is 2-carpellate and produces a 2-celled capsule 12-14 mm long. By contrast, *Ruellia* in the same family is barely bilateral and has 4 stamens. Flowers May-August in water and wet places; Georgia-Texas and north into Vermont-Wisconsin.

cularia gibba

Ruellia humilis

Ruellia caroliniensis

Justicia americana

PLANTAGINACEAE
(Plantain Family)

Plantago lanceolata L. **English Plantain**

This plantain and *P. major* or common plantain represent most of those in our area. The latter has large ovate leaves on long petioles. English plantain has flowers regular or radially symmetrical with a corolla tube 2-3 mm long with 4 spreading, pointed lobes 1.7-2.3 mm long. The 4 stamens, with long, white filaments, are attached to the corolla tube. The pistil is 2-celled and the fruit is a special capsule, not splitting, but with a domelike lid which pops off to release 2 tiny seeds. The calyx has 4 lanceolate teeth. These features place the plantains in position near the preceding several families. A basal rosette of oblanceolate leaves, 5-30 cm long by 1-2.5 cm wide, produces 5-channeled or ribbed scapes even to 75 cm tall, terminated by short, blunt spikes elongating to 10 cm long by 1.5 cm thick in fruit. Flowers April-frost in open fields and waste places over much of the United States and Canada.

RUBIACEAE
(Madder Family)

Cephalanthus occidentalis L. **Buttonbush**

This comomon round-shaped shrub, much branched, with opposite leaves grows 1-4 m high and is mostly limited to water edges of ponds and streams. The ovate-lanceolate, smooth-margined, petioled, deciduous leaves are 8-15 cm long by 3-7 cm wide. *Cephalanthus* means "head-flowers" and refers to the pendant, 2.5-4 cm compact, globose heads or "buttons" of many 8-10 mm long fragrant white tubular flowers, each corolla with 4 short triangular lobes. The 4 short stamens are attached within the 4-toothed corolla tube. The long slender style of the pistil extends twice the length of the tube, presenting the fuzzy appearance of the head. The 4-toothed calyx cup extends up around, and is attached to, the 2-celled, wholly or partially inferior ovary which becomes a 1-2 seeded, dry, reddish brown achene. Flowers June-August near edges of ponds and streams over most of the eastern United States and Canada.

RUBIACEAE
(Madder Family)

Diodia virginiana L. **Buttonweed**

This erect to creeping, glabrous to pubescent plant 15-60 cm long is a herbaceous perennial. The sessile opposite leaves are elliptic-lanceolate, 2-7.5 cm long by 5-12 mm wide. The 1-2 axillary white flowers have a corolla tube 7-9 mm long with 4 spreading lobes 3-4 mm long, pubescent on the upper surface. The stigma of the pistil is deeply divided and the inferior ovary produces a 4-9 mm long pubescent 2-celled dry fruit, topped by 2 calyx teeth 4-6 mm long (photo). Another species, *D. teres,* with pink flowers and 4 calyx teeth, is also found in our area. Flowers June to frost on low, moist ground and wet areas; Florida-Texas and north into New England-Illinois-Missouri.

RUBIACEAE
(Madder Family)

Mitchella repens L. **Partridge Berry**

This trailing perennial evergreen plant, 10-40 cm long, rooting at the stem nodes, has opposite, petioled leaves 1-2 cm long. It often makes a thick ground cover in rich deciduous woods and along stream banks. Tubular white flowers 9-14 mm long have 4 lobes 3-4 mm long, and appear in pairs in leaf axils along the stem. These paired flowers are partly to completely fused together in a common calyx cup. There are 4 stamens on the corolla tube and the stigma of the pistil is 4-lobed at the top. The 2 ovaries are completely fused and become a fleshy drupe containing 8 hard seeds. The red, rarely white, fruits are 7-10 mm in diameter and persist through the winter into the next flowering time, as seen in the photo. Flowers May-July; Florida-Texas and into Newfoundland-Minnesota.

Cephalanthus occidentalis

Diodia virginiana

Plantago lanceolata

tchella repens

RUBIACEAE
(Madder Family)
Houstonia pusilla Schoepf. **Bluets, Innocence**

This species is one of the more common harbingers of spring, along with spring beauty, *Claytonia virginica*. This winter annual 2-10 cm high has opposite, petioled ovate-spatulate leaves, 8-13 mm long. Single flowers, only 3-5 mm long and 6-8 mm across, terminate the branching stems. The calyx is half the length of the corolla tube and, with the calyx teeth, about equals the length of the compressed, globose 4-5 mm broad, 2-celled capsule, half covered by the calyx cup. The corolla is blue-purple with a darker or red "eye." There are 4 short stamens deep within the corolla tube. Flowers March-April in sandy-rocky open places; Florida-Texas and north into Virginia-Missouri-Oklahoma.

RUBIACEAE
(Madder Family)
Houstonia caerulea L. **Bluets, Innocence**

This species grows 5-17 cm high with erect, branching filiform stems from a basal rosette of oblong-spatulate, petioled leaves 5-15 mm long. Stem leaves are shorter and narrower. Blue to white, 4-lobed tubular flowers are twice the size of *H. pusilla* 5-10 mm long by 9-13 mm across, and have a yellow "eye." Two flowers are on peduncles 1.5-7 cm long, terminating the branching stems. The calyx cup encloses the lower half of the 2-celled compressed capsule, 2-3.5 mm long, shorter than the 4 lanceolate calyx teeth. Flowers March-May in moist, grassy, and open deciduous woodland; Georgia-Alabama-Missouri and north into Nova Scotia-Wisconsin.

RUBIACEAE
(Madder Family)
Houstonia purpurea L. **Large Houstonia**

This herbaceous perennial grows 10-30 cm tall from a basal rosette of leaves not seen at flowering time. Stems are 4-angled and have sessile, opposite leaves which are ovate-lanceolate, 1.5-4.5 cm long by 0.5-3.5 cm wide and mostly glabrous. Stems branch upward into terminal flower clusters of few-many purple-white tubular flowers with 4 flaring lobes. The linear-lanceolate calyx lobes are shorter than the corolla tube which is twice the length of the corolla lobes. Total flower length is nearly 1 cm. The ovary is partially inferior and the calyx lobes adhere to the 2-lobed, compressed globose capsule in maturity. Flowers May-July in clearings, open woods, and slopes; Georgia-Oklahoma and north into Delaware-Iowa.

RUBIACEAE
(Madder Family)
Houstonia purpurea var. *calycosa* Gray **Bluets**

Authorities hardly agree as to whether some closely similar forms or varieties of bluets are distinct species. *H. longifolia, H. lanceolata* and this variety are closely similar. The leaves in this variety are somewhat wider than the other two, being mostly ovate-lanceolate. Terminal flat-topped clusters of flowers have a long-tapered bract at the base of each flower. White to pinkish-lavender flowers 7-10 mm long have gradually flaring tubes with 4 lobes tapered to points. The calyx lobes are about as long as the corolla tube whose lobes are nearly as long as the tube. The lower half of the somewhat compressed capsule is enclosed by the calyx cup. Flowers June-August on drier soils; Georgia-Alabama-Oklahoma and north into Maine-Illinois.

Houstonia pusilla

stonia caerulea

Houstonia purpurea

ıstonia purpurea var. calycosa

RUBIACEAE
(Madder Family)

Galium aparine L. **Bedstraw, Cleavers**

This is a weak or reclining annual with mostly 8 leaves in whorls at the stem nodes. Branching plants 20-100 cm long have recurved bristly hairs on both stems and leaves. Leaves 2-4.5 cm long by 2-6 mm wide are linear to narrowly oblanceolate and abruptly pointed at their tips. Tiny flowers, 1-several in axillary clusters, have no sepals, a 3-5 lobed corolla of united petals 2-3 mm across, 4 short stamens and a 2-celled ovary, at maturity becoming 2 nutlets about 2 mm long, covered with short, hooked bristles. Flowers May-September in meadows, open woodlands, and waste places throughout most of the United States, apparently a naturalized weed from Europe.

CAPRIFOLIACEAE
(Honeysuckle Family)

Lonicera japonica Thunb. **Japanese Honeysuckle**

This pubescent, high-climbing or trailing perennial is beautiful and very fragrant, but is a pest where not wanted. The opposite leaves are short petioled, ovate-elliptic, nontoothed, rounded at the base, and 3-7.5 cm long. White flowers, turning yellow, appear in pairs in the axils of the near-terminal leaflike bracts. The tubular corolla is 2-lipped, 4 lobes above, 1 below, 3-4 cm long, with the pubescent tube being 1.5-2 cm of that length. The 5 stamens are attached to the tube and are long exserted but not as long as the style with its capitate stigma. The completely inferior ovary is well below the 5 slender calyx teeth. The black, fleshy, subglobose several-seeded berries, 5-6 mm long, are usually seen in pairs. Birds eat the fruits and aid in dissemination of the plant. Flowers April-August in low woodlands, thickets, and fence rows; Florida-Texas and north into New York-Indiana-Kansas.

CAPRIFOLIACEAE
(Honeysuckle Family)

Lonicera sempervirens L. **Trumpet Honeysuckle, Coral Honeysuckle**

This is a semievergreen climbing vine with elliptic-ovate, opposite, short-petioled leaves, glaucous white over a dark green upper surface; they are 5-7.5 cm long. The upper 1 or 2 pairs of leaves are joined by their bases around the stem, perfoliate, and are somewhat bowl-shaped. Sessile, red-yellow flowers arise in terminal whorls at the last few nodes of the stem. The gradually expanding corolla is scarcely 2-lipped, only one of the 5 lobes is slightly larger; the tube is 3-5 cm long and the flared lobes are 4-8 mm long. The calyx cup with no teeth surrounds the inferior ovary and the fruit is an orange to scarlet, several-seeded berry 6-8 mm long. Flowers March-July in woods and thickets; Florida-Texas and north into Maine-Nebraska.

CAPRIFOLIACEAE
(Honeysuckle Family)

Lonicera flava Sims. **Yellow Honeysuckle**

This twining, evergreen, shrubby vine has whorls of 6 stalkless yellow flowers terminating the stems. Just beneath the flower cluster, the upper pair or two of ovate-round leaves are completely joined together around the stem. The sessile, opposite lower leaves are glabrous, dark-green above, gray-green below, elliptic to broadly oval and are 4-6.5 cm long, by 1.5-5.5 cm wide. The 2-lipped yellow corolla with 4 upper, 1 lower, lobes 1-1.5 cm long, has a tube 1.5-2 cm long that is not swollen at the base. The 5 glabrous stamens are exserted and attached to the corolla tube. The inferior 2-3 celled ovary becomes a globose, several-seeded, yellow to orange-red berry 7 mm in diameter. Flowers April-May in rocky woodlands and thickets; Georgia-Alabama-Arkansas and north into North Carolina-Missouri-Oklahoma.

Galium aparine

icera japonica

Lonicera flava

cera sempervirens

CAPRIFOLIACEAE
(Honeysuckle Family)
Lonicera periclymenum L. **European Woodbine**

This honeysuckle appears to be a garden escape and may be trailing or high climbing. Its opposite, ovate-oblong leaves, 4-6 cm long are petioled below to sessile toward the branch tips, none are joined together around the stem. Flowers 4-5 cm long are in several terminal whorls forming close clusters. The tubular, 2-lipped corolla is purple and pubescent on the outside, white within turning yellow with age. The upper lip is 4-lobed while the lower is long and narrow. Stamens and pistils are longer than the corolla to which the 5 stamens are attached. The inferior ovary is of 3 carpels, but the stigma is not 3-lobed and the fruit is a several-seeded red berry. Flowers May-June in thickets and roadsides; West Tennessee-Mississippi.

CAPRIFOLIACEAE
(Honeysuckle Family)
Sambucus canadensis L. **Black Elderberry**

This coarse shrub may grow to 10 m high and has a large white pith area inside the stems. The opposite leaves are pinnately compound 10-30 cm long, with 5-11 elliptic-lanceolate leaflets 5-15 cm long with finely serrated teeth and rounded bases. Flowers are in flat-topped clusters, 8-25 cm across which are followed by purplish-black 7 mm diameter berries. The small white flowers are only 5-7 mm across, having petals united into a short tube, flaring abruptly into 5 similar lobes. There are 5 exserted stamens attached to the corolla tube. The berrylike drupe from an inferior ovary is eaten by birds and also used in making pies, jelly, and wine. Flowers May-July in lowland areas and roadside ditches; Florida-Texas and north into Canada.

VALERIANACEAE
(Valerian Family)
Valerianella radiata (L.) Dufr. **Corn-salad, Cow-salad**

This succulent, mostly glabrous, herbaceous annual, 15-60 cm tall, has nearly sessile, opposite basal leaves that are spatulate with rounded tips and smooth margins. The upper leaves are mostly ovate, 1.5-3 cm long by 1-2 cm wide and are widely toothed. The square stems fork in pairs throughout and into the flat-topped flower clusters. Tiny 1.5 mm long irregular tubular white flowers are nearly equally 5-lobed. There are usually 3 stamens attached to the corolla tube. The inferior 3-celled ovary is topped by a calyx ring without teeth and forms only a 1-seeded, flattened dry fruit about 1.5 mm long. Further details of this family differ only slightly from the Honeysuckle Family. Flowers April-May along roadsides and in meadows; Florida-Texas and north into New Jersey-Kansas.

CUCURBITACEAE
(Cucumber Family)
Sicyos angulatus L. **Bur-Cucumber**

This pubescent annual climbing vine, 3-8 m long, with branching tendrils opposite or beside its alternate, palmately lobed, simple leaves has flowers clustered at ends of long stalks in leaf axils. *Sicyos* is Greek for "cucumber" and *angulatus* refers to the 5-angled star-shaped leaf; the stems are also angled. Plants are monoecious, i.e., having separate male and female flowers on the same plant. Greenish-white petals are united into a slender tube spreading immediately into an ovate 5-equal-lobed face 8-12 mm across; the lobes of males flowers seen here are linear. The 1-celled ovary is completely enclosed in a calyx tube which is slender-spiny and becomes a 1-seeded, indehiscent, burlike fruit 10-12 mm long. Pumpkin, squash, and melons are also in this family. Flowers June-frost in alluvial woods and thickets; Florida-Texas and north into Maine-Minnesota.

Lonicera periclymenum

lerianella radiata

Sambucus canadensis

icyos angulatus

CAMPANULACEAE
(Bellflower Family)
Specularia perfoliata (L.) A.DC. **Venus' Looking-glass**

This square-stemmed alternate-leaved annual usually branches below into several single stems 20-100 cm tall. The broadly ovoid leaves 5-25 mm broad are broad-toothed and clasp the stem with the blade. There are 1-3 axillary, sessile flowers at each node. Lower, self-fertilizing flowers are small and have rudimentary petals shorter than the 3-5 lobed calyx cup. Upper flowers are showy, with the 5-lobed, radial, united petal, blue-violet corolla 15-22 mm across. There are 5 separate stamens and a 3-celled inferior ovary, a 3-lobed stigma and a capsule 4-6 mm long, each cell opening by a lateral, elliptic pore releasing the seeds. Flowers April-July in open woods, fields and gardens over most of this country and beyond. *S. biflora* is a similar, smaller species without leaves clasping.

CAMPANULACEAE
(Bellflower Family)
Campanula americana L. **Tall Bellflower**

This biennial plant, from a weak taproot, grows erect, 20-200 cm tall, and has elliptic-lanceolate, finely-toothed, alternate, petioled leaves 5-18 cm long by 1-6 cm wide. Blue to violet flowers are borne in loose or dense, leafy-bracted terminal spikes 30-60 cm long. Its united petals form a saucer-shaped, 5-pointed lobed corolla 2.5 cm broad. The 5 stamens, broadened at their bases, are free from the corolla tube. The pistil with a completely inferior 3-celled ovary has a declined, upward curving style, 3-parted at the tip. The 5 linear sepals remain atop the club-shaped 6-13 mm long capsule which opens by pores at its tip, releasing many 1-mm long flat brown seeds. Flowers June-September in deciduous woodlands; Florida-Alabama-Arkansas and north into Maine-South Dakota.

CAMPANULACEAE
(Bellflower Family)
Campanula divaricata Michx. **Southern Harebell**

This erect to branching perennial, 20-75 cm tall, is mostly glabrous and has alternate, lanceolate leaves, pointed at both ends, with sharply toothed margins, 3-7 cm long by 1-2.5 cm wide. Loosely branched terminal flower clusters in axils of leaflike bracts bear drooping blue-violet bell-shaped flowers. Corollas are 7-10 mm long with 5 short reflexed lobes and a long exserted style. The inferior ovary is topped by 5 persistent short calyx teeth on the "top-shaped" capsule which opens by pores near the middle. Flowers July-September in dry, rocky woodlands; Georgia-Alabama and north into North Carolina-Kentucky.

CAMPANULACEAE
(Bellflower Family)
Lobelia cardinalis L. **Cardinal Flower**

This is our only red lobelia, the others are bluish or white. This herbaceous, seldom branched, perennial has alternate, ovate to lanceolate, finely-toothed leaves 5-15 cm long by 1-4 cm wide on stems to 1.5 m tall, and terminal flowering spikes to 40 cm long. The 5 petals are united into a scarlet 2-lipped corolla with a tube 2 cm long and lips 1.5-2.5 cm long. The upper lip has 2 linear lobes and the lower broad lip has 3 ovate-pointed lobes. The 5 stamens are free from the corolla tube but are joined together by their filaments, forming a red tube 1.8-3.5 cm long around the style and topped by anthers which are bearded with white tufts of hairs. The inferior ovary is topped by 5 slender calyx teeth and becomes a 2-celled many-seeded capsule opening at the top. Flowers July-September in low wet stream beds, marshes, and meadows; Florida-Texas and north into Canada.

Specularia perfoliata

Campanula divaricata

Campanula americana

Lobelia cardinalis

CAMPANULACEAE
(Bellflower Family)

Lobelia siphilitica L.

Great Blue Lobelia

This sparsely pubescent perennial has several unbranched stems 5-130 cm long from a basal crown, with nearly sessile alternate leaves, lanceolate to oblong, finely toothed and 5-15 cm long by 1-5 cm wide. The upper 10-60 cm of the stem produces blue flowers 2.3-3.3 cm long in axils of leafy bracts. Individual flower stalks have 2 slender bracts below the calyx of 5 ovate-lanceolate, pubescent sepals 6-12 mm long. The tubular corolla is 2-lipped, the upper 2-lobed erect; the longer lower lip is 3-lobed, spreading and white at the base. The 5 stamens are united by the filaments into a tube 12-14 mm long around the pistil. The ovary produces a 2-celled, many-seeded, broadly ovoid capsule 8-10 mm long. Flowers August-October in low woodlands and swamps; Georgia-Texas and north into Maine-Minnesota.

CAMPANULACEAE
(Bellflower Family)

Lobelia puberula Michx.

Downy Lobelia

This mostly unbranched perennial to 1.2 m tall is similar to great lobelia but is not as large, is more finely pubescent, and its flowers are not as densely clustered. Elliptic-lanceolate to oblong, pubescent leaves are alternate, short petioled to sessile, finely toothed and 3-12 cm long by 1-4 cm wide. Flowers are in loose, spikelike racemes which may get 50 cm long, with each flower subtended by a leaflike bract. The blue, 2-lipped, 2-cm long corollas have a white "eye" on the lower lip as does great lobelia. The filament tube is only 5-10 mm long, about the length of the corolla tube. The inferior ovary results in a capsule similar to other species of lobelia; see *L. cardinalis* for comparison. Flowers July-October in low, moist woodlands and openings; Florida-Texas and north into New Jersey-Illinois-Kansas.

CAMPANULACEAE
(Bellflower Family)

Lobelia spicata Lam.

Pale Spiked Lobelia

This mostly unbranched, densely pubescent stemmed perennial 20-120 cm tall has almost sessile, thickish, elliptic-oblanceolate leaves 3-11 cm long by 1-5 cm wide, with finely toothed margins. Loosely to densely flowering racemes may get 45 cm long and have bracts longer than each pedicel. The blue flowers are 2-lipped, with the corolla tube 4-6 mm long and the 5 lobes 5-8 mm long. The 5 stamens, free from the corolla tube, form a filament tube 2-3 mm long around the style. The calyx tube surrounding the inferior ovary has 5 slender teeth atop the "top-shaped" 4-7 mm broad capsule. Flowers June-August in dry, open woods, and meadows; Georgia-Louisiana-Arkansas and north into Maine-Minnesota.

ASTERACEAE
(Composite Family)

Ambrosia trifida L.

Giant Ragweed

This coarse rough-hairy annual, 1-5 m high, has opposite palmately 3, seldom 5, deeply-lobed, serrate, petioled leaves often 25-30 cm wide. Plants have separate male and female flowers on the same plant. There are 5-20 male flowers in a head 5-10 mm across which is surrounded by several 3-ribbed involucral bracts. Heads of male flowers are in racemes 8-30 cm long as seen in the photo. Each male flower has 5 stamens growing from a 5-toothed green tubular corolla about 2 mm long. Female heads are few in axils of the bractlike upper leaves, each flower having no corolla, only a forked pistil with an inferior ovary surrounded by a 5-7 ribbed calyx tube which becomes a beaked achene, 6-13 mm long with each rib terminated by a sharp point. Many persons are allergic to pollen from this plant when flowering, July to frost in alluvial bottom lands and waste places; Florida-New Mexico and north into Canada.

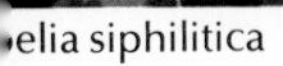
elia siphilitica

Ambrosia trifida

Lobelia puberula

Lobelia spicata

ASTERACEAE
(Composite Family)
Xanthium strumarium L. **Cocklebur**

This coarse, freely-branched, tap-rooted 50-150 cm tall annual is pubescent and has triangular-ovate somewhat 3-lobed, alternate, long-petioled leaves 5-15 cm long and about as wide. Male and female flowers are in separate heads in branching terminal and axillary clusters. The male flowers with only stamens are toward the tips, while 1-3 separate heads of 2 female flowers each are lower. These have only 2 bilobed pistils with their inferior ovary and each produces an achene in the surrounding fused spiny involucral bracts. This bur is 1.5-3 cm long by 1-2 cm broad at maturity. One of the 2 seeds in each bur germinates 1 year, the other the next. A similar species, *X. spinosum,* has a 3-branched 2-2.5 cm long spine at each node of the stem. Flowers July-frost mainly in low fields and waste places; Florida-Texas and north into Massachusetts-North Dakota.

ASTERACEAE
(Composite Family)
Cichorium intybus L. **Common Chicory**

This perennial tap-rooted herb with freely-branched, nearly leafless hollow stems 30-100 cm tall has a basal rosette of dandelionlike, pinnately lobed leaves, 10-30 cm long by 2-7 cm wide. Alternate stem leaves are similar but smaller and clasping. Bright blue flower heads, rarely pink or white, are 2.5-3 cm across and are borne 1-3, sessile or stalked, in bract axils. All are ray flowers (none tubular or disk) and are 5-toothed at their square tips. The pappus on top of the achene is of 2-3 rows of short scales as seen with a hand lens. The involucre is 2 rows of leafy bracts, 1-1.5 cm long, the outer row of 5 are spreading and the inner of 8-10 are more upright. This European import is widely naturalized. Flowers May-frost on roadsides, old fields and waste places; Florida-Mississippi-Missouri and north into Maine-Minnesota. *Lactuca floridana,* wild lettuce, a tall leafy plant with milky juice and many 1-cm broad heads of blue flowers (all ray), may be found in rich woodlands and openings July-frost.

ASTERACEAE
(Composite Family)
Sonchus asper (L.) Hill **Spiny Sow-thistle**

This annual, glabrous herb with milky juice grows during winter and sends up stems to 2 m high as spring approaches. Its alternate leaves are lanceolate-oblanceolate with rounded, earlike lobes clasping the stem, sharply spiny toothed, and 6-30 cm long by 3-10 cm wide. Pale yellow flowers are not showy and the conical heads have perfect ray flowers only, as in chicory. Heads are 2-3 cm across and 1.3-1.6 cm high with 9-12 mm long, narrow overlapping involucral bracts in several series. The pappus of the flat, ribbed, 2-3 mm long achene is of many unbranched capillary bristles. The similar *S. oleraceus* has pointed rather than rounded leaf base lobes. Flowers May-November in our area on roadsides, fields, and waste places; mainly Florida-Texas and north to Maryland-Kansas, but is present in many parts of the world as a weed among crop plants, having been naturalized from Europe.

ASTERACEAE
(Composite Family)
Taraxacum officinale Wiggers **Common Dandelion**

There are several differences between dandelion and false dandelion. Dandelion has no stem leaves, only basal; the unbranched flower stalk or scape is leafless and hollow, bearing a single flower. Dandelion has several series of involucral bracts, reflexing in maturity. As in false dandelion, there are only ray flowers, but they are yellow on the upper surface and purplish below. The achenes are spiny ridged, not just ridged, and the pappus of many capillary bristles is white rather than the tan of the false dandelion. The photo shows the 2-lobed stigma of each flower curling back where it may pick up pollen from its own anthers which are united around the style as a yellow cylinder just below the black stigmas. Young dandelion leaves are eaten as "greens" and the flowers make a delicate wine. Flowers February-frost over most of the United States, naturalized from Europe.

Cichorium intybus

nthium strumarium

Sonchus asper

Taraxacum officinale

ASTERACEAE
(Composite Family)
Dwarf Dandelion

Krigia dandelion (L.) Nuttall
Krigia biflora (Walt.) Blake

Although the Krigias are called dwarf dandelion, only one in our area, *K. occidentalis* can qualify as dwarf. They differ from the common dandelion, *Taraxacum officinale* in having a nonbeaked achene and a pappus of both scales and bristles, while *T. officinale* has a long-beaked achene and only numerous, long capillary bristles. Two of the more common Krigias in our area are treated here. These 2 are perennials with milky juice, have a basal rosette of leaves and yellow-orange flower heads of only ray flowers. Their vertical ribbed achenes are topped by a pappus of 2 series, the outer of 10-15 broad, short scales and the inner of 10-20 unbranched long bristles. Contrasting features of the two species are as follows:

K. dandelion	*K. biflora*
a. flowering stems unbranched, 15-50 cm tall, not leafy	a. flowering stems branched at nodes, 20-70 cm tall, clasping leaves
b. basal leaves linear-lanceolate	b. basal leaves spatulate-oblanceolate
c. flower heads 2-2.5 cm across	c. flower heads 2.5-4 cm across
d. fibrous rooted, 1 or more potatolike tubers	d. fibrous rooted, no attached tubers

Of other species *K. occidentalis* grows only 15 cm high, has only 5-8 involucral bracts and a pappus of 5 scales and 5 bristles. *K. virginica* is an annual and has 5-7 of each, scales and bristles. *K. dandelion* flowers March-May in open woodlands and fields; Florida-Texas and north into New Jersey-Kansas; *K. biflora,* May-August less common southward in open woodlands and fields; Georgia-Oklahoma and north into Massachusetts-Missouri.

ASTERACEAE
(Composite Family)
False Dandelion

Pyrrhopappus carolinianus (Walt.) DC.

This annual or biennial grows to 90 cm high, is freely branched and has both basal and alternate stem leaves. Basal leaves are pinnately lobed, somewhat toothed, oblanceolate to narrowly elliptic in outline, 10-25 cm long by 2-5 cm wide and narrowing into a winged petiole. Stem leaves are sessile to partly clasping, seldom toothed, long lanceolate, and are smaller to bractlike above. Flower heads are 1-several on a usually branched stem. The cylindric heads have linear inner involucral bracts bilobed at their tips, 2-2.5 cm long and shorter loose-spreading outer ones below. Only yellow ray flowers, spreading above, are present, 2-2.5 cm long, toothed at their tips. Achenes are cylindric, grooved and tapered at both ends 1.2-1.5 cm long including the beak. The pappus atop the beak is of many tan capillary bristles 8-10 mm long. Flowers April-October in fields, roadsides, and waste places; Florida-Texas and north into Delaware-Kansas.

ASTERACEAE
(Composite Family)
Butterweed

Senecio glabellus Poir.

This glabrous annual, erect, hollow stemmed leafy plant 30-100 cm tall branches at the top, producing many 1.5-2.2 cm broad heads of yellow flowers. Alternate leaves, 5-25 cm long are pinnately round-lobed and divided, the terminal segment larger. *Senecio* has species with both disk and ray flowers and some with only disk flowers. In all species, the involucral bracts are erect in 1 series. Here, there are 6-12 female ray flowers with rays 1-1.3 cm long, their achenes without a pappus. The disk is 3-4 mm across, its tubular flowers perfect and producing achenes 1.5 mm long topped with a white bristled pappus about 5 mm long. An abundant, showy weed in alluvial woods, fields and meadows. Flowers March-May; Florida-Texas and north into North Carolina-Missouri.

Krigia dandelion

Krigia biflora

ʼyrrhopappus carolinianus

Senecio glabellus

ASTERACEAE
(Composite Family)

Senecio plattensis Nutt. **Prairie Ragwort**

This perennial, mostly basal-leafed plant, 15-40 cm high, has mostly persistent, white matted hairs on its clustered stems and petioles. Basal leaves are mostly unlobed, shallowly toothed, long-petioled with ovate to oblong blades 2-8 cm long by 1-5 cm wide, tapering to rounded at their bases and white tomentose underneath. Several upper stem leaves, becoming bractlike above, are clasping at their bases, long tapered and usually sharply toothed at their margins. Showy yellow heads, with disk and ray flowers, are 2.4-2.6 cm broad and loose or compact in terminal branching clusters. Involucral linear-lanceolate bracts 5-6 mm long are in a single series. The pappus atop the achene is of unbranched bristles. Flowers April-July on dry rocky bluffs and prairies; Georgia-Arizona and north into Canada.

ASTERACEAE
(Composite Family)

Senecio tomentosus Michx. **Woolly Ragwort**

This perennial ragwort with woolly patches on the several stems grows 15-60 cm tall, with both basal leaves and stem leaves somewhat woolly beneath. Basal leaves are long-petioled, ovate-lanceolate, blunt tipped and round toothed, 5-15 cm long by 2-8.5 cm wide, rarely they are deeply cut at the base. Stem leaves are few, much smaller, linear lanceolate, coarse toothed to cut-lobed. Terminal branching flower clusters have heads of both disk and 10-15 ray flowers, yellow to orange in heads 2-2.5 cm broad. There is a single ring of linear involucral bracts 8-10 mm long. The finely spiny achenes 2-2.5 mm long are topped by a pappus of many white capillary bristles in one ring. Flowers April-June in moist sandy or rocky soils in open woods and clearings; Florida-Texas and north into New Jersey-Arkansas.

ASTERACEAE
(Composite Family)

Erechtites hieracifolia (L.) Raf. **Fireweed**

This erect, coarse, mostly glabrous annual 20 cm to over 3 m high branches above into many slender flower stalks with heads of only disk flowers. The stem is grooved and has alternate elliptic to lanceolate, irregularly sharply-toothed leaves 5-20 cm long by 1-6.5 cm wide, decreasing and clasping above. The tubular flowers are cream-pinkish, all fertile with marginal ones being female, in erect cylindric heads, swollen at the base in bud, 1.2-2.2 cm tall by 1 cm across. Involucral bracts are green to purplish, in 1 series. Tiny brown achenes are ribbed and topped by soft, white capillary bristles 1-1.4 cm long. *Erechtites* is a name given by Dioscorides to a *Senecio*-like plant and *hieracifolia* refers to leaves like *Hieracium* or hawk-weed, another Composite. "Fireweed" refers to its invasion of fire-burned fields. Flowers July-frost, in thickets, woodlands, and waste ground; Florida-Texas and north into Newfoundland-Minnesota.

ASTERACEAE
(Composite Family)

Centaurea americana Nutt. **Star-thistle**

This rough, little-branched annual 60-180 cm tall has lower leaves spatulate-oblong, alternate, 5-10 cm long by 2.5-4 cm wide and slightly or not at all toothed at the margins. Lower leaf blades taper into petioles while the upper leaves are oblong-lanceolate and sessile. Flower heads are 5-10 cm across and have several series of yellowish ovate-lanceolate involucral bracts with many lateral, linear teeth. All flowers are tubular disk flowers with 5 narrow, elongate lobes varying from white to pinkish purple. The stem is thickened and wing-ridged just below the head. The flattened achenes are topped with a pappus of many unequal capillary bristles. Flowers May-August in open woods and plains; Louisiana-Mexico and northward into Arkansas-Kansas. Both star-thistles herein are naturalized from Europe.

Senecio plattensis

Senecio tomentosus

Erechtites hieracifolia

Centaurea americana

Erechtites hieracifolia

ASTERACEAE
(Composite Family)

Centaurea maculosa Lam. **Spotted Star-thistle**

This stiff, much-branched, pubescent to glabrous biennial grows 30-100 cm high and has 10-20 cm long lower leaves deeply pinnatifid cut into 5-7 elliptic to linear lobes. Upper leaves are smaller and have linear lobes. Lavender to pink flower heads terminate the branchlets, are 1.5-2.5 cm across, and have several series of involucral bracts ribbed and with 5-7 narrow long teeth at their tips. "Maculosa" means spotted and each involucral bract is black-tipped. Each tubular flower of the head has a long, slender tube with 5 linear lobes; the outer flowers are sterile and longer than the inner fertile flowers. Dark brown 3 mm long achenes are topped by unequal capillary bristles averaging 2 mm long. Flowers June-August in fields, roadsides, and waste places; spreading into our area from West Virginia-Missouri-Kansas and beyond.

ASTERACEAE
(Composite Family)

Cirsium discolor (Muhl.) Spreng. **Field Thistle**

This stout, branching biennial, 1-3 m tall, has alternate, deeply pinnate, spiny lobed, elliptic-lanceolate leaves 10-30 cm long by 3-4.5 cm wide, rolled under at their margins and white pubescent beneath. Upper leaves are smaller, more linear-lanceolate, bractlike near the flower heads. The purple flower heads at branch ends are about 4 cm high and broad, and made up of only tubular disk flowers, each with 5 long, linear lobes. The involucral bracts in several series, except for the innermost, are each tipped with a horizontal or recurved spine 4-7 mm long. Achenes are smooth and topped with several series of white plumose pappus bristles 1.8-2.5 cm long, not capillary unbranched bristles as in star-thistles. Flowers July-October in prairies, pastures, and woodland edges; Georgia-Mississippi and north into Canada. (Some authorities prefer the name *Carduus* to *Cirsium*.)

ASTERACEAE
(Composite Family)

Cirsium horridulum Michx. **Yellow Thistle**

This robust single-stemmed biennial grows 0.2-1.5 m high. It may reach 60 cm across with alternate, sessile to clasping, pinnately lobed, strongly spined leaves to 30 cm long by 10 cm wide. Yellow, purple or even white heads to 7 cm across may be 1-10 clustered at the top of the stem. Closely subtending each head is a ring of linear leaf bracts 4-5 cm long, edged with spines. Involucral bracts are scarcely spine tipped. Tubular corollas are 2-2.5 cm long including 5 short linear lobes. There are no ray flowers. The smooth achenes are topped by a plumose bristled pappus 3-4 cm long. Also called *Carduus spinosissimus* by some. The yellow form is mostly limited to the coastal plain. Flowers March-August in sandy soil, meadows, and marshes; Florida-Texas and north into Maine and Pennsylvania.

ASTERACEAE
(Composite Family)

Vernonia noveboracensis (L) Michx. **New York Ironweed**

This erect, branching, pubescent-glabrous perennial herb is 1-3 m tall, has alternate lanceolate-oblong leaves tapered at both ends, 13-30 cm long by 1.5-4 cm wide and finely toothed margins. Terminal flat-topped branches to 30 cm across bear 30-50 deep purple 1-1.5 cm broad heads of 5 long linear-lobed disk flowers only. Involucral bracts 8-12 mm long, about that wide, in several series, have long-tapered recurving tips. Achenes, 4-5 mm long have 8-10 spinulose ridges and are topped by a purple pappus of 2 rings of bristles, the outer of short scales or stout bristles and the inner of many rough, capillary bristles 5-7 mm long. Flowers August-October in low, wet woodlands, meadows, and marshes; Georgia-Mississippi and north into Masachusetts-Ohio. (See Joe-Pye-weed for contrast)

Cirsium discolor

Centaurea maculosa

um horridulum

Vernonia noveboracensis

Liatris aspera Michx.
Liatris spicata (L.) Willd.
Liatris scabra (Greene) K. Shum.
Liatris squarrosa (L.) Michx.

ASTERACEAE
(Composite Family)
Blazing-star, Gayfeather

This genus of erect, 1-several simple-stemmed perennials, 60-150 cm high from a tuberous base have alternate, nontoothed, mostly linear leaves. Pink to purple flower heads are in terminal, spikelike, loose to dense clusters to 75 cm long. These prairie type plants go by the name of blazing-star, also given to some other genera. The flowers are all tubular or disk, with 5 lobes, a pistil with a 2-parted stigma, and an inferior ovary producing a 10-ribbed achene topped with a pappus of 15-40 either plumose or barbed capillary bristles. The 4 species described here have the latter type of pappus. The involucral bracts around the head are overlapping in several series, the outer ones shorter. The contrasting and diagnostic features of the 4 species shown here follow:

L. aspera
Stems: glabrous to pubescent
Spikes: loose to dense, heads sessile to 1 cm stalks
Heads: 16-35 flowered, 1-1.5 cm long, 1-2 cm broad
Bracts: rounded, spreading, swollen, white-pink
Pappus: 6.5-7.5 mm long
Flowers August-October in dry, often sandy soil; Florida-Texas north into South Carolina-North Dakota.

L. spicata
Stems: glabrous or nearly so
Spikes: dense, heads mostly sessile
Heads: 5-18 flowered, 10-12 mm long, 6-8 mm broad
Bracts: round-tipped, appressed, purple, 6-10 mm long
Pappus: 4-4.5 mm long
Flowers July-September in wet meadows, marshes, and damp slopes; Florida-Louisiana north into New Jersey-Wisconsin.

L. scabra
Stems: rough, gray pubescent, also on flower stalks
Spikes: loose, heads on 1-1.5 cm long stalks
Heads: 20-35 flowered, 1.5-2 cm long, same broad
Bracts: green, rounded, lower recurved, upper appressed
Pappus: 8-10 mm long
Flowers August-October in dry open woods and barrens; Alabama-Louisiana-Oklahoma north into Ohio-Illinois.

L. squarrosa
Stems: pubescent-glabrous
Spikes: axillary in terminal leaves
Heads: 25-40 flowered, 1-3 cm long and broad
Bracts: green-purple, lanceolate, recurved, 1.5-2 m long
Pappus: 1-1.5 cm long
Flowers June-August in upland open woodlands or clearings; Florida-Mississippi north into Delaware-Illinois-Missouri.

s aspera

Liatris spicata

iatris scabra

Liatris squarrosa

ASTERACEAE
(Composite Family)

Eupatorium species. **Joe-Pye-weed, Snakeroot, Bone set**

The Eupatoriums, over 15 species in our area, are late summer and autumn flowering plants along with the Goldenrods. They are large, 0.6-2 m tall, erect-branching perennial herbs with opposite or whorled—rarely alternate, simple—rarely compound leaves, and have large much-branched clusters of mostly 5-20 disk flowers per head. There are no ray flowers and disk flowers are white, pink to purple, with 1 species being blue. Overlapping involucral bracts are in 2-several series. The achene fruits are 5-angled, 1.5-5 mm long, and topped by a pappus of 3-5 mm long capillary bristles in one ring. Most of these are found in dry to moist open woodlands and edges, flowering July-frost; Florida-Texas and north into New Jersey-Michigan-Nebraska.

The contrasting and diagnostic features of some of the more common species of *Eupatorium* may be determined below:

With leaves in whorls of 3-7, flowers pink to purple.
- Whorls of 4-7, stem hollow, 5-8 flowers per head. *E. fistulosum* 1.
- Whorls of 3-5, stem solid, 3-7 flowers per head. *E. purpureum* 2.

With leaves opposite.
- Leaves petioled.
  - Leaves ovate, flowers white, 15-30 per head. *E. rugosum* 5.
  - Leaves lanceolate, flowers white, 10-20 per head. *E. serotinum* 4.
  - Leaves triangular, flowers blue, 40-55 per head. *E. coelestinum* 6.
- Leaves sessile, perfoliate, flowers white, 7-15 per head. *E. perfoliatum* 3.

1. *Eupatorium fistulosum* Bar. (no photo) **Joe-Pye-weed**
   Stems to 2.5 m tall, flower cluster to 50 cm broad, round-topped, in damp thickets and meadows.
2. *Eupatorium purpureum* L. **Sweet Joe-Pye-weed**
   Odor of vanilla when bruised, leaves lanceolate to ovate, flowers creamy white to pale purple.
3. *Eupatorium perfoliatum* L. **Boneset**
   Leaves opposite, long-tapering, prominent veined, bases joined around stem. Low wet woods and fields.
4. *Eupatorium serotinum* Michx. **Late-flowering Boneset**
   Leaves broadly lanceolate to narrowly ovate, long-petioled and subtending axillary clusters, involucral l bracts white-margined, flowers white to pale lilac.
5. *Eupatorium rugosum* Houtt. **White Snakeroot**
   Leaves broadly ovate, long tapering, coarsely and sharply toothed, petioles 1.5-6 cm long. Mostly in rich woodlands and openings.
6. *Eupatorium coelestinum* L. **Blue Boneset, Ageratum**
   Flat-topped, compact flower clusters, blue, sometimes white. Leaves square to cordate at base, 4.5-9 cm long by 2-6 cm wide. Plants are 30-100 cm tall.

Eupatorium perfoliatum

Eupatorium rugosum

patorium purpureum

Eupatorium coelestinum

Eupatorium serotinum

ASTERACEAE
(Composite Family)
Carolina Elephant's-foot

Elephantopus carolinianus Willd.

This is a freely, loosely-branching perennial with 1-several pubescent stems 20-80 cm long, bearing alternate, ovate-obovate, shallow-toothed, nearly sessile leaves 8-20 cm long by 5-10 cm wide, becoming smaller above. Terminal, 2.5 cm broad clusters of only 2-5 flowered heads are subtended by 2-3 leaflike ovate bracts 1-3 cm long. The few tubular disk flowers are pink to purple, rarely white, and are about 1 cm long, with 5 pointed lobes. Involucral bracts in 2 series, the outer short, the inner 1 cm long, are scalelike. Achenes 3.5-4 mm long are 10 ribbed and topped by a persistent pappus of a few stiff, rough, awllike bristles 6-10 mm long. Flowers August-October in dry woods and thickets; Florida-Texas and north into New Jersey-Kansas.

ASTERACEAE
(Composite Family)
Gumweed

Grindelia lanceolata Nutt.

This slender glabrous, branching perennial, 50-80 cm tall, has simple, alternate sessile or clasping leaves 2-8 cm long by 1-2.8 cm wide with spine-toothed margins. Flower heads 1.7-2 cm broad are borne terminally on leafy bracted branching stems. Yellow rays, 25-35, are narrowly linear, 10-15 mm long and the 8-10 mm broad disk is yellow flowered. Involucral bracts 8-10 mm long are linear-lanceolate in several series, spreading but not reflexing, and they are hardly gummy. Achenes 4-6 mm long are topped with a pappus of 2 awns 4-7 mm long. This plant is rarely found in isolated rocky prairie islands and does not have the sticky involucral bracts of more western species. Flowers August-October; Louisiana-Texas and north into Tennessee, Missouri-Kansas.

ASTERACEAE
(Composite Family)
Climbing Hempweed

Mikania scandens (L.) Willd.

This is one of the rare viny species of Composites, being found as a pubescent perennial climbing 2-5 m long over bushes or water's edge thickets. The opposite leaves, 4-12 cm long by 2-9 cm wide, have triangular-cordate blades with long-tapering tips and edges remotely shallowly lobed, on petioles to 10 cm long. Flower heads resemble those of *Eupatorium* and the plant is also called climbing boneset. Flower heads have only 4 linear-lanceolate involucral bracts 5-6 mm long and 4 disk flowers, white to pinkish, 8-10 mm long, found in long, branching axillary clusters 2-8 cm broad. The achenes are 5-angled, 2-2.2 mm long, and topped by a pappus of barbed capillary bristles 2.5-3 mm long. Flowers July-October in swamps, wet woods, and lake edges; Florida-Texas and north into Maine-Minnesota.

Elephantopus carolinianus

Grindelia lanceolata

Mikania scandens

ASTERACEAE
(Composite Family)

Pluchea rosea Godfrey **Marsh-fleabane**

This single-stemmed, 40-100 cm tall, quite hairy perennial has alternate, elliptic-oblong, sessile clasping leaves 3-9 cm long by 1-3.5 cm wide, with short thickened teeth. Terminal and lateral flowering branches produce dense clusters of sessile or nearly so heads of pink to rose disk flowers. Involucral bracts in several series are 3-6 mm long and pointed. Achenes are 5-angled, 0.5-1 mm long, topped by a pappus of white capillary bristles 3-4 mm long. Flowers June-July along ditches, plains, and low woodlands around the coastal plain; North Carolina-Florida-Mississippi. This species is rather uncommon and should be protected.

ASTERACEAE
(Composite Family)

Antennaria plantaginifolia (L.) Richards **Pussy-toes**

This hoary pubescent stoloniferous perennial resembles everlasting. An upright stem 5-45 cm tall from a basal rosette produces a terminal globose cluster of 3-30 heads of disk flowers only. Plants are of separate sexes, the female the larger and fertile. Basal leaves are obovate-spatulate, distinctly 3-veined, dark green above, silvery beneath, 4-7.5 cm long by 2-4 cm wide and tapering into a petiole. Stem leaves are oblong-lanceolate, decreasing in size upward and sessile. Involucral bracts are in several series, greenish, white-margined, linear-lanceolate, and 5-7 mm long. Heads are 6-8 mm broad with white to red flowers. Achenes are 1-1.5 mm long and topped by a ring of capillary bristles 4-5.5 mm long. Flowers March-June in dry woodlands and openings; Florida-Texas and north into Maine-Minnesota.

ASTERACEAE
(Composite Family)

Gnaphalium obtusifolium L. **Everlasting, Cat-foot**

This white woolly-stemmed biennial may reach over 1 m in height and have 30 or more alternate, linear-lanceolate, sessile leaves 2.5-8 cm long by 2-8 mm wide. Leaves have rolled-under, wavy edges, are dark green, glabrous above and white woolly beneath. First year basal leaves in a rosette are oblanceolate-spatulate and pubescent. The much-branched top produces numerous 6-7 mm broad heads of several disk flowers surrounded by several series of white papery, lanceolate bracts 6-7 mm long. Achenes are under 1 mm long and topped by a pappus of a ring of 5-mm long capillary bristles. Often used in dry flower arrangements. Flowers August-October in dry fields and clearings; Florida-Texas and north into Canada.

ASTERACEAE
(Composite Family)

Gnaphalium purpureum L. **Cudweed**

This annual composite branches at the base into several erect stems with less than 15 alternate, sessile, clasping, round-tipped leaves 2-7 cm long by 0.5-1.5 cm wide. Basal leaves are spatulate with winged petioles while stem leaves are similar but reduce in size upward. Stems and leaves are white-hairy, thickly so beneath the leaves. Stems are 10-50 cm tall, the top few cm being a bracted spike of many 5-7 mm high flower heads with several series of 3-4 mm long, lanceolate involucral bracts yellowish-brown to purple. Flowers are all disk-type with a pappus of a single ring of capillary bristles, united by their bases at the top of an achene of 0.5-0.7 mm long. Flowers mostly April-June in dry sandy soils; Florida-Texas and north into Maine-Illinois.

:hea rosea

Antennaria plantaginifolia

phalium obtusifolium

Gnaphalium purpureum

ASTERACEAE
(Composite Family)
Pterocaulon pycnostachyum (Michx.) Ell. **Black-root, Rabbit-tobacco**

This plant's name (*ptero* "wing," *caulon* "stem," and *pycno* "crowded," *stachyum* "spike") describes quite well the wing-stemmed perennial growing from a large, dark rootstock. One to several erect stems grow from a crown 40-80 cm tall, with alternate, linear-lanceolate leaves 5-10 cm long by 1-4 cm wide, continuing winglike down the white hairy stem. Leaves with finely-toothed margins are white-felted beneath, glabrous and dark green above. The 3-7 cm long spike is of many compacted heads of pink to white disk flowers as in *Gnaphalium*. Densely hairy involucral bracts are in several series. Achenes are 4-5 angled and topped by a single ring of capillary bristles. Flowers mainly April-June in coastal plains, sandy barrens; North Carolina-Florida-Mississippi.

ASTERACEAE
(Composite Family)
Erigeron philadelphicus L. **Daisy Fleabane**

Is it an *Erigeron* or an *Aster*? When in doubt, *Erigerons* bloom mostly in spring, have involucral bracts in a single series and a single ring pappus of capillary bristles, rarely 2 rings with the outer one short. *Asters* mostly bloom in late summer and fall, and have several series of overlapping involucral bracts, and a single ring pappus of capillary bristles, rarely 2 rings with all bristles long. This *Erigeron* is a perennial 30-90 cm tall from a rosette of basal, ovate-spatulate; toothed leaves 4-16 cm long and 7-15 smaller, lanceolate stem leaves round and clasping at the base. Branching tops bear few to many nodding buds and erect flower heads 1.5-2.5 cm across with 100-150 white to pinkish narrow rays, 5-10 mm long. Tubular disk flowers are 2.5-3.5 mm long. Similar *E. pulchellus* has about 50 ray flowers. Flowers March-July in low moist areas over most of continental United States.

ASTERACEAE
(Composite Family)
Erigeron strigosus Muhl. **Daisy Fleabane**

This common annual, 30-100 cm tall, plant is pubescent with hairs appressed to the surface (strigose) on stems and leaves. Basal toothed leaves to 15 cm long are narrowly oblanceolate-spatulate, the blade tapering to a long petiole. Sessile stem leaves 5-8 cm long are not usually toothed, may be oblanceolate-linear lanceolate and slightly strigose to glabrous. Stems may branch profusely above, tipped with few to 20 heads of flowers with yellow disks 6-12 mm broad and 40 or more white-purplish ray flowers whose rays are the approximate length of the disk width. Involucral bracts in a single series are narrow, 3-5 mm long and nearly glabrous. The pappus on the ray flower achenes is of short bristles or scales; the pappus on the achene from disk flowers has a ring of short scales and an inner ring of many long capillary bristles. Flowers May-October in open woods, fields, and waste places over most of the United States.

ASTERACEAE
(Composite Family)
Aster pilosus Willd. **Frost Aster**

This usually much-branched, soft-hairy (pilose) to glabrous aster to 1.5 m tall has small sub-rigid narrow leaves which are quite inconspicuous by flowering time. Few to many heads of white ray and yellow disk flowers are scattered on one side of long, arching stem branches. There are 15-25 ray flowers and 20-40 disk flowers in heads to 2.5 cm broad, white but sometimes purple. If disk flowers are 10-20 and heads are under 2 cm broad, the species is likely *A. ericoides,* white heath aster. The two are quite variable and perhaps should not be separated. Achenes are 0.7-1.3 mm long, topped by a white pappus of barbed capillary bristles 4-5 mm long. Compare this species with *Erigeron philadelphicus.* Flowers August-November often in dense stands in fields and meadows; Georgia-Arkansas and north into Maine-Minnesota.

;eron philadelphicus

;eron philadelphicus

;eron strigosus

Pterocaulon pycnostachyum

Aster pilosus

ASTERACEAE
(Composite Family)

Aster dumosus L. **Bushy Aster**

This aster closely resembles *A. pilosus* but its branches are not long hairy (pilose) and the 2-12 cm long leaves are 2-8 mm wide vs. 2-15 mm wide. Contrasting features *A. dumosus* vs. *A. pilosus* are as follows: flowers are often pink-purple *vs.* mostly white; disk flowers of both may be pink; rays are fewer, 14-20 *vs.* 20-30; involucral bracts are blunt-tipped *vs.* long tapered; both have a green mid-vein and white margins; achenes are 1.2-2.3 mm long topped with pappus of white bristles 3-4 mm long *vs.* achenes 0.7-1.3 mm long and tan pappus bristles 4.5-5.5 mm long. Flowers August-October in fields, marches, and thickets; Florida-Texas and north into Maine-Illinois.

ASTERACEAE
(Composite Family)

Solidago species. **Goldenrod**

Goldenrods are erect perennials, often woody at the base, little-branched, and with simple, alternate, toothed or smooth-margined leaves. Flowering is later summer and fall. Flower heads are 8-20 flowered and very small. Ray flowers are pistillate only, while disk flowers are perfect. Involucral bracts are in several series. Achenes are usually ribbed, 1-2 mm long and topped by simple barbed capillary bristles 3-5 mm long in 1 or 2 rings. Flower heads may be clustered in leaf axils or terminal, in small or large clusters. Flower heads may be on the upper side of the branches as in most, or equally arranged around the stems. Terminal clusters may be pyramidal or spreading and flat-topped.

	S. nemoralis	*S. ulmifolia*	*S. altissima*
Stems:	15-130 cm tall	30-150 cm tall	100-250 cm tall
	gray pubescent	glabrous	gray pubescent
Leaves:	oblanceolate	elliptic-lanceolate	narrowly lanceolate
	7-15 cm long 1.25 cm wide	7-15 cm by 1-4 cm	6-15 cm by 1-3 cm
	axillary leaflet tufts	no tufts	no tufts
	1 main vein	1 main vein	3 veins
	crowded on stem	distant on stem	crowded on stem
Flowers:	pyramidal, arching	wide arching	wide arching, large
	5-9 ray, 3-6 disk	4-6 ray, 4-6 disk	9-15 ray, 5-8 disk
Clusters:	1-sided	1-sided	1-sided
Habitat:	dry open fields	moist woodlands and thickets	dry open fields

Solidago nemoralis Ait. **Early Goldenrod**

Flowers July-November; Florida-Texas and north into Canada.

Solidago ulmifolia Muhl. **Elm-leafed Goldenrod**

Flowers July-September; Georgia-Texas and north into Nova Scotia-Minnesota.

Solidago altissima L. **Tall Goldenrod**

Flowers August-November; Georgia-Texas and north into Maine-Ontario.

Aster dumosus

;o nemoralis

Solidago ulmifolia

;o altissima

ASTERACEAE
(Composite Family)

Polymnia canadensis L. **Leaf-cups**

This rather uncommon coarse-leaved perennial, glandular hairy, somewhat branching plant, 0.8-1.5 m tall, has mostly alternate, sharply pinnately lobed or divided leaves 10-30 cm long by 10-27 cm wide. Opposite lower leaf petioles appear cuplike around the stem. Leaves are toothed and 3-5 triangular-lobed or divided. Terminal clusters have few flower heads 1-1.4 cm broad with no or 5-8 white ray flowers with 5-15 mm long rays 3-lobed at their tips. A yellow disk of flowers is 6 mm broad. Involucral bracts, 5-8 in 1 ring, are ovate-lanceolate and 6-11 mm long. Achenes are 3-ribbed, 3-4 mm long, and have no pappus. *P. uvedalia* has yellow ray flowers with pointed rays unlobed. Flowers July-October mainly in calcareous woods and edges; Florida-Arkansas and north into Vermont-Minnesota.

ASTERACEAE
(Composite Family)

Silphium laciniatum L. **Rosinweed**

This very rough, bristly, and coarse unbranched perennial plant, 1-3.5 m high, has alternate, deeply pinnately lobed and divided blades. Laciniate refers to the narrow, deeply cut, pointed lobes. Lower compound leaves are 30-90 cm long by 5-25 cm wide, sessile or petioled, and clasping the stem. Several flower heads 5-12 cm across are sessile or nearly so along the leafless upper stem with 20-30 linear rays 2.5-5 cm long. Disk flowers are perfect but sterile. Involucral bracts in 2-3 series are ovate-lanceolate, 2.5-4 cm long, strongly recurved, and resinous pubescent. Flat, winged achenes are 10 mm long, notched at the top, and have no pappus. Since leaves usually point north-south this has been called compass plant. Flowers July-September in dry open areas, prairies; Alabama-Texas and north into Ohio-Minnesota-North Dakota.

ASTERACEAE
(Composite Family)

Rudbeckia species. **Coneflowers**

Coneflowers are perennial or biennial, few are annual. Stems are mostly bristly hairy with alternate leaves simple, lobed or not, to pinnately compound. Ray flowers are mostly yellow and sterile. Disk flowers, elevated hemispherical to conelike, are usually purplish-black and fertile. Style branches are usually hair-tufted. Ovary is inferior, covered by the calyx tube making a dry achene fruit. Achenes are 4-ribbed with a pappus of only 2-4 very tiny teeth in a ring or completely absent. Heads are many-flowered, and involucral bracts are in 2-4 series. Flowers mostly late summer to frost, some in open woodlands but more in open grasslands, often in showy abundance. Four of about twelve species in our area may be determined from the following table.

Rudbeckia laciniata L. **Green-headed Coneflower**

The leaves are irregularly divided and lobed into 3, 5 or 7 segments with few pointed teeth, thus describing the term laciniate. Flowers July-October in moist woodlands, stream banks, and meadows; Florida-Texas and north into Quebec-Montana-Idaho.

Rudbeckia triloba L. **Thin-leaved Coneflower**

Clumps of several stems arise from the basal crown. Lower leaves are often palmately lobed into 3 or more lobes but become palmately compound. Flowers June-October in open woodlands and fields; Florida-Louisiana-Oklahoma and north into New York-Minnesota.

mnia canadensis

Silphium laciniatum

lbeckia laciniata

Rudbeckia triloba

Rudbeckia amplexicaulis Vahl. **Clasping-leaf Coneflower**

Amplexi means "clasping," *caulis*, "stem." This has the tallest of cones in the group, but compare this with cones of *Ratibida columnifera*. Flowers in June; Georgia-Texas and north into Missouri and Kansas.

Rudbeckia hirta L. **Black-eyed Susan**

Hirta means "rough," describing the bristly hairs on the plant. Clumps of several stems arise from the basal crown. This species includes *R. serotina* Nutt., sometimes given separate standing. Flowers June-October; Georgia-Texas and north into Massachusetts-Illinois.

	R. laciniata	*R. triloba*	*R. amplexicaulis*	*R. hirta*
Stems:	50-300 cm tall glabrous perennial	30-160 cm tall glabrous-hairy annual or biennial	30-60 cm tall glabrous annual	30-100 cm tall bristly hairy perennial
Leaves:	5-7 compound and 3-5 narrow lobed	3-lobed not compound	upper simple, ovate-lanceolate clasping stem	simple, elliptic-lanceolate
Heads:	6-10 cm broad few, terminal	to 5 cm broad many in branching clusters	to 5 cm broad solitary and terminal	5-10 cm broad few, solitary and terminal
Rays:	6-10 reflexing 2-10 cm long yellow	8-12, yellow 1.5-3 cm long	5-9 yellow, brown at base 1-2.5 cm long drooping	12-20 orange-yellow 2-4 cm long
Disks:	greenish-yellow low, becoming 1.5-3 cm high	purplish-black 1-1.5 cm high	brown-purple 1.5-3 cm high	brown-purple 1-1.5 cm high
Achenes:	flat, 5-6 mm long 4 short teeth	minute crown	no pappus	no pappus

ASTERACEAE
(Composite Family)

Ratibida columnifera (Nutt.) Woot. & Stand. **Prairie Coneflower**

Clumps of stems branch from a basal perennial crown to 30-60 cm high, and have 5-9 linear leaflets to a pinnately compound leaf 5-10 cm long by 2.5-5 cm wide. Disk flowers are in a cone or cylinder to 4 cm high, they are gray with black stamens and are fertile. Involucral bracts in 2-3 series are linear-lanceolate, 5-8 mm long and soon spreading. Rays, 4-10, are yellow, purple-brown at base or wholly so, drooping, 1.5-2.5 cm long by 7-14 mm wide and notched at the tip. Achenes are flattened and the obscure pappus is of minute teeth or scales. This plant is entering our area from the western prairies. Flowers June-October in rich prairie soils; Alabama-New Mexico and north into Illinois-Montana.

ASTERACEAE
(Composite Family)

Borrichia frutescens (L.) DC. **Sea Ox-eye**

This coastal shrubby (frutescent) perennial spreads by creeping stems and forms branching colonies 30-120 cm high. The opposite, mostly oblanceolate-spatulate leaves are finely gray-pubescent, thick, leathery, smooth-margined, and are 3-8 cm long by 1-3 cm wide. Flower heads are borne terminally and singly on opposite branches, are about 2.5 cm broad with 15-25 lemon-yellow ray flowers and a flat disk 6-9 mm across. Disk flowers are tubular, 5-lobed, and yellow-green with black anthers. Involucral bracts in 2-3 series are ovate taper-pointed and spreading. Achenes are 3-4 sided, 3-4 mm long, and topped by an obscure pappus ring of tiny teeth. Flowers April-October in brackish wet depressions and on sand ridges around the outer coastal plain; Virginia-Florida-Texas-Mexico.

udbeckia amplexicaulis

Rudbeckia hirta

richia frutescens

Ratibida columnifera

ASTERACEAE
(Composite Family)
Echinacea purpurea (L.) Moench. **Purple Coneflower**

This perennial, glabrous to bristly hairy as seen here, grows 60-135 cm tall with alternate, ovate-tapered, toothed-margined leaves 7-20 cm long by 2.5-7.5 cm wide, and round or square at the base, on long stalks. Upper leaves are smaller, 3-veined, nearly sessile, and often smooth margined. Flower heads are terminal on few-branched stems. There are 15-20 purplish, spreading to drooping ray flowers with rays 4-6.5 cm long notched at the tip. A rounded dome of disk flowers has intermingled spines exceeding the disk flowers, the spines orange-tipped and straight. Achenes are 4-sided and topped with an obscure pappus of a ring of teeth. In the similar *E. pallida* the spines are short and curved; also its leaves are linear-lanceolate. *Echinate* means "spiny," hence the generic name. Flowers June-October in open woods and prairies; Georgia-Louisiana and north into Pennsylvania-Iowa.

ASTERACEAE
(Composite Family)
Helianthus species. **Sunflowers**

Sunflowers are mostly coarse, erect branching plants with simple, alternate, opposite or both, leaves; bearing heads with yellow sterile ray flowers and usually purplish fertile disk flowers. Involucral bracts in several series are large and often long-tapering. Among the disk flowers are chaffy awl-shaped scales, being shed with the achenes, often used in identification; note old heads of *H. debilis* in photo. Achenes taper to the bases, are somewhat flattened and topped with a pappus of 2 opposite, awnlike short scales, hardly the length of the achenes. There are about 12 species of sunflowers in our area. Three of these may be distinguished by special features indicated below:

	H. angustifolius	*H. giganteus*	*H. debilis*
Stems:	single, erect, branching 1-2 m perennial	single, erect, branching 0.7-3 m	sprawling-erect annual, mottled purple 0.5-2 m
Leaves:	linear, 10-20 cm long, 6-15 mm wide margins roll under	lanceolate, sessile to petiole under 1.5 cm long	deltoid, triangular alternate long-petioled
Heads:	5-7.5 cm broad on red-brown stems	4-6 cm broad few at top	6-8.5 cm broad
Disks:	1 cm broad red-purple	2 cm broad yellow	1 cm broad red-purple
Involucral Bracts:	8-13 mm long, 12-17 mm broad at base, linear	1.5-2 cm long linear, loose spreading	1.3-1.7 cm long broad base, loose spreading
Achenes:	2.5-4 mm long	3.5-5 mm long	3.5-4 mm long
Pappus:	2 awns, 1-2 mm long	2 awns, 2.7-3.5 mm long	2 awns, 2.5-3 mm long

Helianthus angustifolius L. **Narrow-leaved Sunflower**

This plant is widespread along the coastal plain and inland, in moist barrens, marshes, fields, and ditches. Flowers July to frost; Florida-Texas and north into New York-Ohio-Missouri.

Helianthus giganteus L. **Tall Wild Sunflower**

This plant may grow over 3 m tall but its flowers are not as large as expected. The long, tapered, green, spreading involucral bracts are obvious. Flowers July-October in damp thickets and roadside ditches; Florida-Mississippi-Colorado and north into Maine-Montana.

Helianthus debilis Nutt. **Spreading Sunflower**

The term *debilis* means "weak," indicated ints spreading, decumbent nature. The purple mottled stem and long-petioled scurfy triangular leaves are typical. Flowers May-October in sandy fields, roadsides, and waste places near the coast; South Carolina-Florida-Texas.

Echinacea purpurea

thus angustifolius

Helianthus giganteus

nthus debilis

ASTERACEAE
(Composite Family)

Verbesina alternifolia (L.) Britt. ex Kern. **Wingstems**

This glabrous to minutely hairy perennial 1.2-2.5 m high has alternate, lanceolate-oblanceolate, toothed, sessile-short petioled leaves 10-30 cm long and 1.5-6.5 cm wide. Leaf blades taper to the wingless petiole, but the stem is usually 2-winged from below each petiole. Lower leaves may be opposite or in whorls of 3. Terminal branches bear many 2.5-5 cm broad flower heads of 20-30 yellow disk and 2-10 sterile ray flowers. Rays are 1.5-3 cm long by 2-3 mm broad. Involucral bracts in 1-2 series are linear to oblanceolate 2-5 mm long, becoming reflexed. Achenes are obovoid, narrowly to broadly winged, 3.5-5 mm long and topped by a pappus of 2 divergent awns. Flowers August-September in woods, fields, and marshes; Florida-Louisiana and north into New York-Iowa-Kansas.

For Key to dinstinguish *Coreopsis* from *Bidens,* see last page of descriptions, following *Chrysanthemum.*

ASTERACEAE
(Composite Family)

Coreopsis lanceolata L. **Lance-leaved Coreopsis**

This 30-80 cm tall, glabrous to pubescent perennial has mostly simple, linear to oblanceolate, sessile to slender, petioled leaves 5-15 cm long. Flowering heads 4-6.5 cm broad, may be solitary or on branching stems and slender stalks 10-40 cm long. Six to ten bright yellow rays, 1.3-3 cm long by 1-1.7 cm wide, are deeply 3-7 tooth-lobed at their tips. Disk flowers are yellow. Outer involucral bracts are lanceolate, 5-10 mm long while inner, larger bracts are 9-17 mm long. Flat achenes are broadly thin-winged on 2 sides and are 2.3-3 mm long, topped by 2 scalelike awns under 0.5 mm long or none evident. Flowers April-July in sandy woods, thickets, and roadsides; Florida-New Mexico and north into New York-Wisconsin.

ASTERACEAE
(Composite Family)

Coreopsis grandiflora Hogg. **Large-flowered Coreopsis**

This usually glabrous perennial, 30-90 cm tall, has mostly pinnately compound leaves with narrow linear to elliptic leaflets, 2-8 cm long by 1-10 mm wide, extending well up the stem, the upper ones 3-5 parted. Flowering heads 4-5 cm broad, are solitary, on slender stalks 7-25 cm long. Yellow rays are 6-10, 1.3-2.5 cm long by 1 cm wide and 3 or more toothed at their tips. Disk flowers are yellow. Outer lanceolate involucral bracts with white margins are 5-10 mm long, are narrower and shorter than the inner ovate-lanceolate 9-17 mm long bracts. Flat achenes are ovoid, 2.3-3 mm long by 1.6-2 mm broad, winged on the sides and topped by 2 scalelike awns under 0.5 mm long. Flowers April-July in open woodlands and prairies; Florida-New Mexico and north into North Carolina-Kansas.

ASTERACEAE
(Composite Family)

Coreopsis tinctoria Nutt. **Golden Coreopsis**

This is a freely branching, mostly glabrous, annual 30-100 cm tall. Its opposite leaves are pinnately divided into linear or narrowly lanceolate leaflets below; the upper leaves may not be divided but are reduced to linear bracts. Flowering heads 2.2-2.5 cm broad are solitary on slender stalks 1-6 cm long on upper branches. Yellow rays have a red base, or may even be all red, are 1-3 cm long by 7-12 mm wide, and are conspicuously 3 tooth-lobed at their tips. Disk flowers are red. Outer involucral bracts are lanceolate, only 1-3 mm long with brown inner bracts 4-7 mm long. Narrow achenes are 1.5-2.2 mm long, both wingless and awnless. Flowers, often in great profusion, June-September in fields and waste places; North Carolina-Georgia-Texas-California and north into Minnesota-Washington.

besina alternifolia

Coreopsis grandiflora

eopsis tinctoria

Coreopsis lanceolata

ASTERACEAE
(Composite Family)
Coreopsis basalis (Diet.) Blake **Calliopsis**

This freely branched annual to 70 cm tall might be mistaken for *C. tinctoria* because of the red-brown blotching of corolla bases and the red-brown disk flowers. Study reveals that rays of *C. basalis* are wider, 1-2 cm *vs.* 7-12 mm; the outer involucral bracts are longer, 4-10 mm *vs.* 1-3 mm; individual flower head stalks are longer, 5-25 cm *vs.* 1-6 cm; and the wingless achenes are 2x the diameter, 1.5-1.7 mm *vs.* 0.6-0.8 mm. More obviously the leaflets of the stem leaves are not linear as in *C. tinctoria* but are broader, elliptic-ovate, similar to but smaller than the basal leaves. This plant is rare and seldom reported. Flowers in dry, open sandy areas around the coastal plain; North Carolina-Georgia-Louisiana-Texas.

ASTERACEAE
(Composite Family)
Coreopsis nudata Nutt. **Swamp Coreopsis**

This glabrous perennial, 60-120 cm high, is unusual in two ways: it has pink ray flowers and its few tubelike leaves are mostly circular in cross section except at the base, the longer ones 7-30 cm long. The few leaves give the plant a nude appearance unlike other species of *Coreopsis* which usually have yellow rays. Single flower heads are borne at the tips of remotely branching bare stems except for a few bracts 4-6 cm long. Flower heads 2.5-3 cm across have about 8 rose-pink rays, 3-5 toothed at the tip, the middle tooth longer than the marginal ones. Disk flowers are yellow in a disk nearly 1 cm wide. Achenes are about 3 mm long, tipped by a pair of pappus awns. Flowers April-June, uncommon along the lower coastal plain in wet pinelands, cypress swamps, and ditches; Florida-Mississippi and north into Georgia.

ASTERACEAE
(Composite Family)
Bidens aristosa (Michx.) Britt. **Tickseed Sunflower**

This much branched pubescent annual, 30-120 cm tall, has opposite pinnately compound, sometimes only lobed, leaves on red-brown stems. Many 2.5-5 cm broad yellow heads are borne in leaf axils on slender stalks 1-15 cm long. Involucral bracts are in 2 series: the 8-12 outer are spreading, linear to spatulate, 3-12 mm long and with or without ciliate hairs; the inner bracts are 5-8 mm long. Golden yellow rays, 6-10, are oblanceolate 1.5-2.5 cm long by 5- mm wide and rounded at the tips. Disks are yellow, 1 cm broad and produce flat to 4-angled beakless and wingless achenes. Pappus awns are 2 (rarely 4), broad based, barbed, and nearly as long as the achenes. Flowers August-October in swampy meadows and marshes, often in great abundance; Alabama-Texas and north into Delaware-Minnesota.

ASTERACEAE
(Composite Family)
Galinsoga ciliata (Raf.) Blake **Peruvian Daisy, Galinsoga**

This weedy bushy-branched annual 10-60 cm tall has coarse, long-pubescent stems with opposite petioled leaves, toothed and ovate to elliptic-ovate, 2-8 cm long by 1-5 cm wide. Small flower heads 8-10 mm broad are produced on axillary and terminal branches on pubescent stalks 1-4 cm long. Tiny white fertile ray flowers, 4-5, have 1-3 mm long and wide 3-toothed-lobed rays. Disk flowers, 8-12, are yellow and fertile. Thin, ovate involucral bracts in 2-3 series are erect. 2-4 mm long by 3-6 mm wide and shed upon maturing. Achenes are densely pubescent, 1-1.5 mm long, black, and topped by a pappus ring of cut-fringed scales or bristles 1-2 mm long. A naturalized garden pest from tropical areas. Flowers May-frost in waste places over much of the United States.

Coreopsis nudata

Coreopsis basalis

Galinsoga ciliata

Bidens aristosa

ASTERACEAE
(Composite Family)

Gaillardia pulchella Foug. **Firewheel, Indian Blanket**

This very pubescent annual, decumbent with ascending branches, has basal and alternate leaves and grows 20-60 cm high. Leaves are pinnately lobed below to simple oblong-lanceolate, sessile and clasping above, 3-8 cm long by 5-20 mm wide. Flower heads 2.5-7.5 cm broad are borne terminally and have 10-20 red to purple, yellow, seldom white, rays with 3 tooth-lobes at their tips. Raised disks have yellow, purple-tipped disk flowers interspersed with chaffy scales 2-3 mm long. Involucral bracts in 2-3 series are green to purple, linear-lanceolate, 1-1.5 cm long and reflexing at maturity. Pubescent 4-sided achenes, 2 mm long, are topped with a pappus of 5-7 awn-tipped scales 4-6 mm long. Flowers April-frost in dry open areas; Florida-Arizona and north into North Carolina-Colorado.

ASTERACEAE
(Composite Family)

Helenium amarum (Raf.) Rock **Bitterweed**

This tap-rooted glabrous annual is much branched above, 15-70 cm tall and has many filiform-linear alternate leaves 2-7 cm long and 1-4 mm wide at flowering time. The plant has a strong odor and imparts a bitter taste to milk when eaten by cows. Flowering heads 1.5-2.7 cm broad are borne on slender stems 3-10 cm long. The 6-9 involucral bracts in 1 ring are 4-6 mm long, linear and reflexing. The 4-8 yellow rays are 6-7 mm long, wedge-shaped, 3-toothed at the tip, and usually drooping. The glabrous yellow disk is 6-8 mm broad. Pubescent achenes 1.5-2 mm long are 4-angled and topped by a pappus of 5-8 shorter, awn-pointed scales. Flowers June-October in open fields and abundant in pastures when overgrazed; Florida-Texas and north into New York-Michigan.

ASTERACEAE
(Composite Family)

Achillea millefolium L. **Yarrow**

This perennial is branching above, 30-60 cm tall, glabrous to loosely pubescent, and has finely dissected compound alternate leaves 2-15 cm long by 0.5-4 cm wide. White flowering heads only 4-5 mm broad are numerous on the terminal branching, stiffly erect stems, making flat-topped clusters 2-10 cm broad. White, sometimes pink, 4-5 ray flowers are fertile and have 3-toothed rays broader than long. Disks are white flowered and fertile. Several involucral bracts are oblong-lanceolate, thin margined, and in 3-4 series 4-5 mm high. Achenes 2-3 mm long are glabrous, slightly compressed and have no pappus. Flowers June-September along roadsides and in fields throughout most of the continent, having become naturalized from Europe.

ASTERACEAE
(Composite Family)

Anthemis cotula L. **Dog-fennel, Mayweed**

This mostly glabrous, much-branched, often decumbent, annual grows 30-60 cm high. It has ill-scented, alternate, finely 3-times dissected leaves, 2.5-6 cm long by 1-3 cm wide. Flowering heads 2-2.5 cm broad are borne singly terminating the stems. The 10-18 white rays are linear-oblong 6-10 mm long and 3-toothed at the tip, the middle tooth shortest. The 8-10 mm broad yellow disks have a short lanceolate scale beside each central tubular disk flower. Involucral bracts are white-margined, pubescent, linear-oblong and overlap in several series. Achenes 1 mm long are rough-ribbed and have no pappus. Flowers June-October in fields and waste places over most of the continent, naturalized from Europe.

aillardia pulchella

Helenium amarum

Achillea millefolium

Anthemis cotula

ASTERACEAE
(Composite Family)

Chrysanthemum leucanthemum L. **Ox-eye Daisy**

This glabrous perennial from a rootstock grows 30-70 cm tall with many basal leaves and alternate pinnately tooth-lobed, oblanceolate, simple leaves 2-10 cm long by 2-15 mm wide. Flower heads of white rays and yellow disks are 2.5-6 cm broad and borne singly on stalks 1-10 cm long. The 20-30 rays, 1.5-2.5 cm long by 2-4 mm wide, are minutely 3-toothed at the tip. Disks are raised convex, yellow, about 2 cm broad and have no scales among the disk flowers. Involucral bracts 4-7 mm long, in several series, are narrowly lanceolate, white margined, and brown lined. Achenes are about 1 mm long, 10 rough-ribbed, and have no evident pappus. Naturalized from Europe and flowering over most of the United States May-November in fields; it is uncommon southward.

Distinguishing *Coreopsis* or tickseeds from *Bidens* or beggar-ticks is not easy, a hand lens may be necessary. There are both ray and disk flowers in *Coreopsis* but some *Bidens* have only disk flowers. Both genera have simple and compound leaves. Leaves are alternate in some *Coreopsis* but are opposite in *Bidens*. Look for contrasting features of the flower heads in table below.

	Coreopsis	*Bidens*
Rays:	mostly 8 tips often tooth-lobed	3-8 when present tips rarely tooth-lobed
Involucral bracts in 2 series:	outer narrower and shorter than inner	outer larger than the inner
Achenes:	flat, under 5 mm long winged on 2 sides	flat to 4-sided, tapered to base, wingless, 6-10 mm long
Pappus:	none, or 2 barbless teeth or awns, under 1.5 mm long	2 or 4 reverse-barbed awns 3-6 mm long

Chrysanthemum leucanthemum

Chrysanthemum leucanthemum

Supplementary Literature

Beck, Charles B. *Origin and Early Evolution of Angiosperms.* New York: Columbia University Press, 1976.

Benson, Lyman. *Plant Classification.* Boston: D. C. Heath, 1957.

Bold, Harold C. *Morphology of Plants.* 3rd ed. New York: Harper & Row, 1973.

Britton, Nathaniel Lord and Addison Brown. *An Illustrated Flora of the Northern United States and Canada.* 2nd ed., 3 vols. 1913. New York: Dover Publications, 1970.

*Cobb, Boughton. *A Field Guide to the Ferns and Their Related Families of Northeastern and Central North America.* Peterson Field Guide Series. Boston: Houghton Mifflin, 1963.

Fernald, M. L. *Gray's Manual of Botany.* 8th ed. New York: American Book Co., 1963.

Gleason, H. H. *The New Britton and Brown Illustrated Flora of the Northeastern United States and Adjacent Canada.* 3 vols. New York: New York Botanical Garden, 1952.

*Harrar, Ellwood S. and J. George Harrar. *Guide to Southern Trees.* 2nd ed., 1946. New York: Dover Publications, 1962.

Hughes, Norman F. *Palaeobiology of Angiosperm Origins.* New York: Cambridge University Press, 1976.

*Peterson, Roger T. and Margaret McKenny. *A Field Guide to Wildflowers of Northeastern and North-central North America.* Peterson Field Guide Series. Boston: Houghton Mifflin, 1968.

*Porter, C. L. *Taxonomy of Flowering Plants.* San Francisco: W. H. Freeman, 1967.

Radford, Albert E.; H.E. Ahles, and C. R. Bell. *Manual of the Vascular Flora of the Carolinas.* Chapel Hill: University of North Carolina Press, 1964, 1968.

*Rickett, Harold W. *Wildflowers of the United States.* 6 vols. in 14 parts. Vol. 2 in 2 parts, *The Southeastern States.* 1967. Vol. 3 in 2 parts, *Texas.* 1969. New York: McGraw-Hill for The New York Botanical Garden.

Scagel, Robert F.; R. J. Bandoni, et al. *An Evolutionary Survey of the Plant Kingdom.* Belmont, Cal.: Wadsworth, 1965.

Stebbins, G. Ledyard. *Flowering Plants: Evolution above the Species Level.* Cambridge, Mass.: Harvard University Press, Belknap Press, 1974.

Steyermark, Julian A. *Flora of Missouri.* Ames: Iowa State University Press, 1963.

*Vines, Robert A. *Shrubs and Woody Vines of the Southwest.* Austin: University of Texas Press, 1960.

*Nontechnical treatment of material.

INDEX

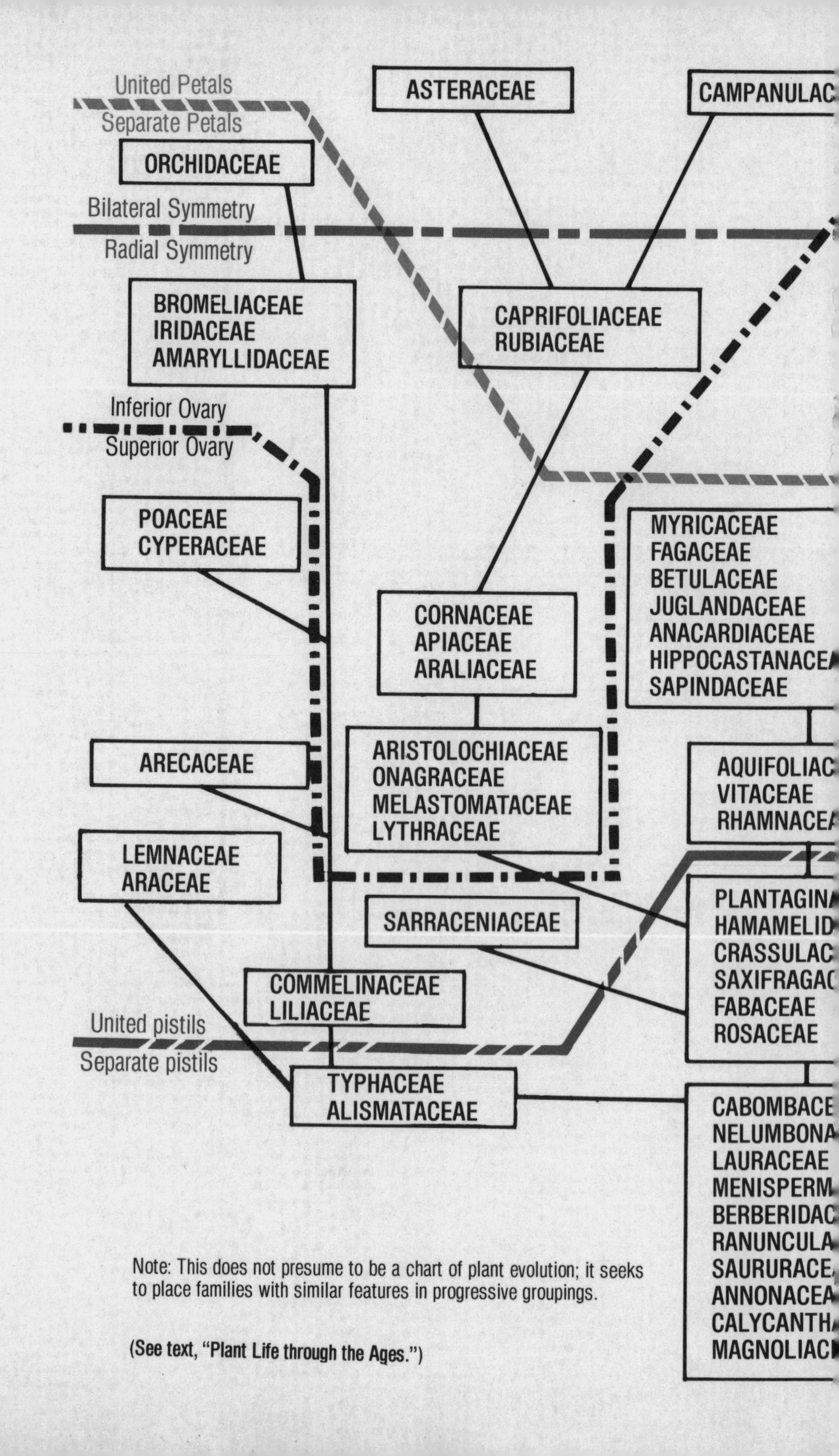

Note: This does not presume to be a chart of plant evolution; it seeks to place families with similar features in progressive groupings.

(See text, "Plant Life through the Ages.")